VAMPEERZ, MY PEER VAMPIRES.

AKILI

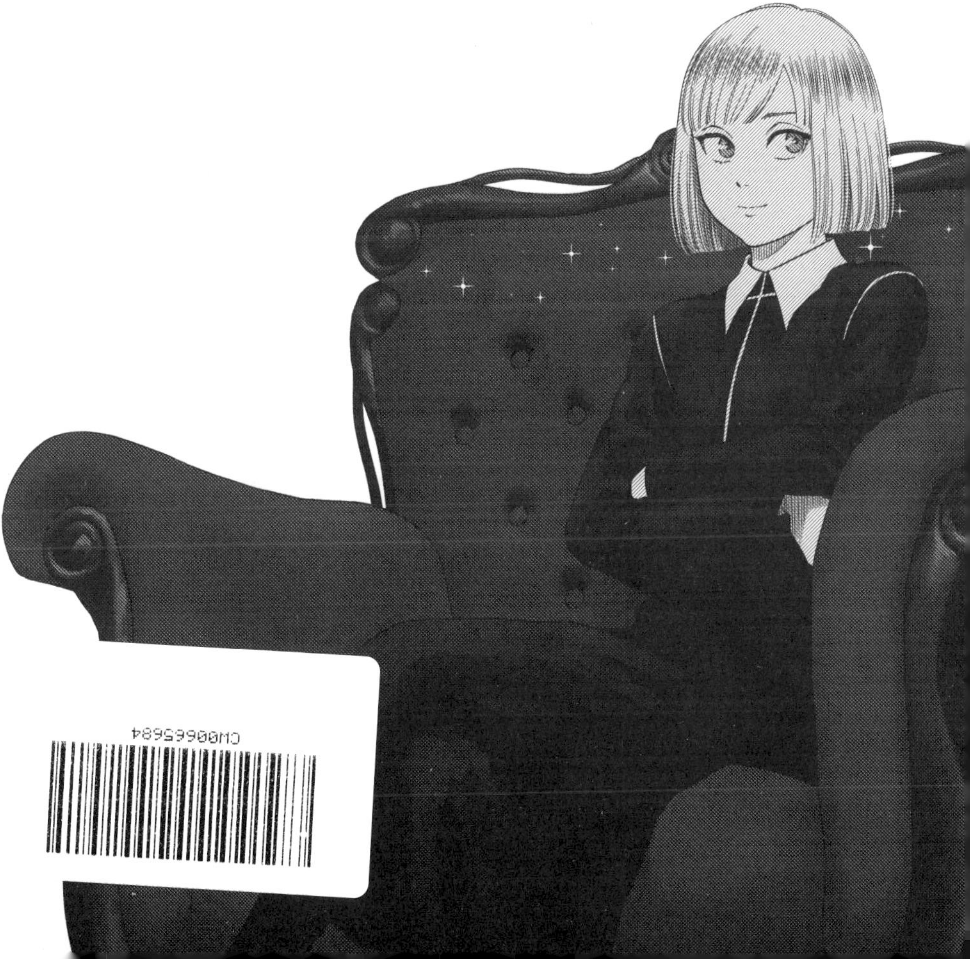

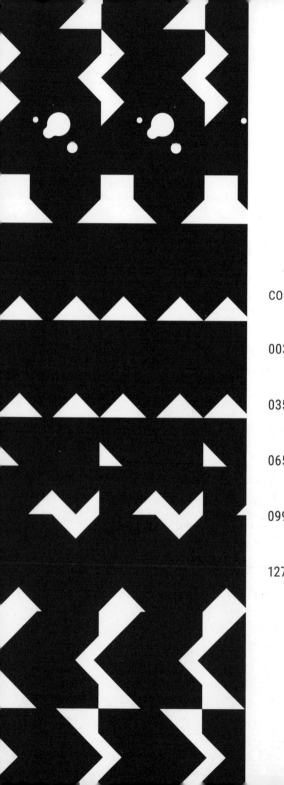

CONTENTS

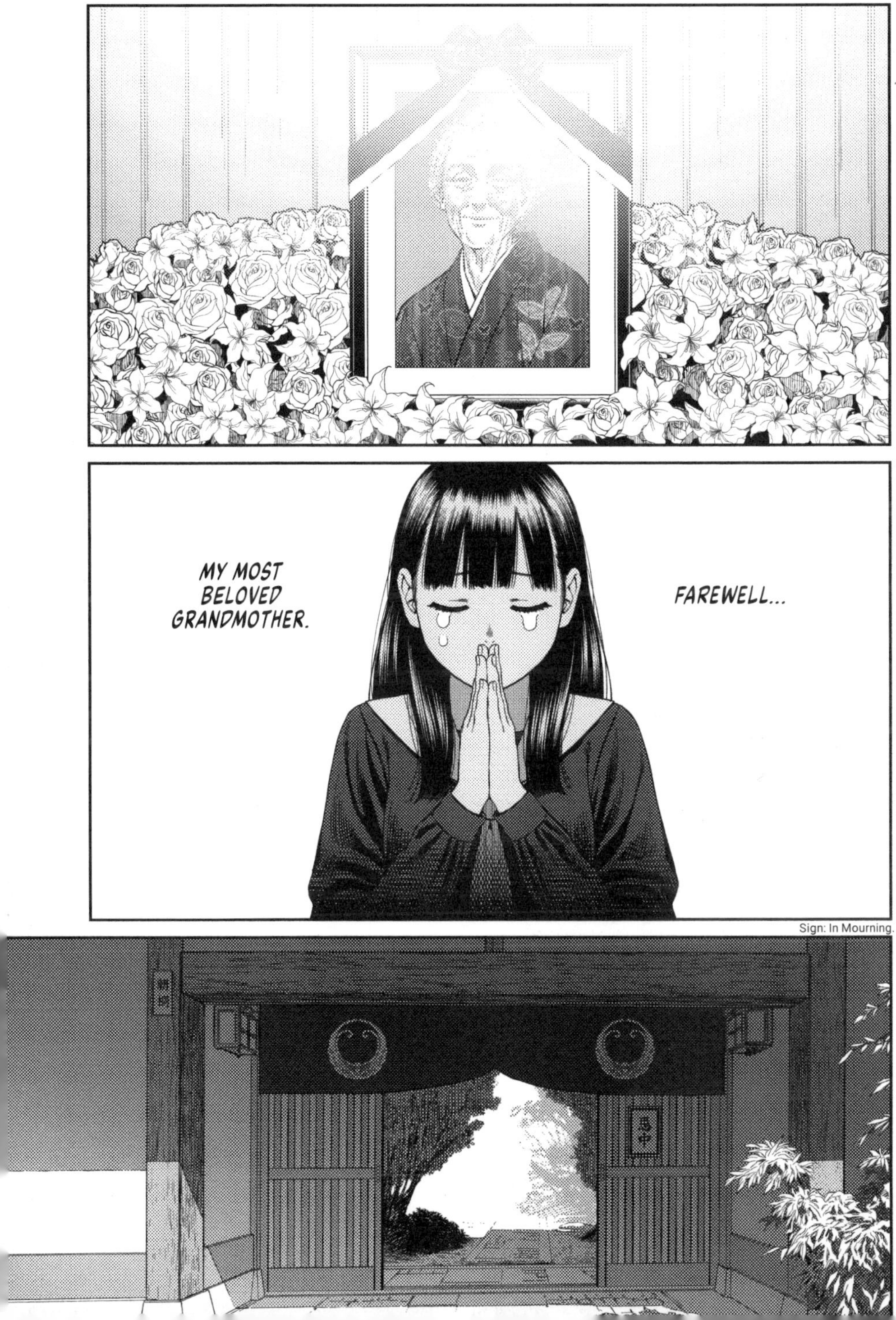
FAREWELL...
MY MOST BELOVED GRANDMOTHER.
Sign: In Mourning.

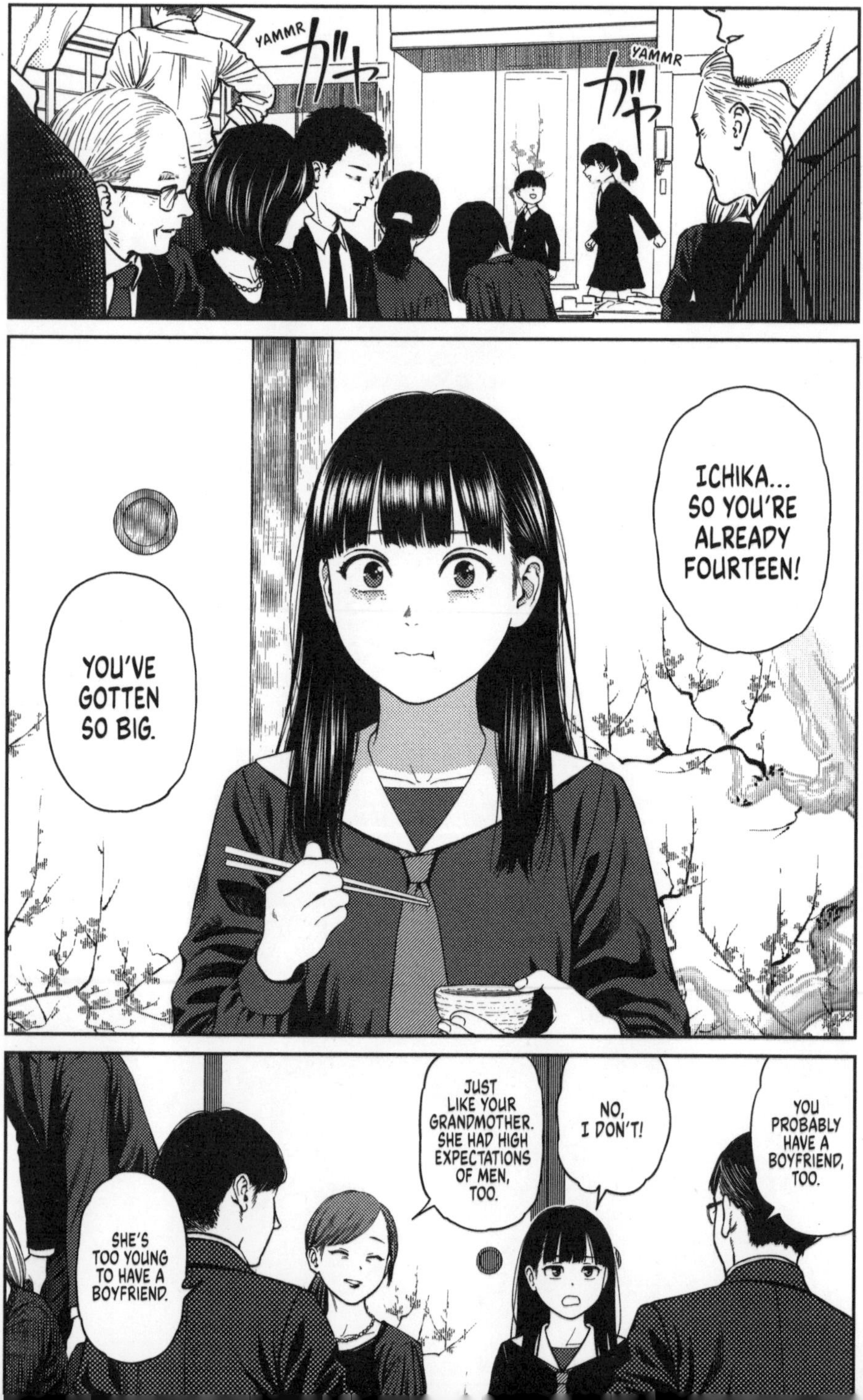

YAMMR
ガヤ
YAMMR
ガヤ
ICHIKA... SO YOU'RE ALREADY FOURTEEN!
YOU'VE GOTTEN SO BIG.
YOU PROBABLY HAVE A BOYFRIEND, TOO.
NO, I DON'T!
JUST LIKE YOUR GRANDMOTHER. SHE HAD HIGH EXPECTATIONS OF MEN, TOO.
SHE'S TOO YOUNG TO HAVE A BOYFRIEND.

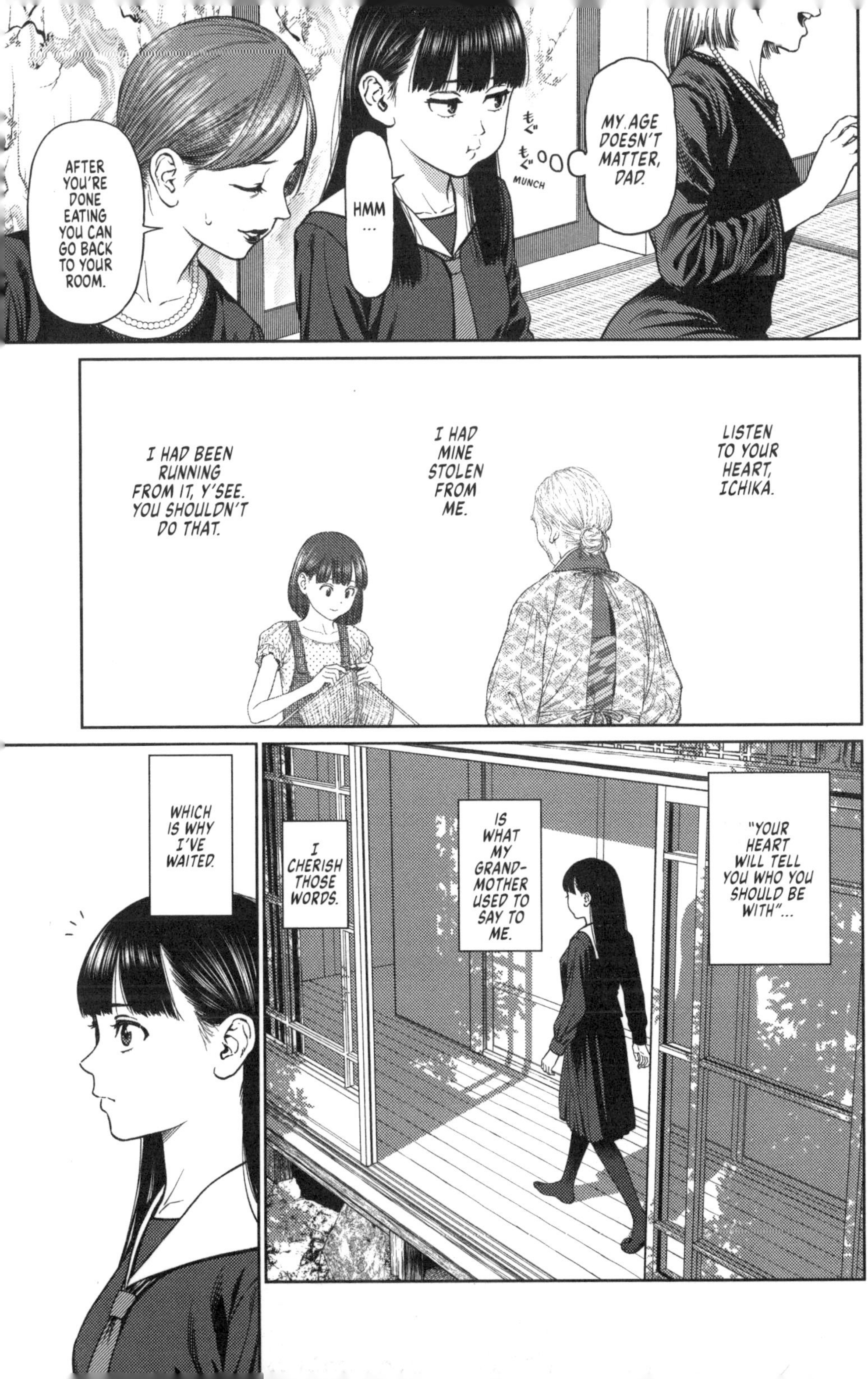
MY AGE DOESN'T MATTER, DAD.
もぐ もぐ
MUNCH
HMM...
AFTER YOU'RE DONE EATING YOU CAN GO BACK TO YOUR ROOM.
LISTEN TO YOUR HEART, ICHIKA.
I HAD MINE STOLEN FROM ME.
I HAD BEEN RUNNING FROM IT, Y'SEE. YOU SHOULDN'T DO THAT.
"YOUR HEART WILL TELL YOU WHO YOU SHOULD BE WITH"...
IS WHAT MY GRANDMOTHER USED TO SAY TO ME.
I CHERISH THOSE WORDS.
WHICH IS WHY I'VE WAITED.

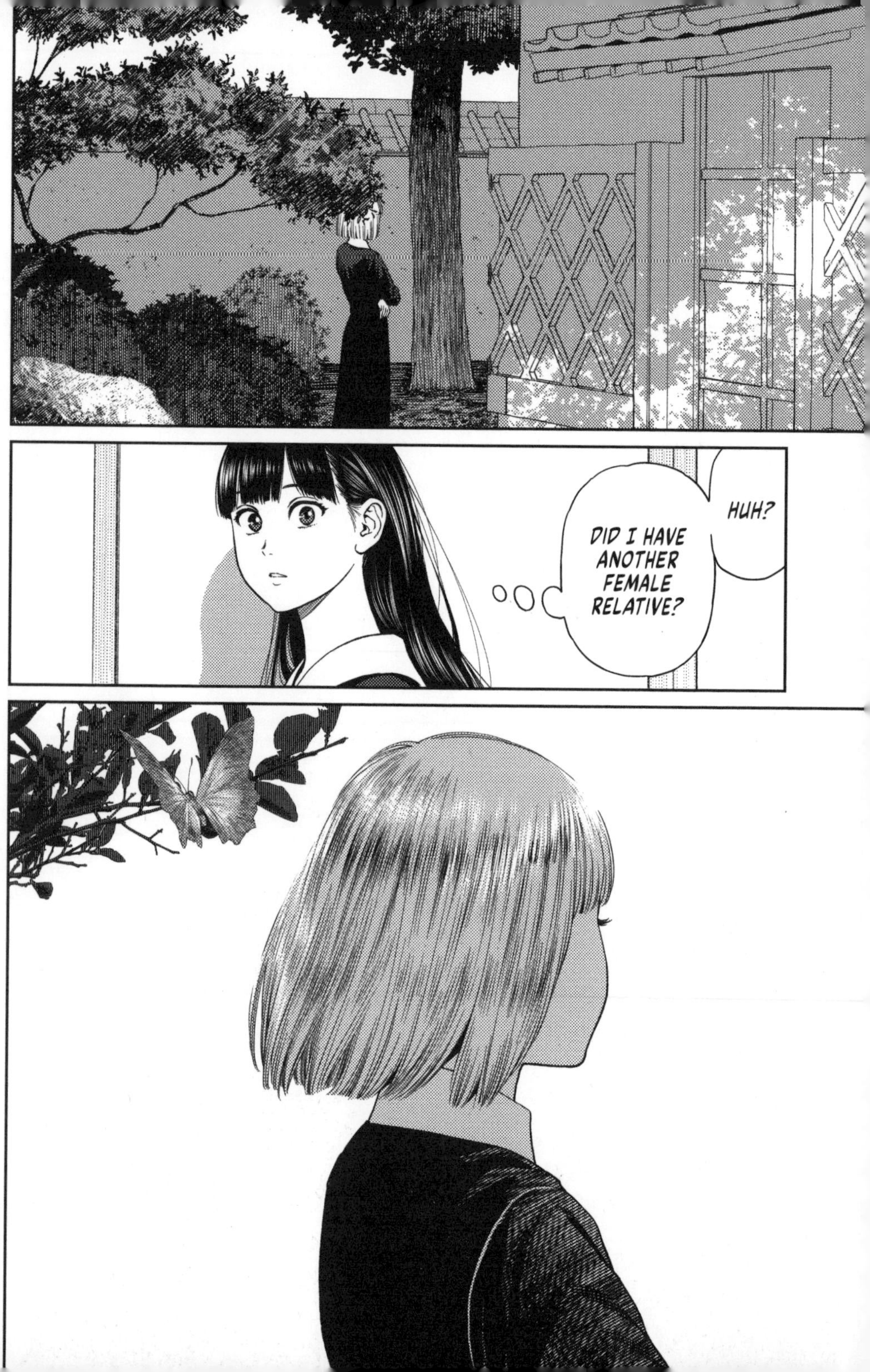
HUH?
DID I HAVE ANOTHER FEMALE RELATIVE?

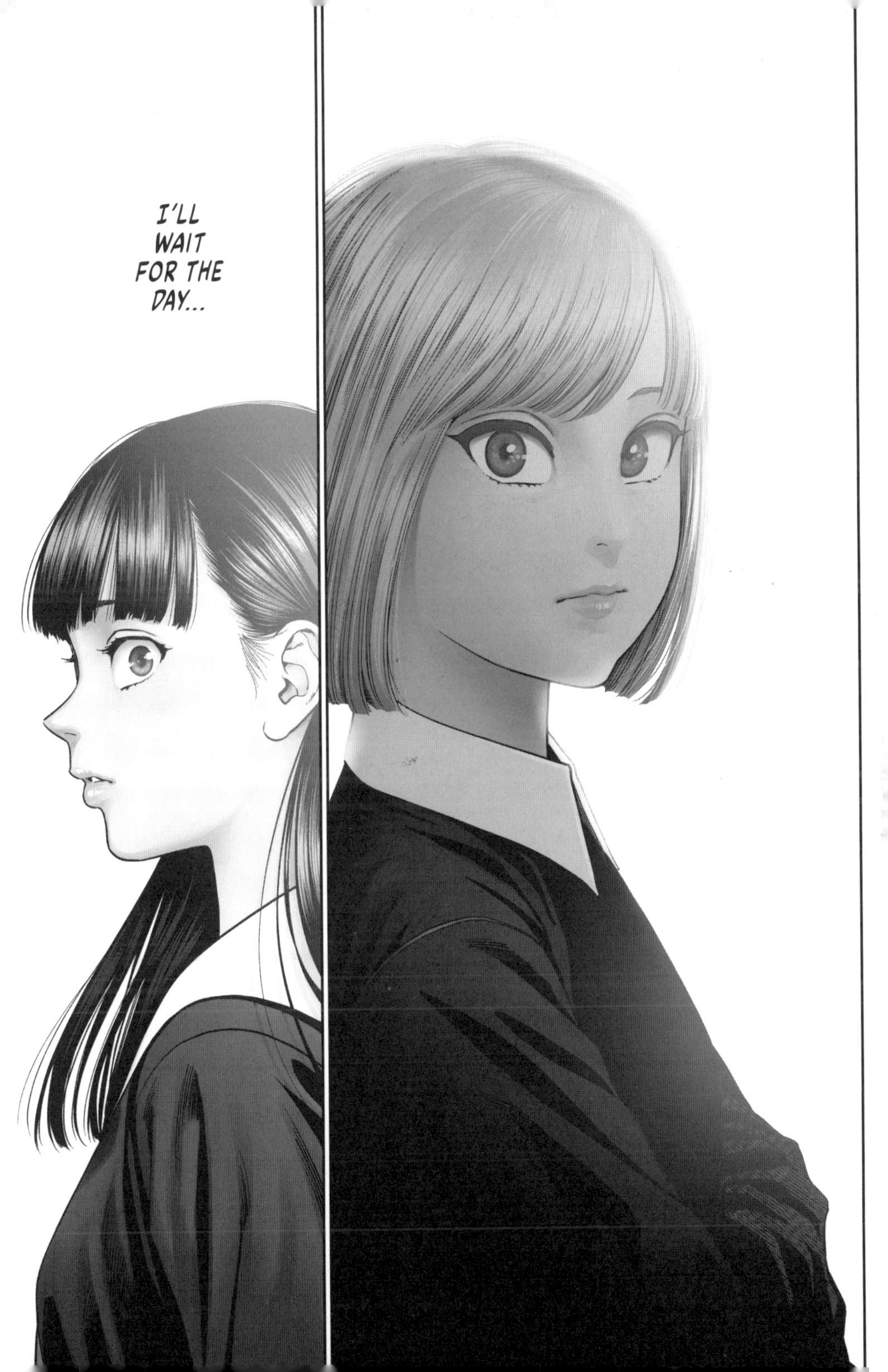
I'LL WAIT FOR THE DAY...

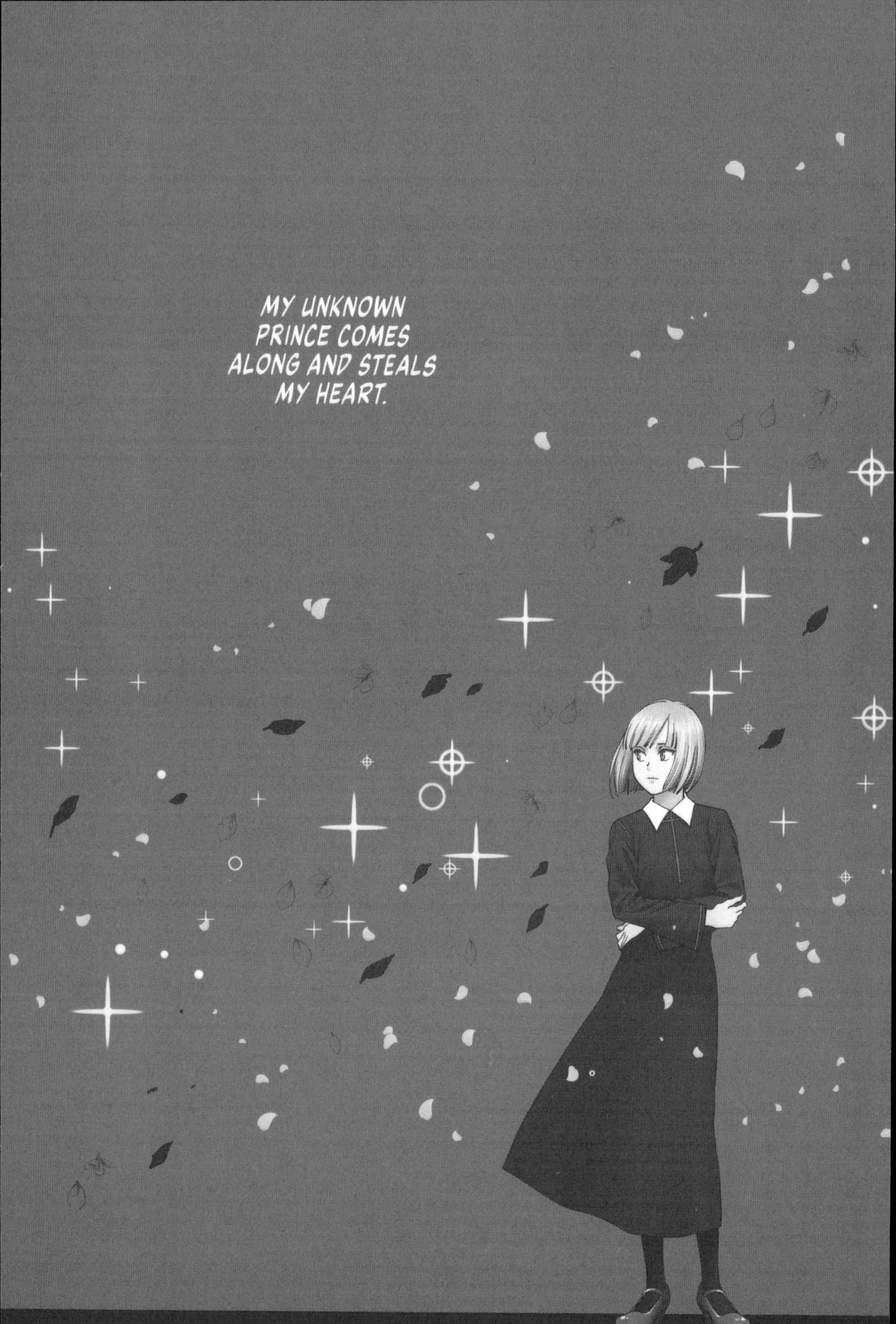
MY UNKNOWN PRINCE COMES ALONG AND STEALS MY HEART.

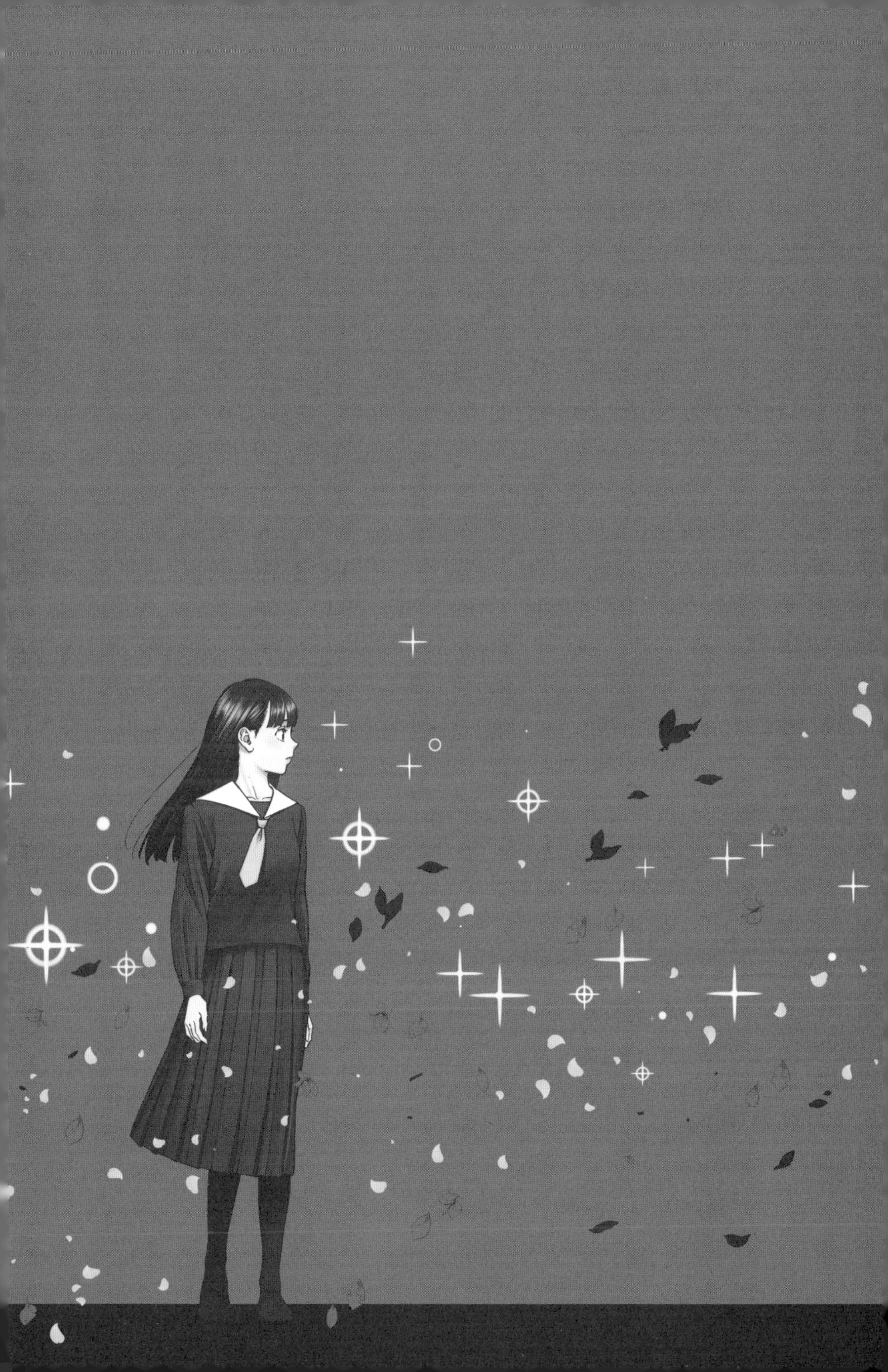

VAMPEERZ

MY PEER VAMPIRES

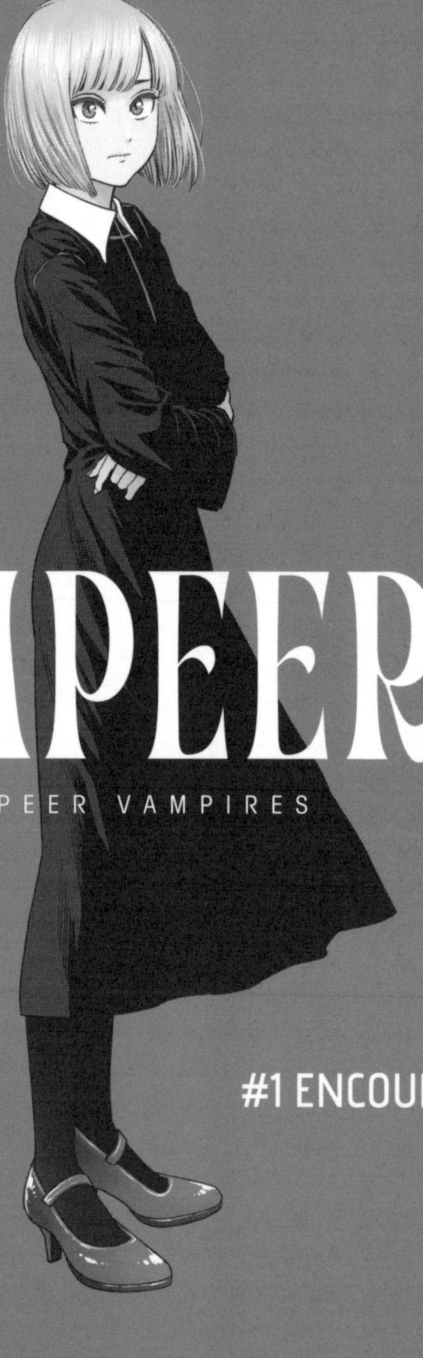

#1 ENCOUNTER

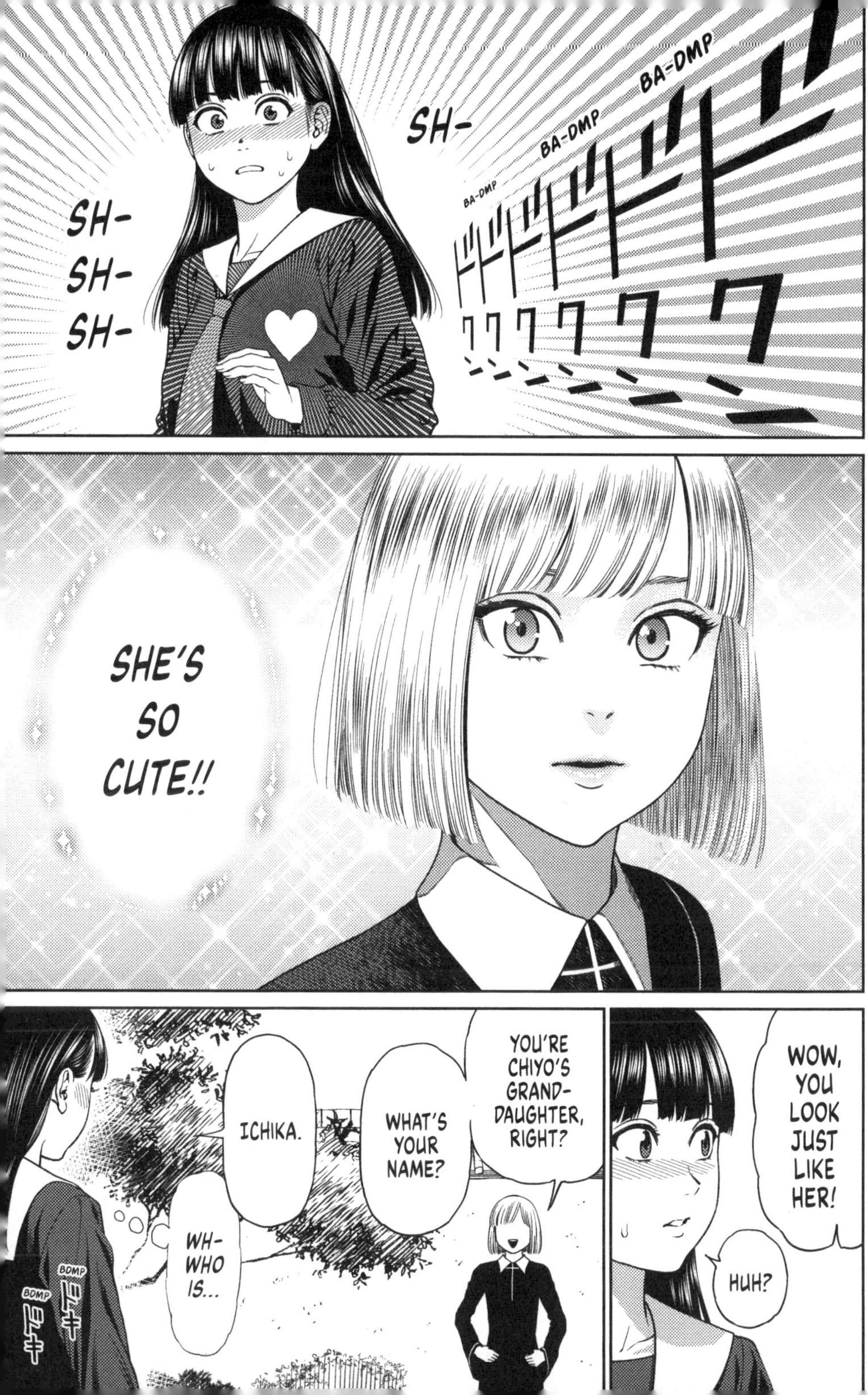
BA-DMP
BA-DMP
BA-DMP
SH-
SH-
SH-
SH-
SHE'S SO CUTE!!
WOW, YOU LOOK JUST LIKE HER!
HUH?
YOU'RE CHIYO'S GRAND-DAUGHTER, RIGHT?
WHAT'S YOUR NAME?
ICHIKA.
WH- WHO IS...
BDMP
BDMP

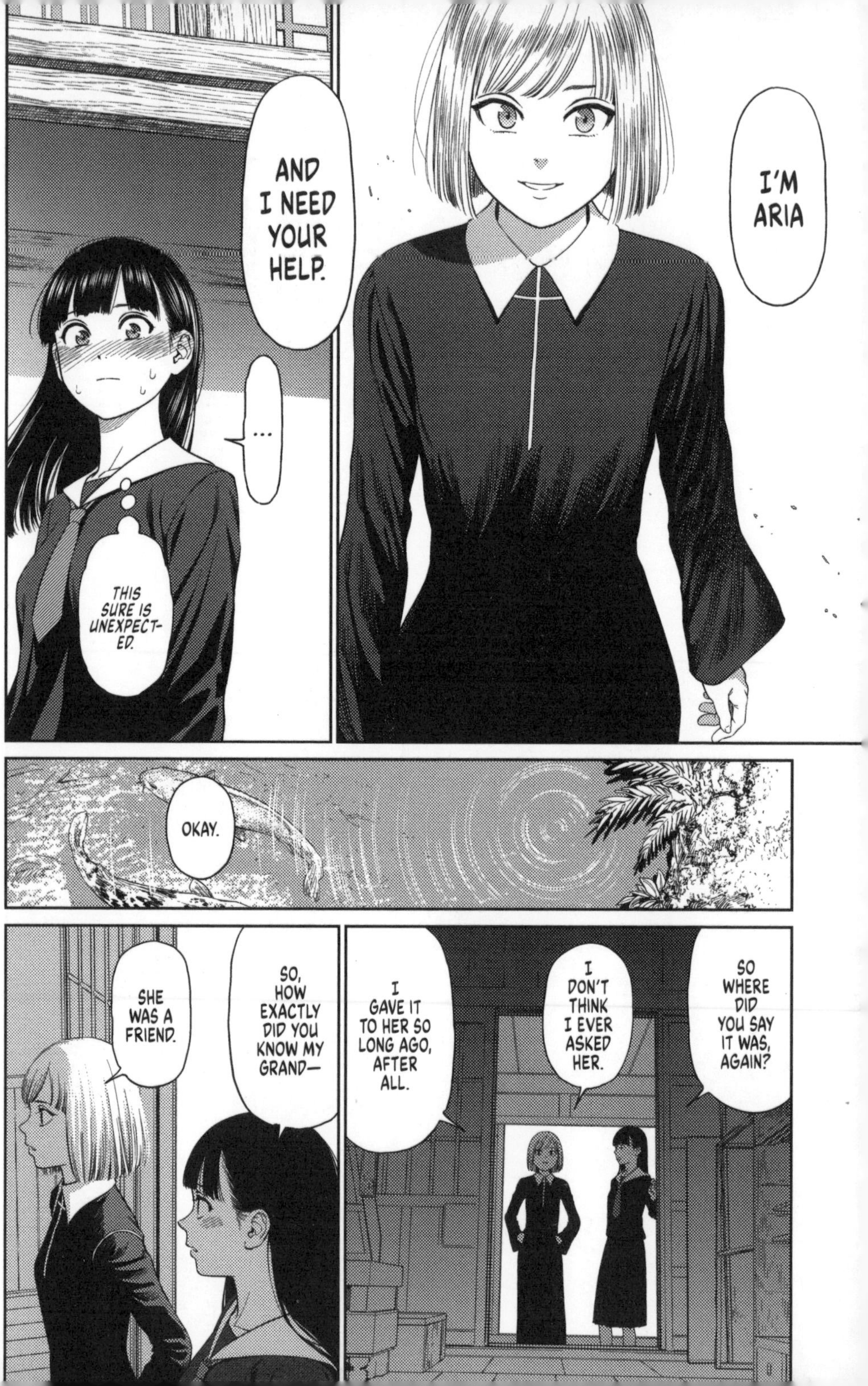
I'M ARIA
AND I NEED YOUR HELP.
...
THIS SURE IS UNEXPECTED.
OKAY.
SO WHERE DID YOU SAY IT WAS, AGAIN?
I DON'T THINK I EVER ASKED HER.
I GAVE IT TO HER SO LONG AGO, AFTER ALL.
SO, HOW EXACTLY DID YOU KNOW MY GRAND—
SHE WAS A FRIEND.

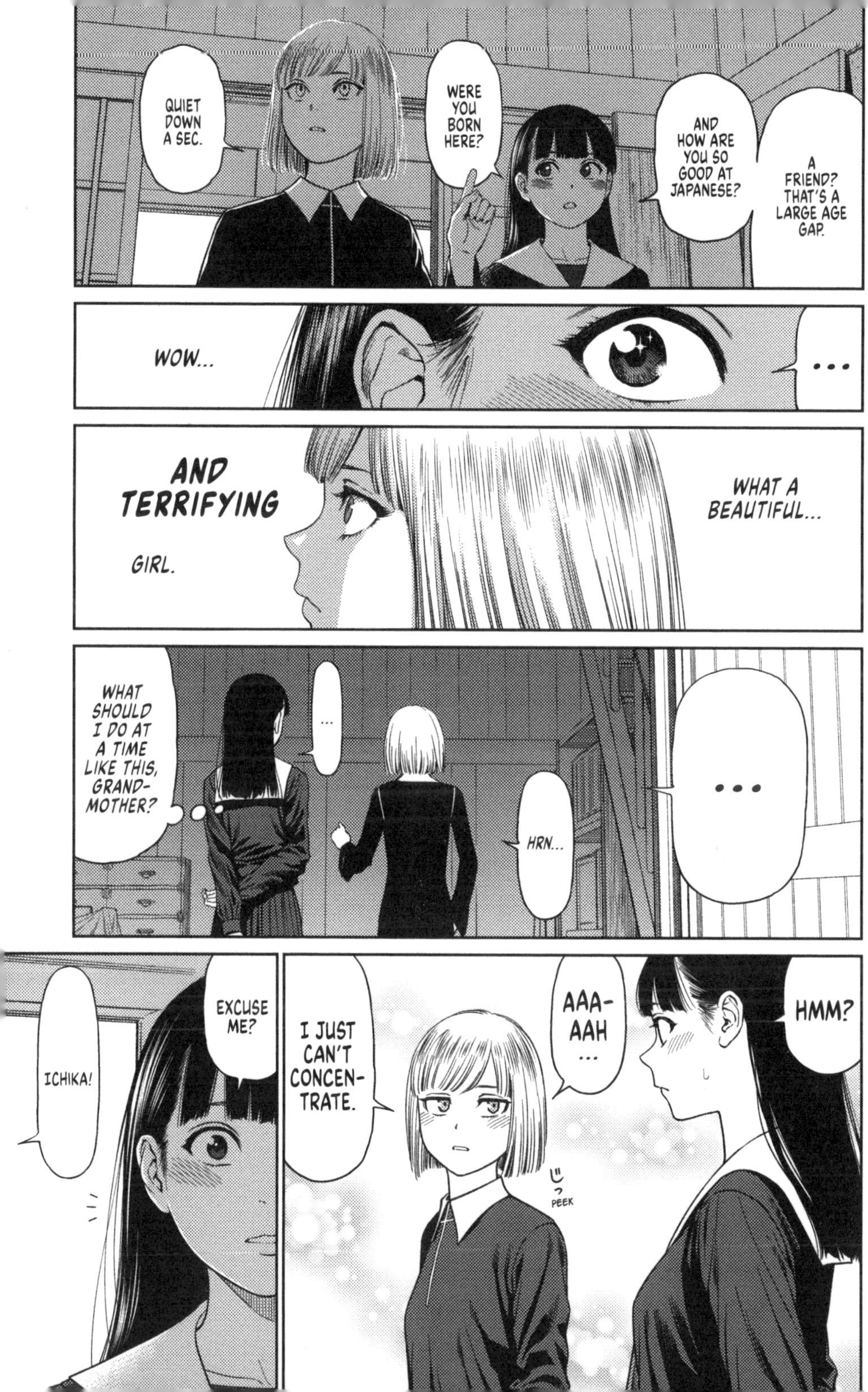
A FRIEND? THAT'S A LARGE AGE GAP.
AND HOW ARE YOU SO GOOD AT JAPANESE?
WERE YOU BORN HERE?
QUIET DOWN A SEC.
...
WOW...
WHAT A BEAUTIFUL...
AND TERRIFYING
GIRL.
...
HRN...
...
WHAT SHOULD I DO AT A TIME LIKE THIS, GRAND-MOTHER?
HMM?
AAA-AAH...
I JUST CAN'T CONCEN-TRATE.
じっ
PEEK
EXCUSE ME?
ICHIKA!

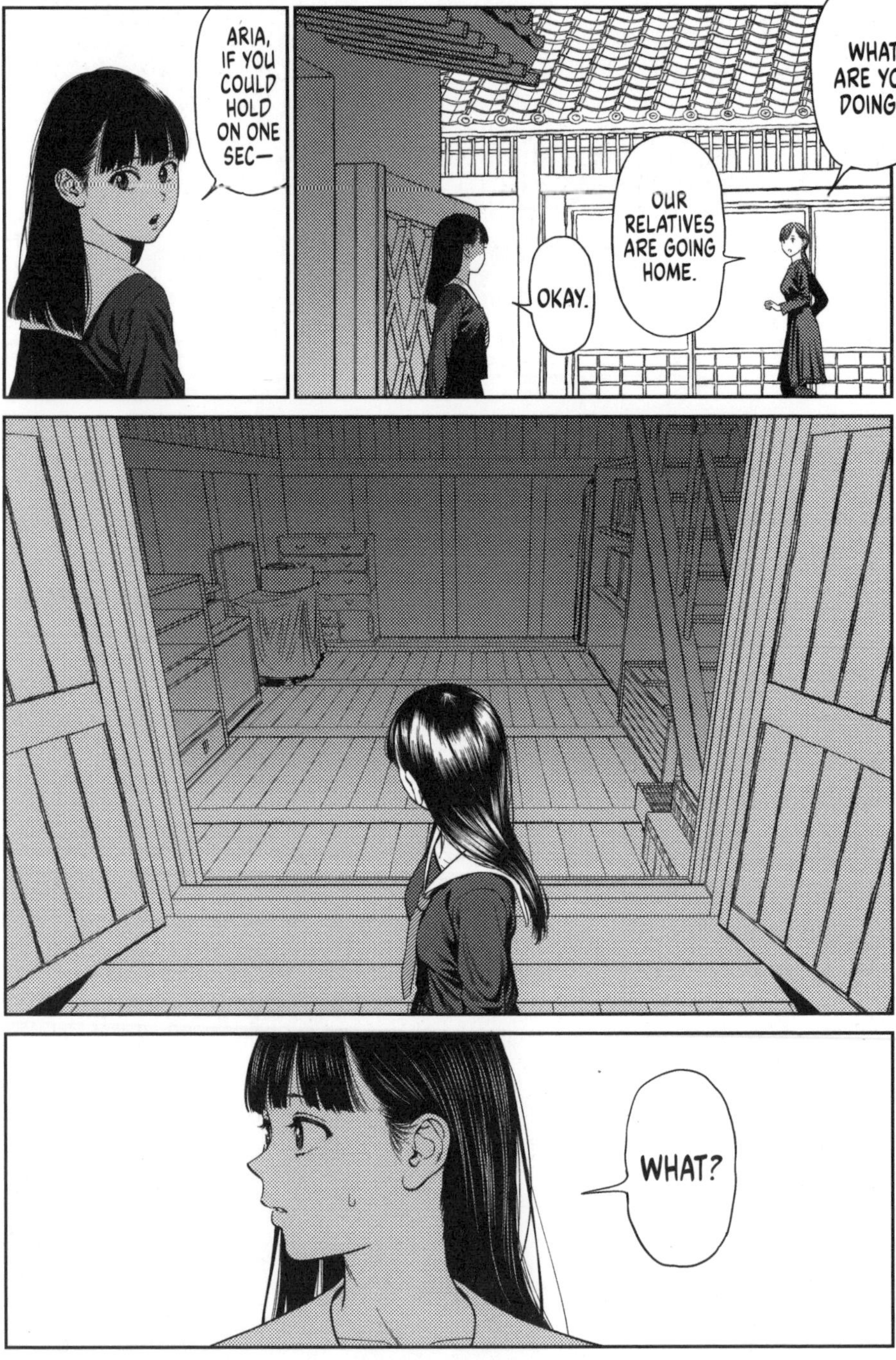
WHAT ARE YOU DOING?
OUR RELATIVES ARE GOING HOME.
OKAY.
ARIA, IF YOU COULD HOLD ON ONE SEC—
WHAT?

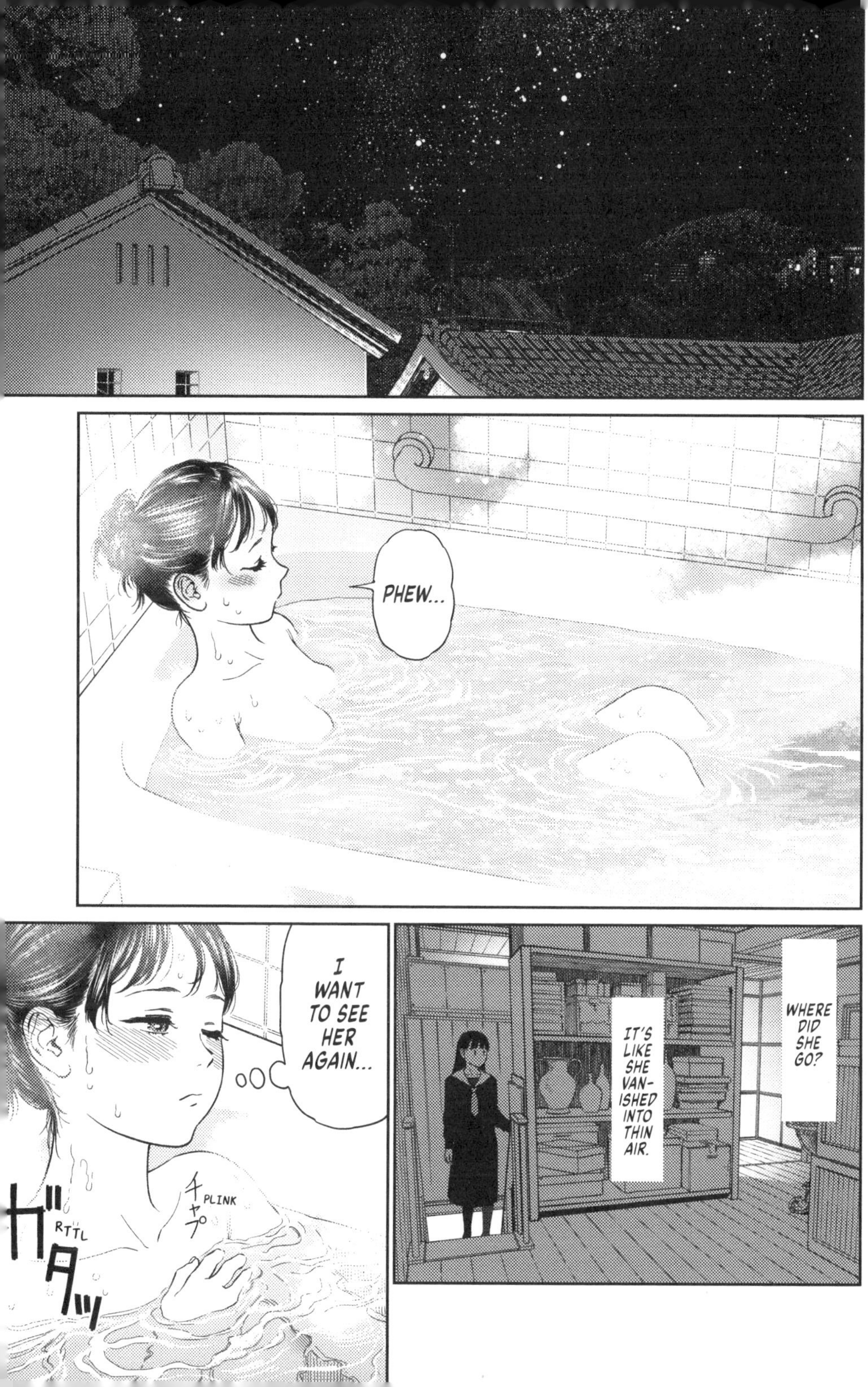
PHEW...
WHERE DID SHE GO?
IT'S LIKE SHE VAN-ISHED INTO THIN AIR.
I WANT TO SEE HER AGAIN...
チャプ PLINK
ガタッ RTTL

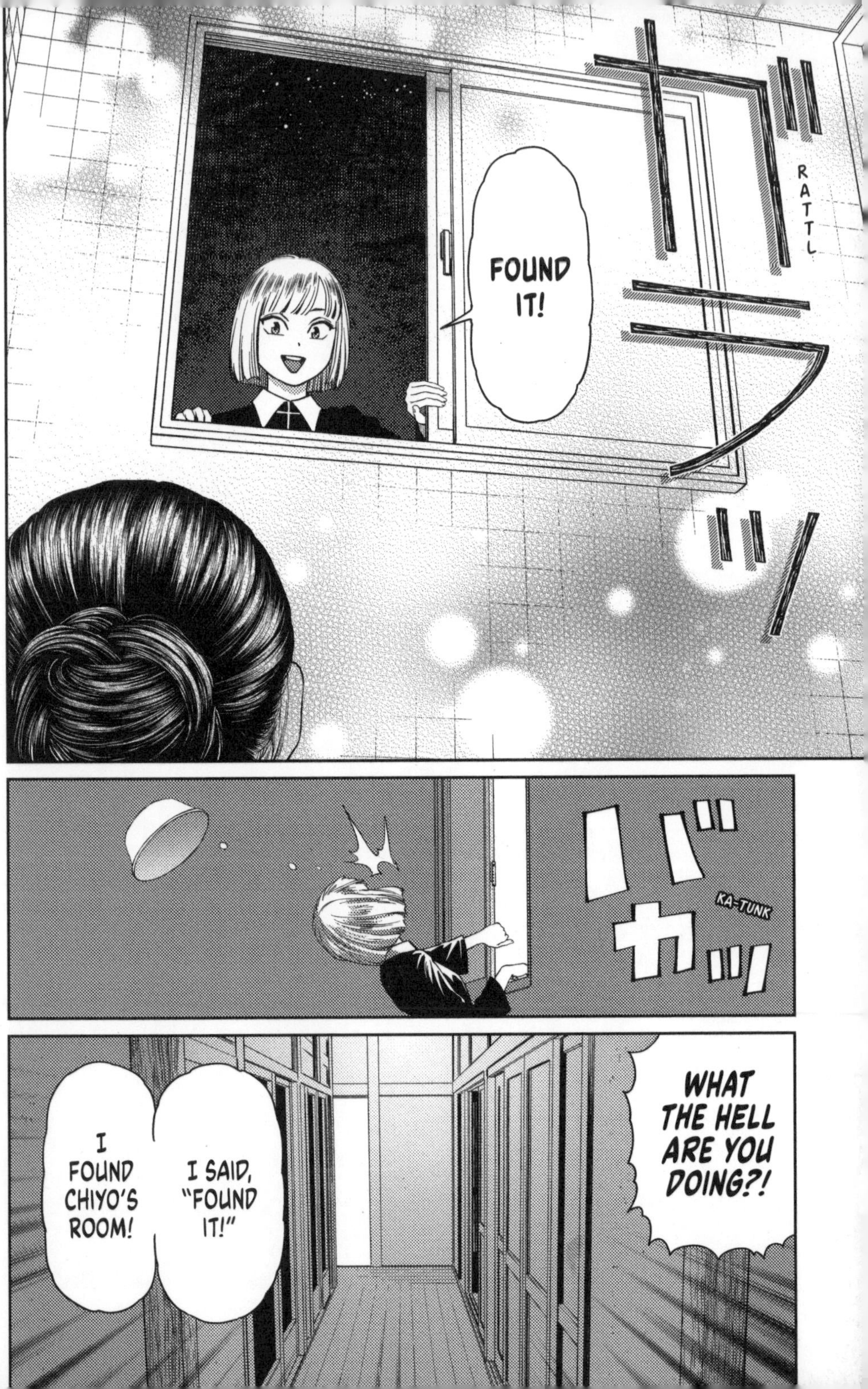
RATTL
FOUND IT!
KA-TUNK
WHAT THE HELL ARE YOU DOING?!
I SAID, "FOUND IT!"
I FOUND CHIYO'S ROOM!

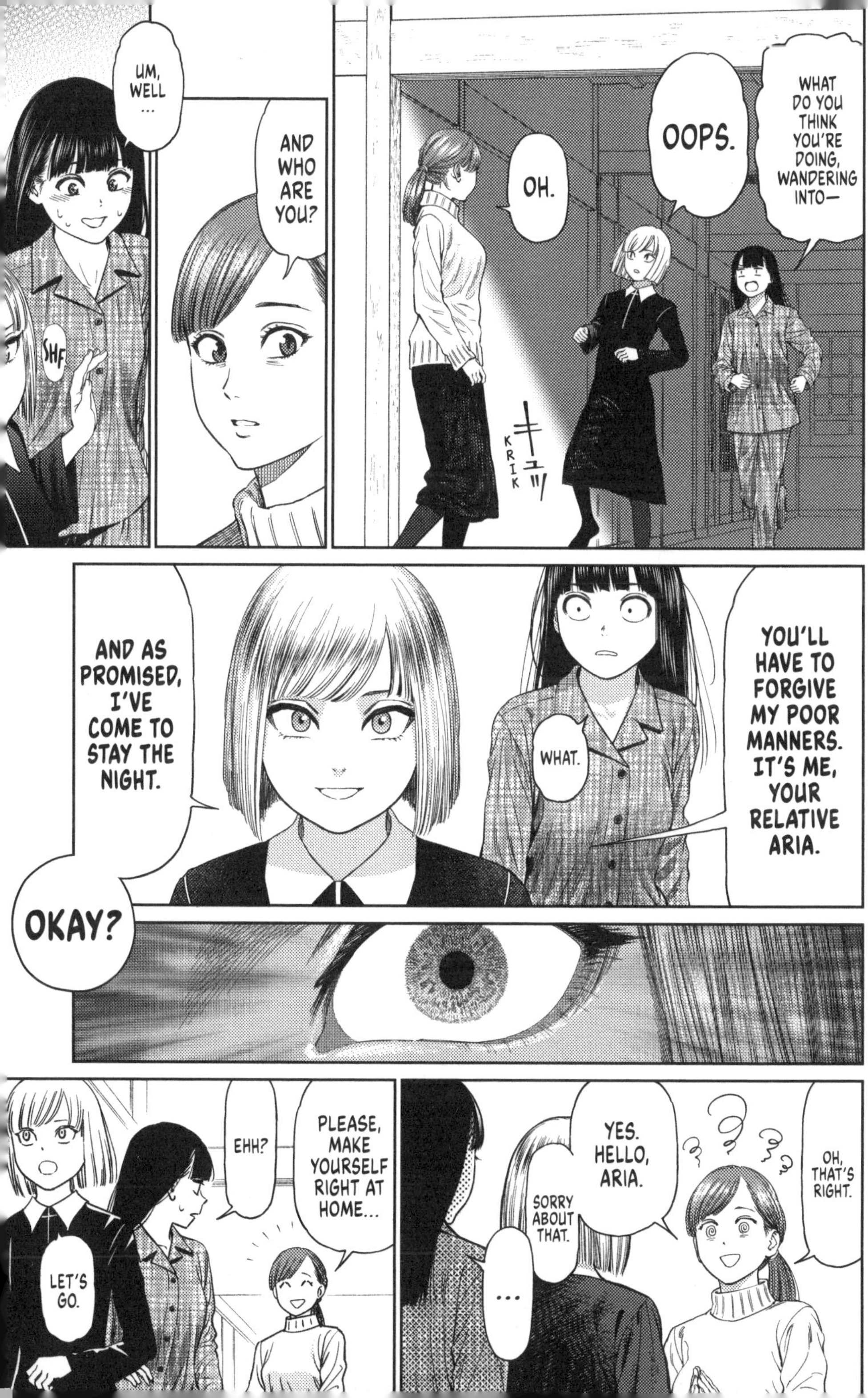
WHAT DO YOU THINK YOU'RE DOING, WANDERING INTO—
OOPS.
OH.
KRIK
AND WHO ARE YOU?
UM, WELL ...
SHF
YOU'LL HAVE TO FORGIVE MY POOR MANNERS. IT'S ME, YOUR RELATIVE ARIA.
WHAT.
AND AS PROMISED, I'VE COME TO STAY THE NIGHT.
OKAY?
OH, THAT'S RIGHT.
YES. HELLO, ARIA.
SORRY ABOUT THAT.
...
PLEASE, MAKE YOURSELF RIGHT AT HOME...
EHH?
LET'S GO.

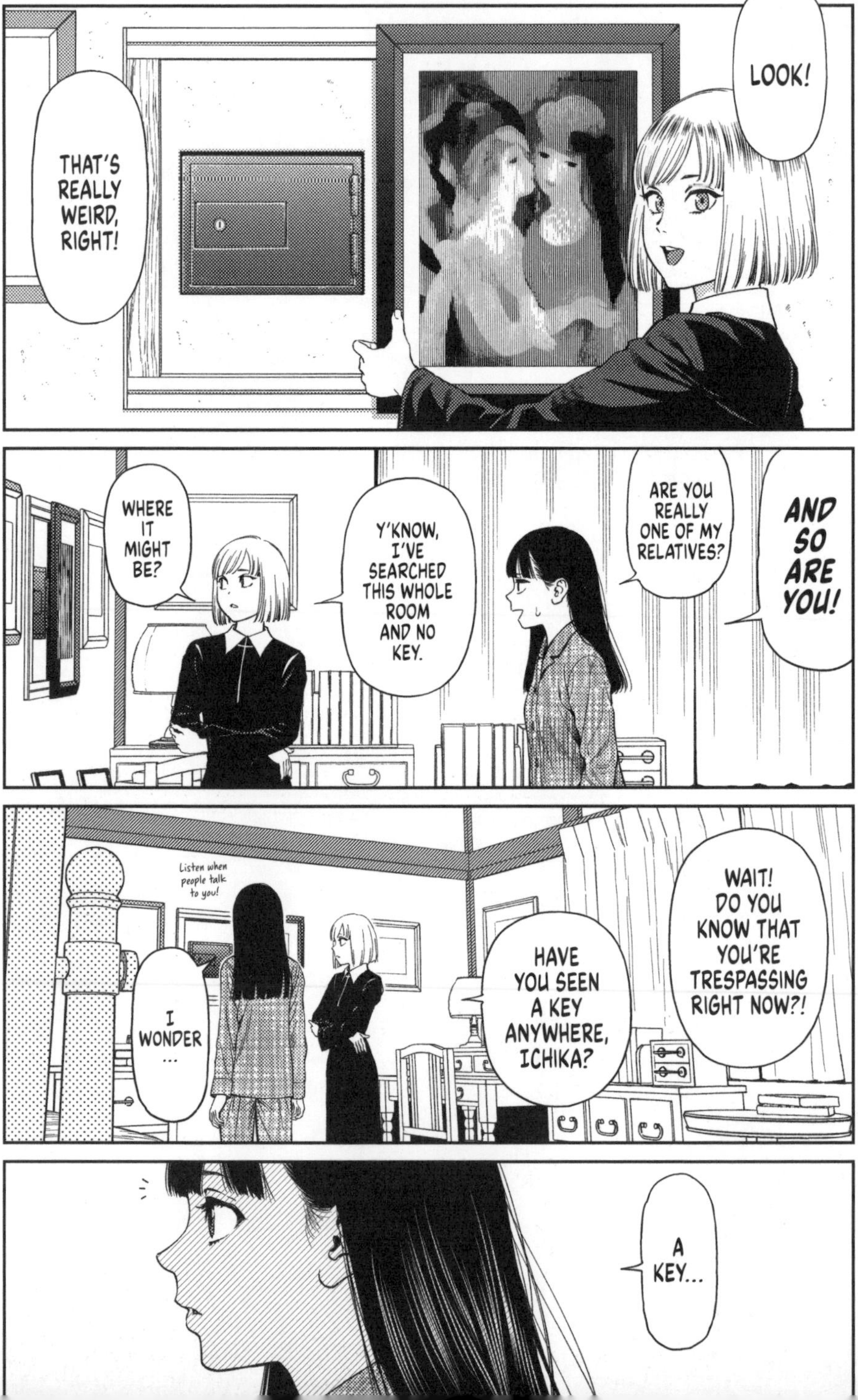
LOOK!
THAT'S REALLY WEIRD, RIGHT!
AND SO ARE YOU!
ARE YOU REALLY ONE OF MY RELATIVES?
Y'KNOW, I'VE SEARCHED THIS WHOLE ROOM AND NO KEY.
WHERE IT MIGHT BE?
WAIT! DO YOU KNOW THAT YOU'RE TRESPASSING RIGHT NOW?!
HAVE YOU SEEN A KEY ANYWHERE, ICHIKA?
Listen when people talk to you!
I WONDER ...
A KEY...

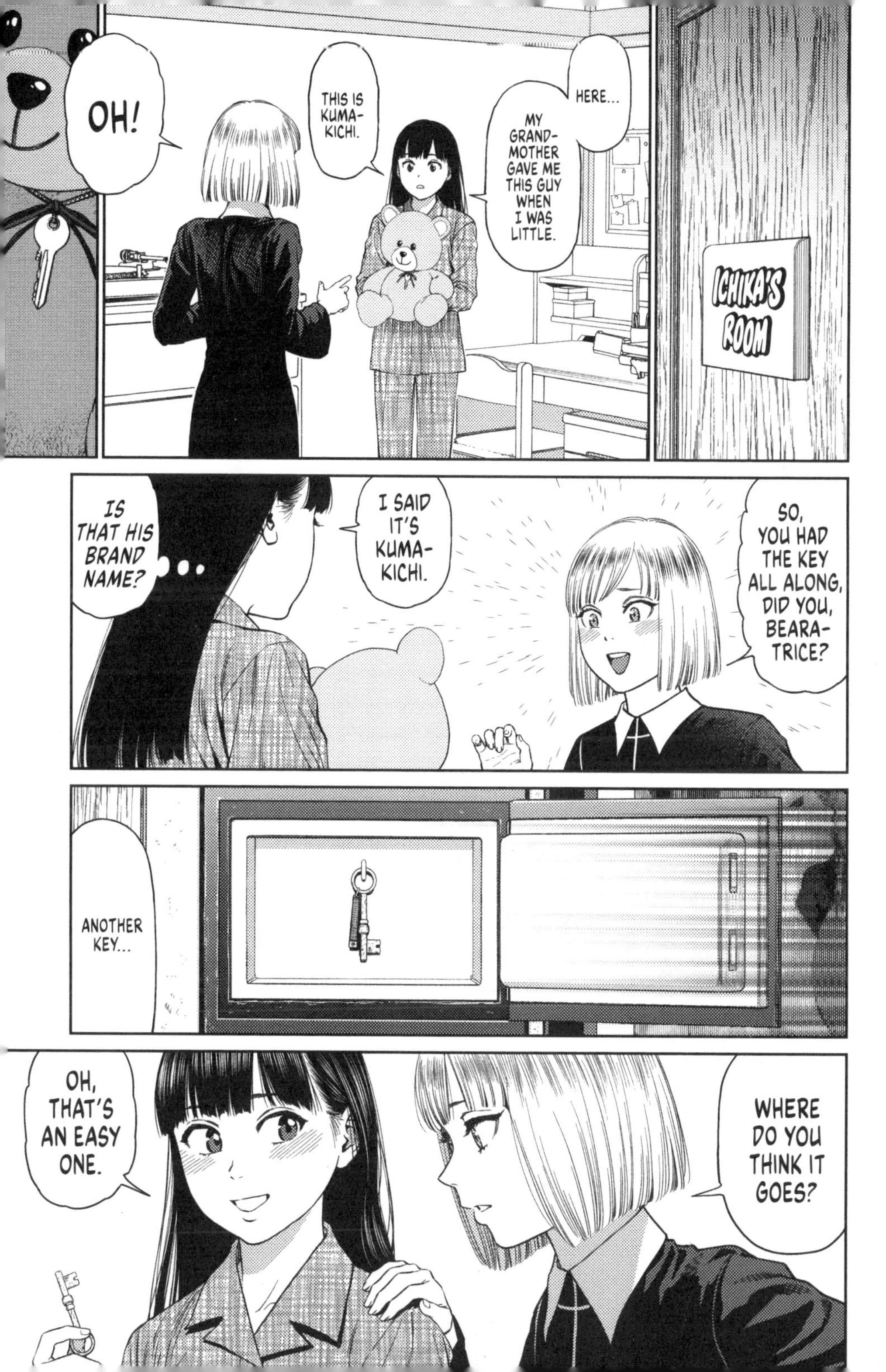
ICHIKA'S ROOM
HERE...
MY GRANDMOTHER GAVE ME THIS GUY WHEN I WAS LITTLE.
THIS IS KUMA-KICHI.
OH!
SO, YOU HAD THE KEY ALL ALONG, DID YOU, BEARATRICE?
I SAID IT'S KUMA-KICHI.
...
IS THAT HIS BRAND NAME?
ANOTHER KEY...
WHERE DO YOU THINK IT GOES?
OH, THAT'S AN EASY ONE.

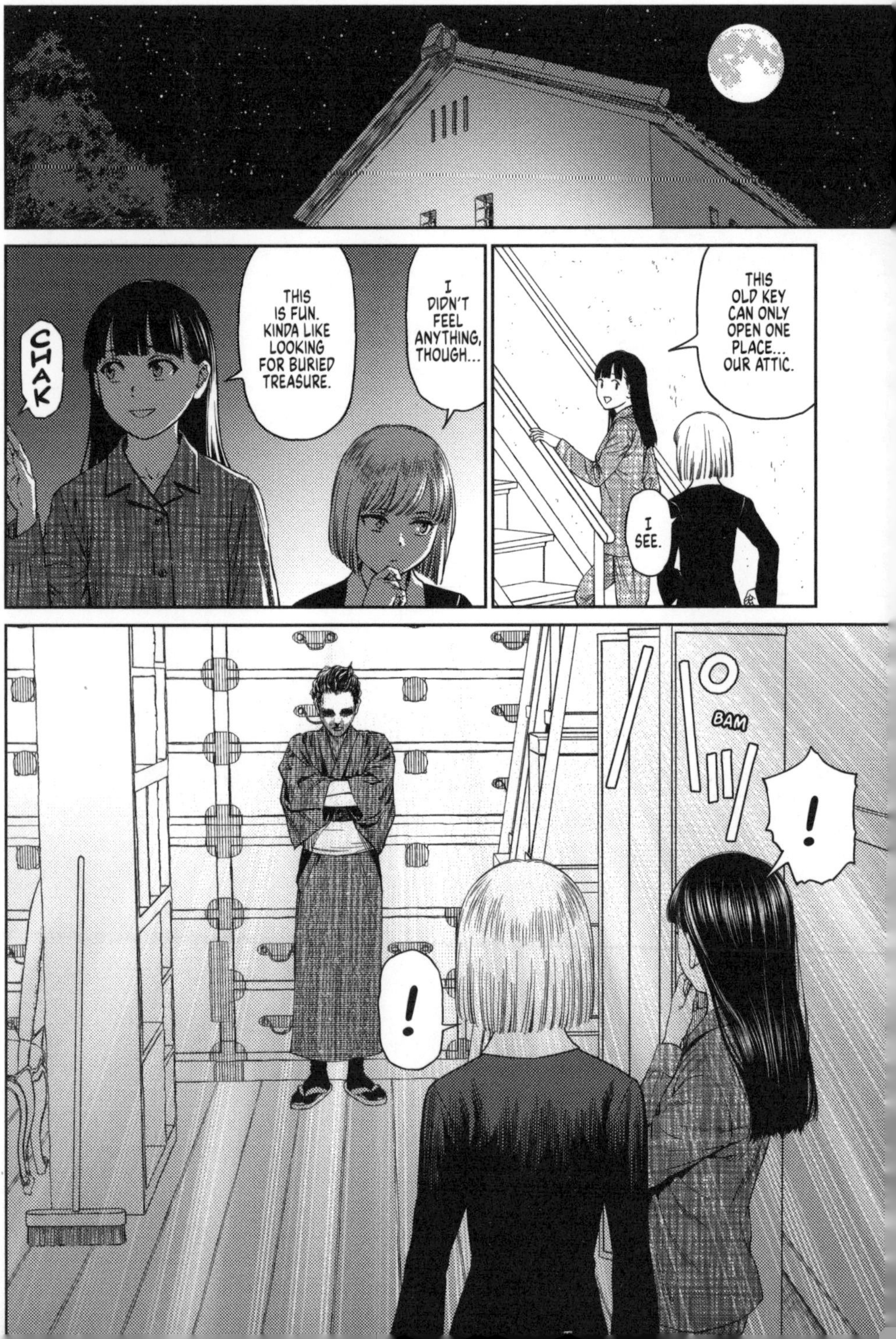
THIS OLD KEY CAN ONLY OPEN ONE PLACE... OUR ATTIC.
I SEE.
I DIDN'T FEEL ANYTHING, THOUGH...
THIS IS FUN. KINDA LIKE LOOKING FOR BURIED TREASURE.
CHAK
BAM
!
!

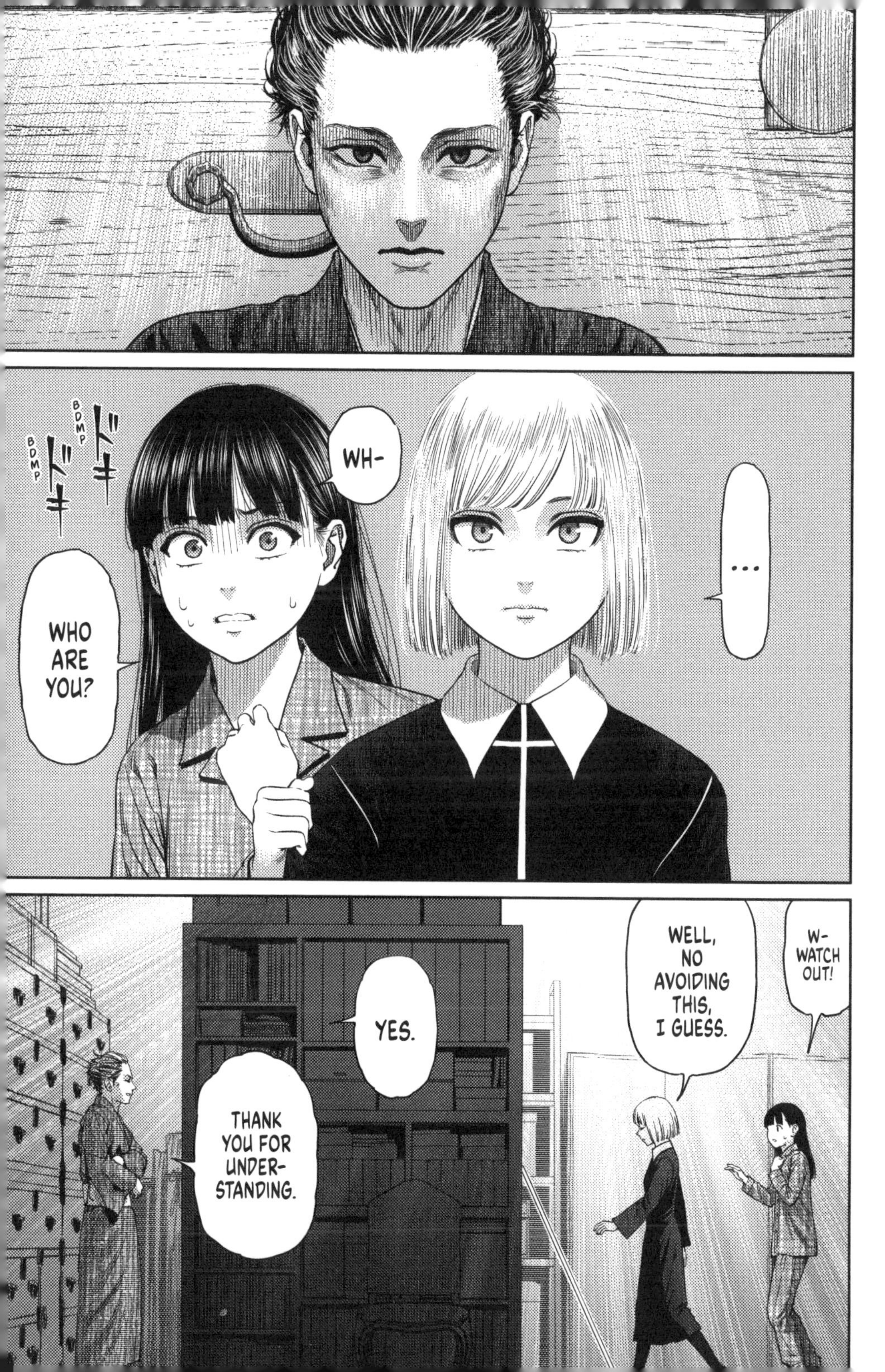
...
WH-
ドキ BDMP
ドキ BDMP
WHO ARE YOU?
W-WATCH OUT!
WELL, NO AVOIDING THIS, I GUESS.
YES.
THANK YOU FOR UNDER-STANDING.

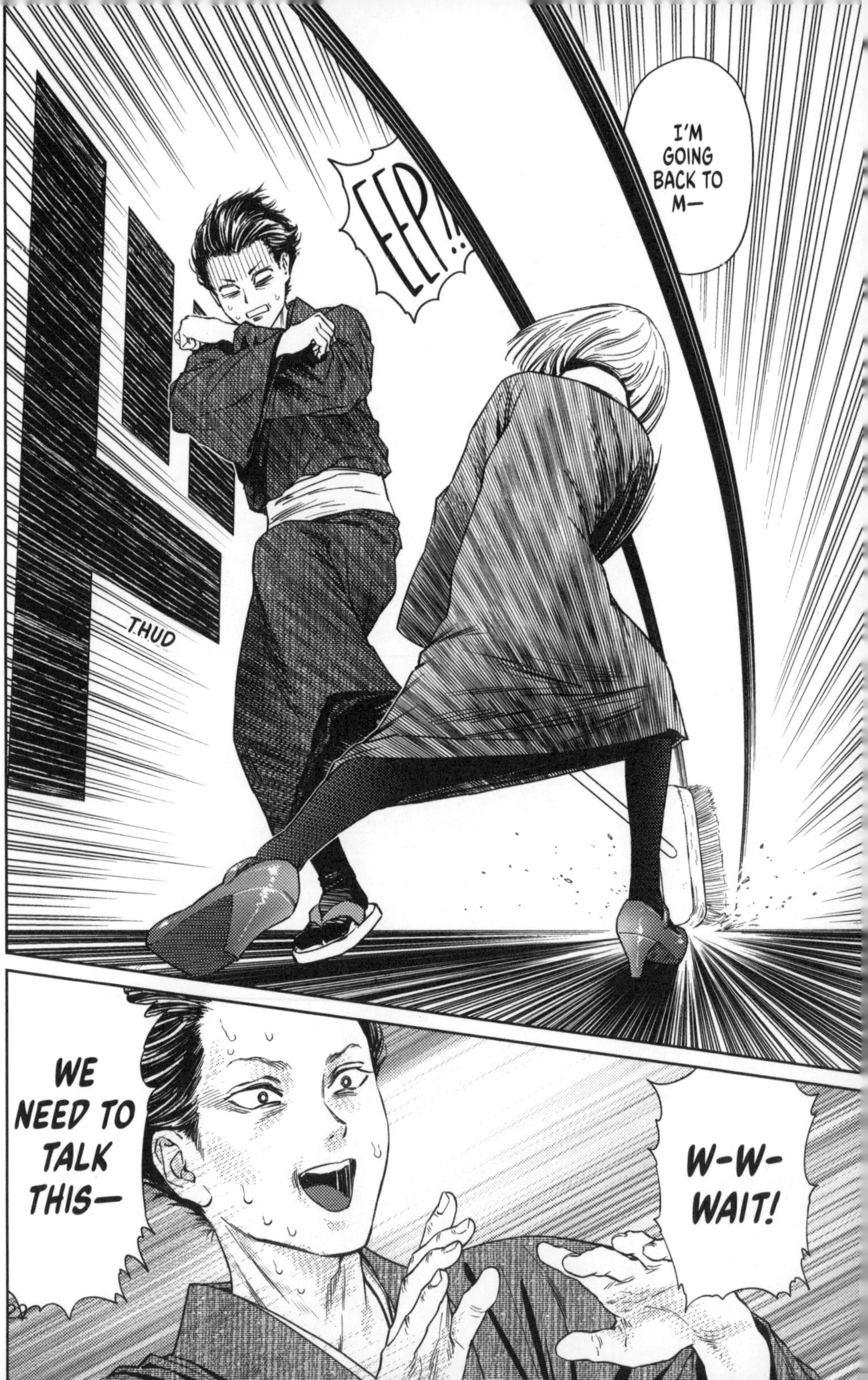
I'M GOING BACK TO M—
EEP!!
THUD
W-W-WAIT!
WE NEED TO TALK THIS—

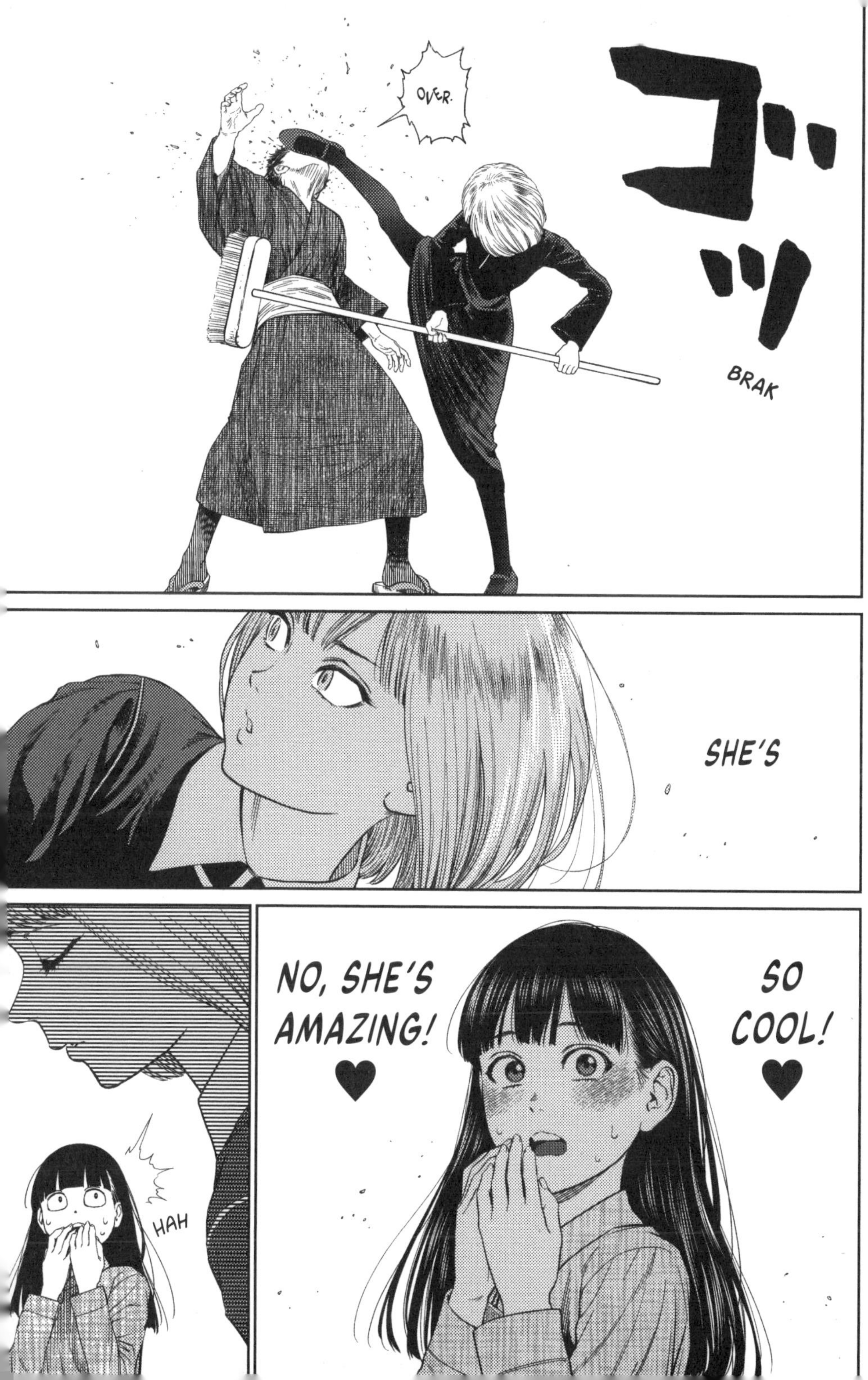
ゴッ
BRAK
OVER.
SHE'S
SO COOL! ♥
NO, SHE'S AMAZING! ♥
HAH

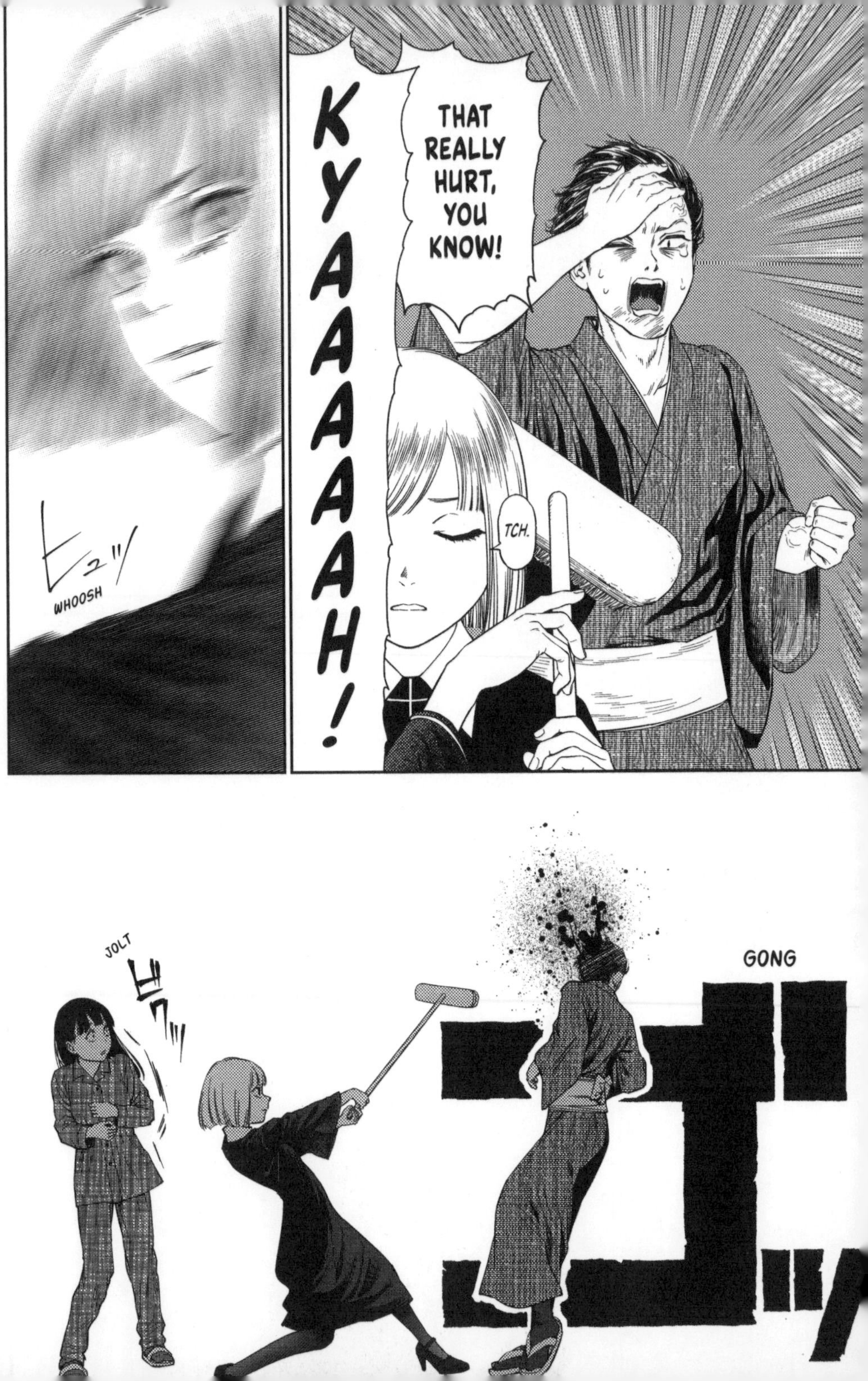
THAT REALLY HURT, YOU KNOW!
KYAAAAAAAH!
TCH.
ヒュッ
WHOOSH
GONG
ゴッ
JOLT
ビクッ

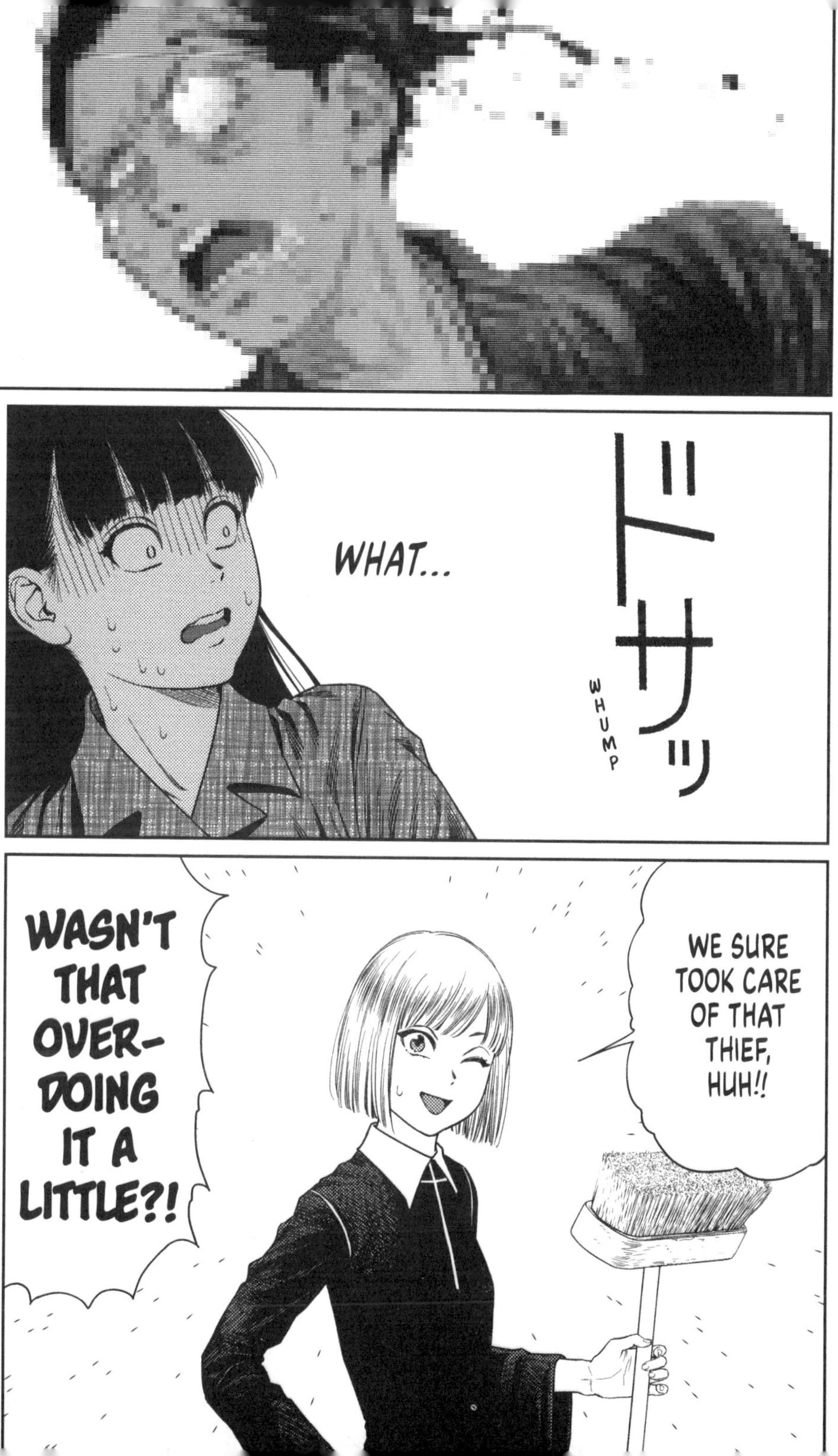
WHAT...
ドサッ
WHUMP
WE SURE TOOK CARE OF THAT THIEF, HUH!!
WASN'T THAT OVER-DOING IT A LITTLE?!

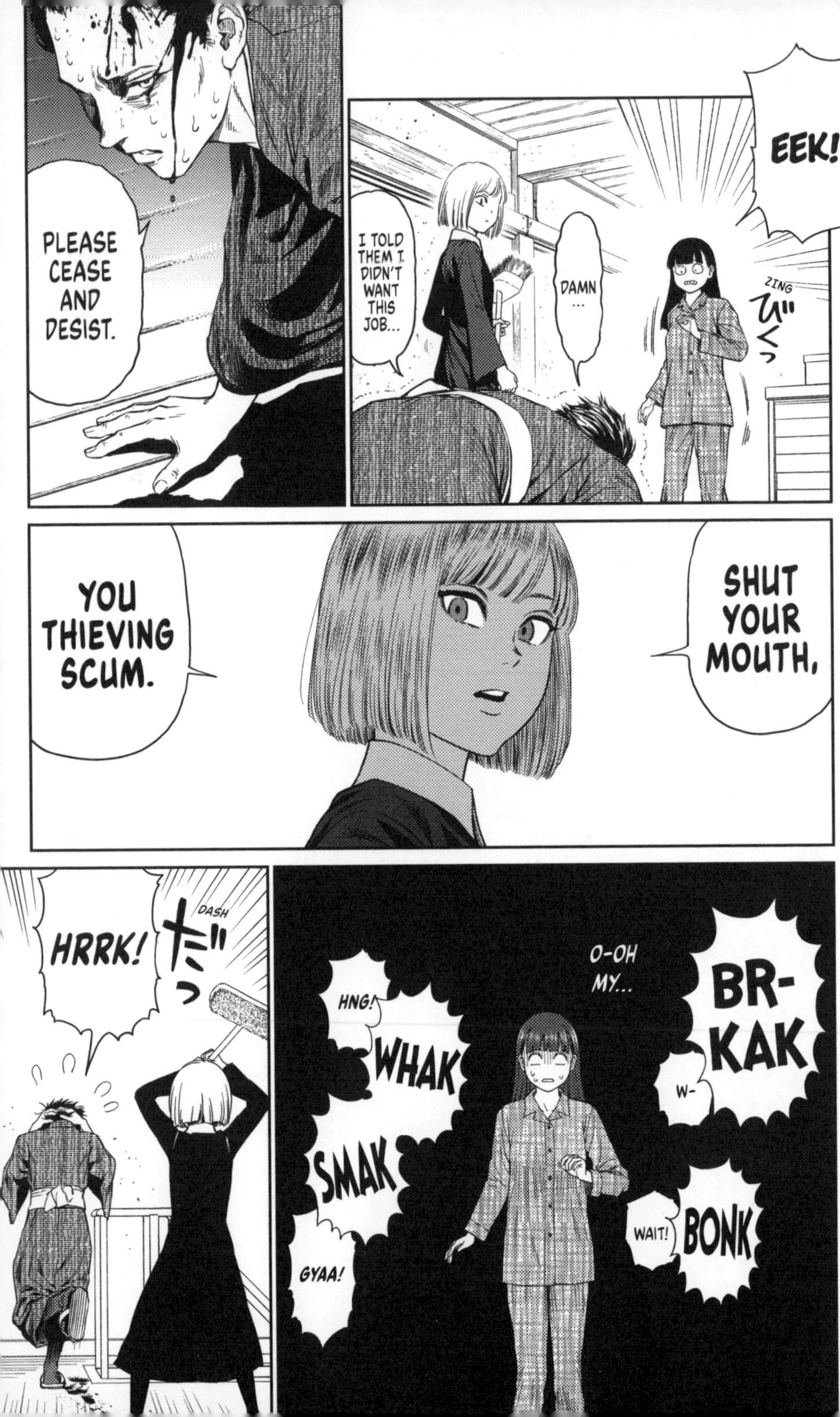
EEK!
ZING
びくっ
DAMN ...
I TOLD THEM I DIDN'T WANT THIS JOB...
PLEASE CEASE AND DESIST.
SHUT YOUR MOUTH,
YOU THIEVING SCUM.
BR-KAK
O-OH MY...
W-
WHAK
HNG!
BONK
WAIT!
SMAK
GYAA!
DASH
だっ
HRRK!

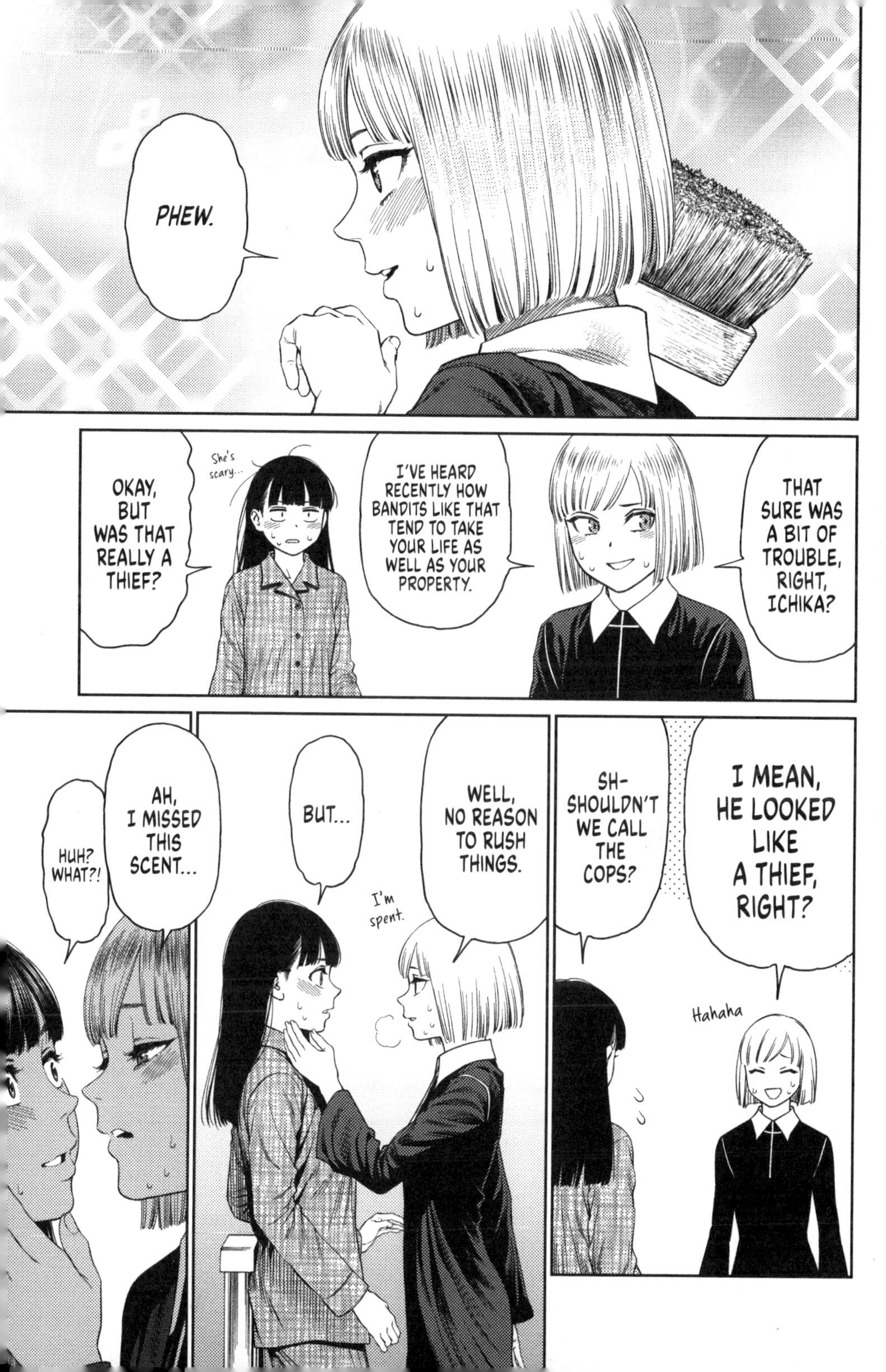
PHEW.
THAT SURE WAS A BIT OF TROUBLE, RIGHT, ICHIKA?
I'VE HEARD RECENTLY HOW BANDITS LIKE THAT TEND TO TAKE YOUR LIFE AS WELL AS YOUR PROPERTY.
She's scary...
OKAY, BUT WAS THAT REALLY A THIEF?
I MEAN, HE LOOKED LIKE A THIEF, RIGHT?
Hahaha
SH- SHOULDN'T WE CALL THE COPS?
WELL, NO REASON TO RUSH THINGS.
I'm spent.
BUT...
AH, I MISSED THIS SCENT...
HUH? WHAT?!

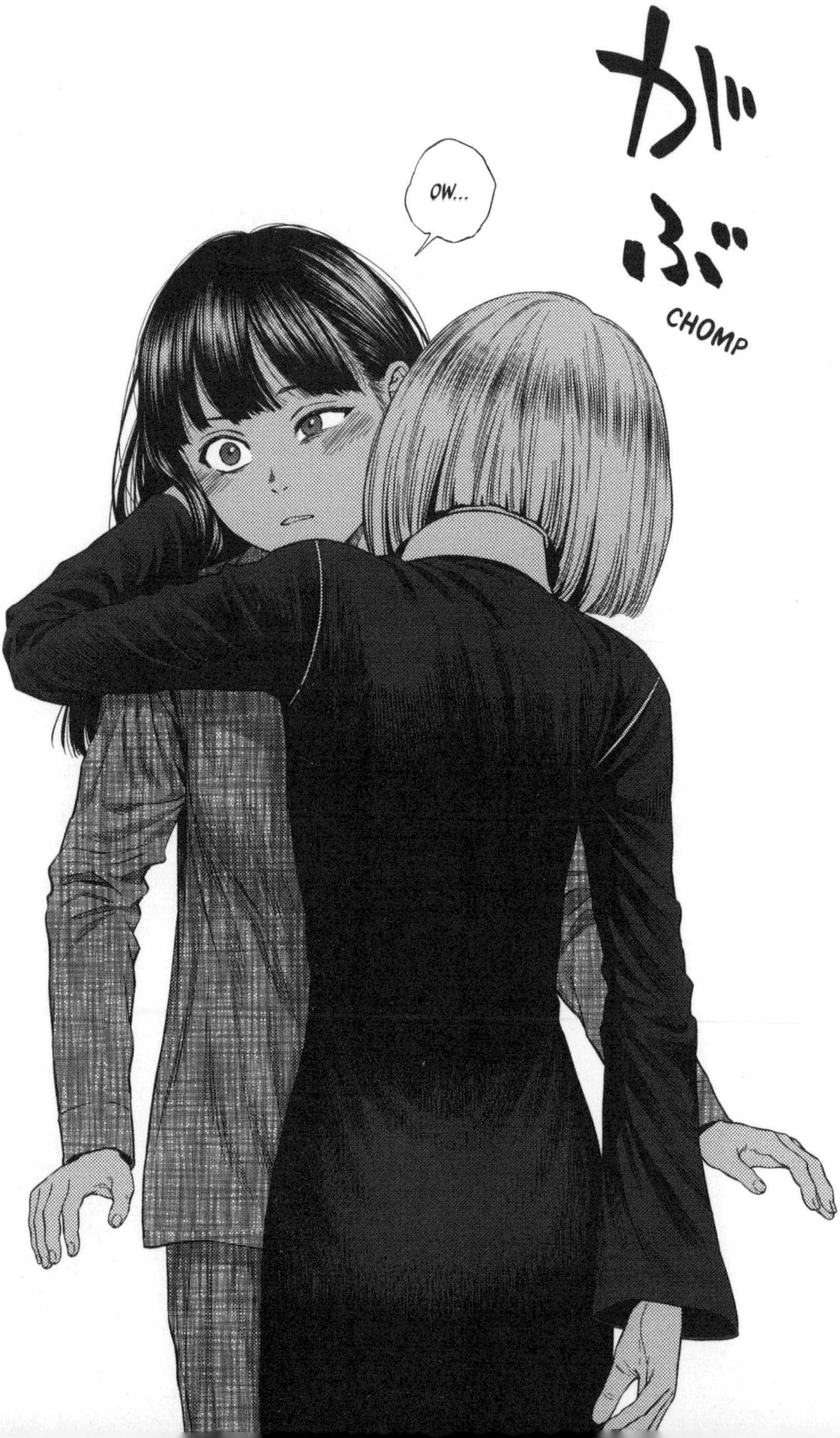
がぶ
CHOMP
OW...

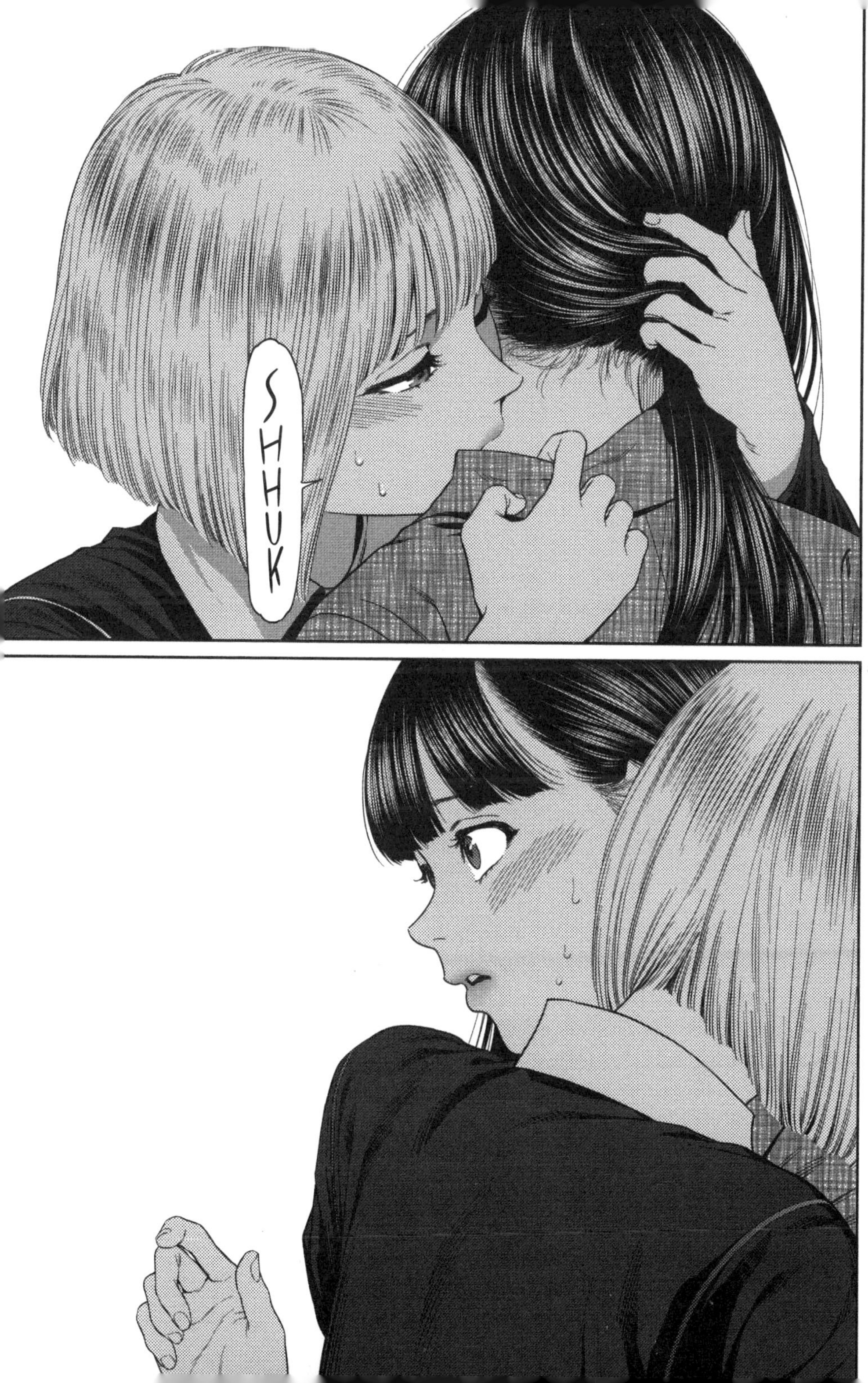
SHHUK

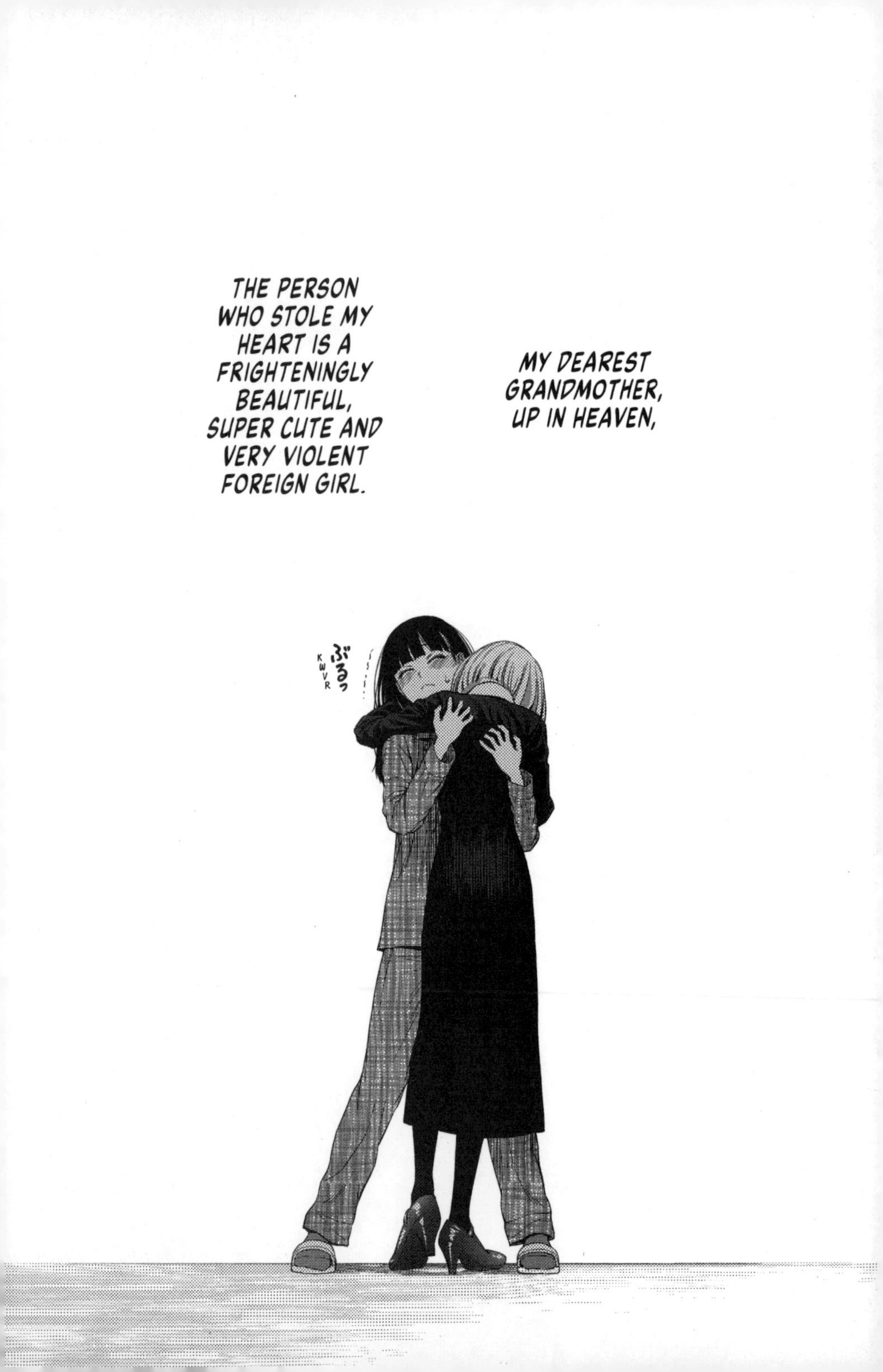
MY DEAREST GRANDMOTHER, UP IN HEAVEN,
THE PERSON WHO STOLE MY HEART IS A FRIGHTENINGLY BEAUTIFUL, SUPER CUTE AND VERY VIOLENT FOREIGN GIRL.
ぶるっ
KWVR

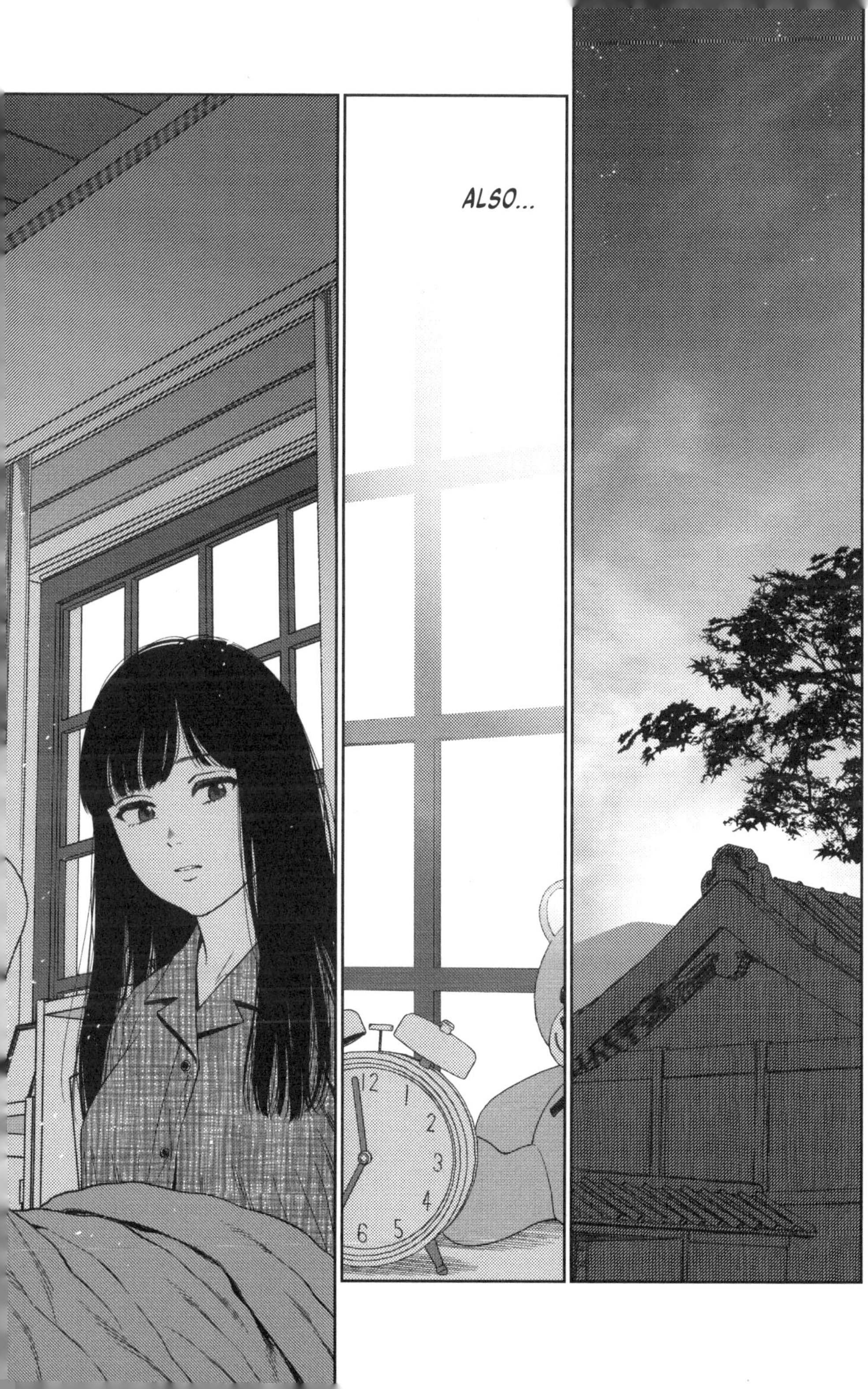
ALSO...

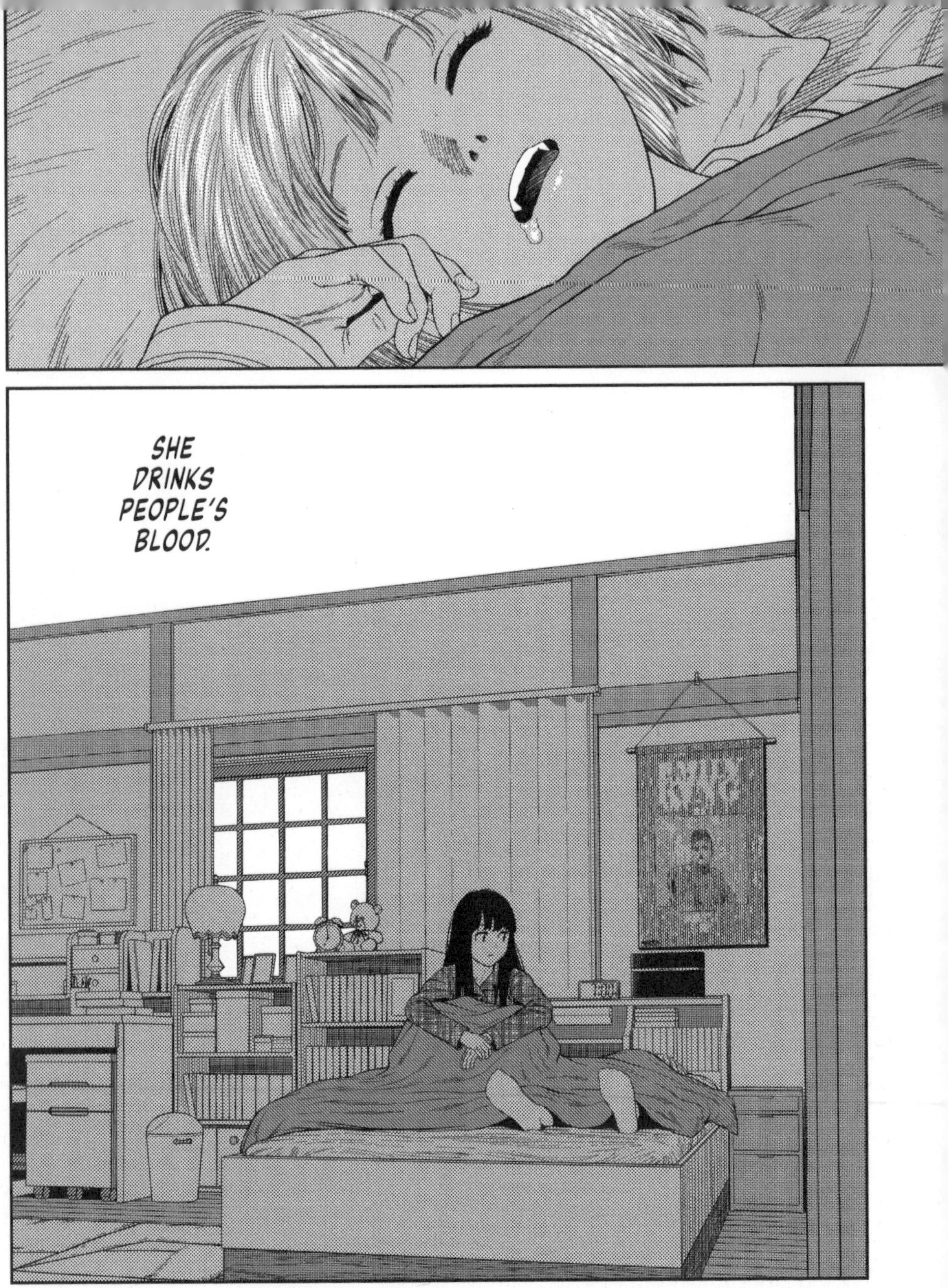
SHE DRINKS PEOPLE'S BLOOD.

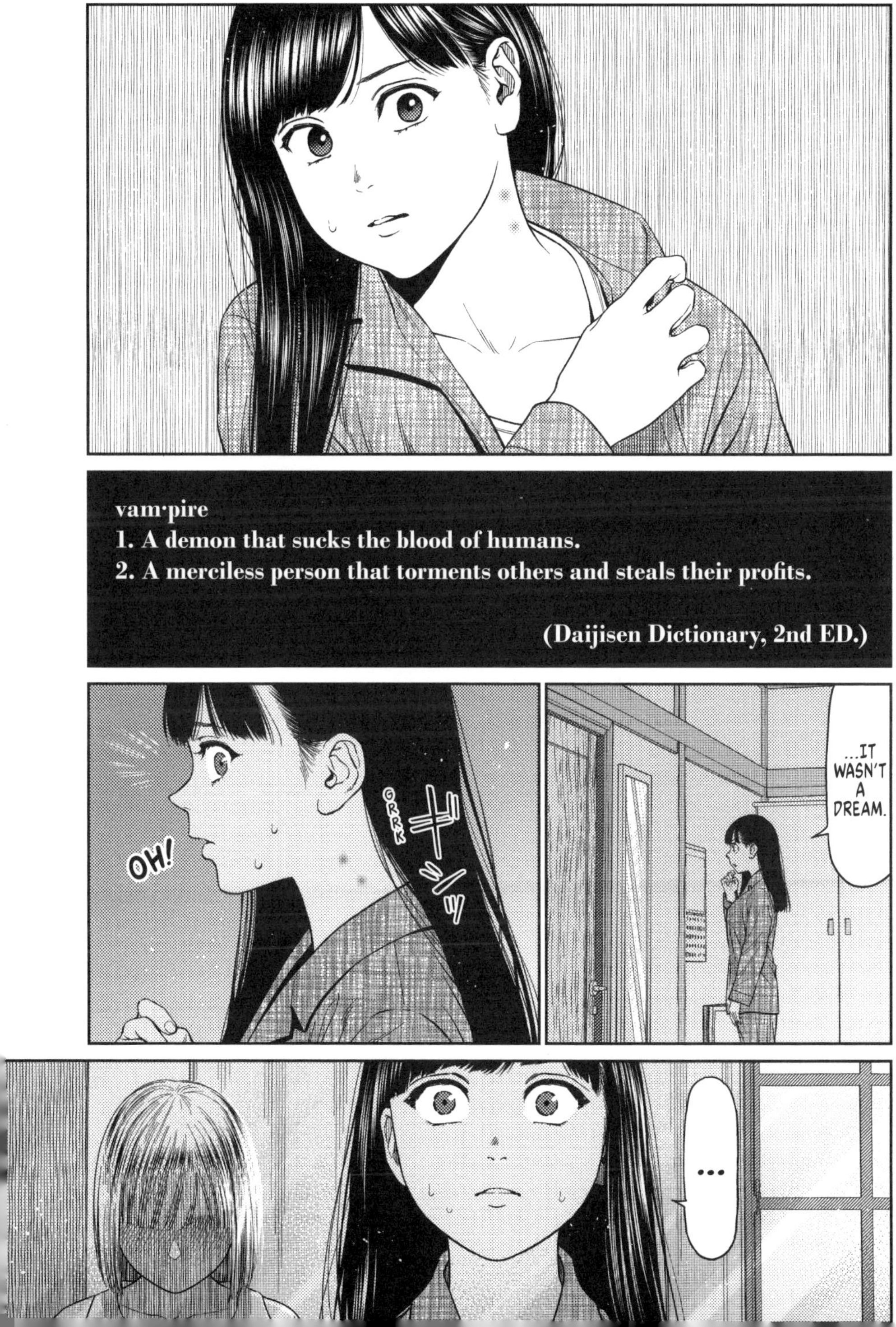
vam·pire
1. A demon that sucks the blood of humans.
2. A merciless person that torments others and steals their profits.
(Daijisen Dictionary, 2nd ED.)
...IT WASN'T A DREAM.
GRRK
OH!
...

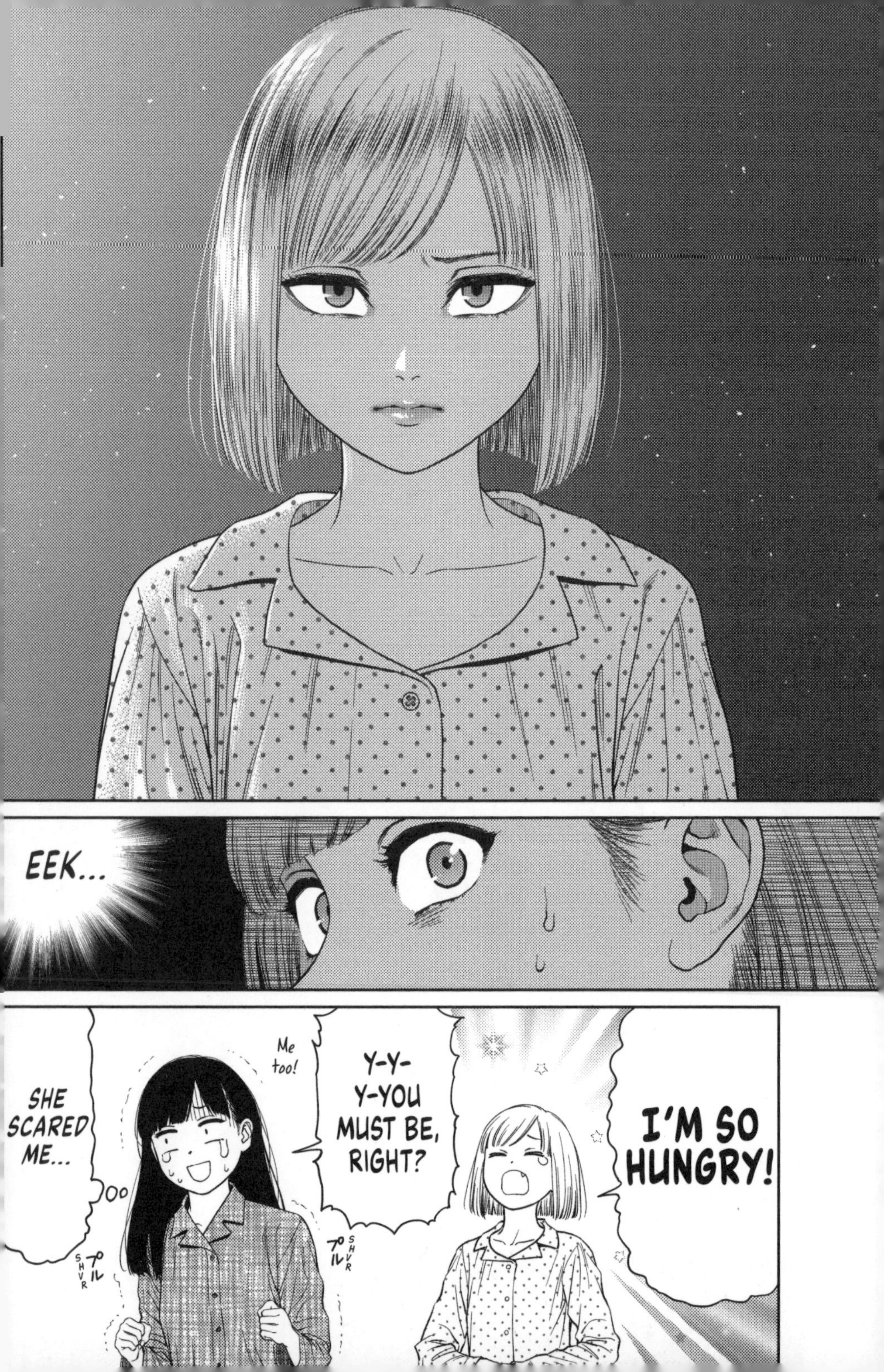
EEK...
I'M SO HUNGRY!
Y-Y-Y-YOU MUST BE, RIGHT?
Me too!
SHVR プル
SHE SCARED ME...
SHVR プル

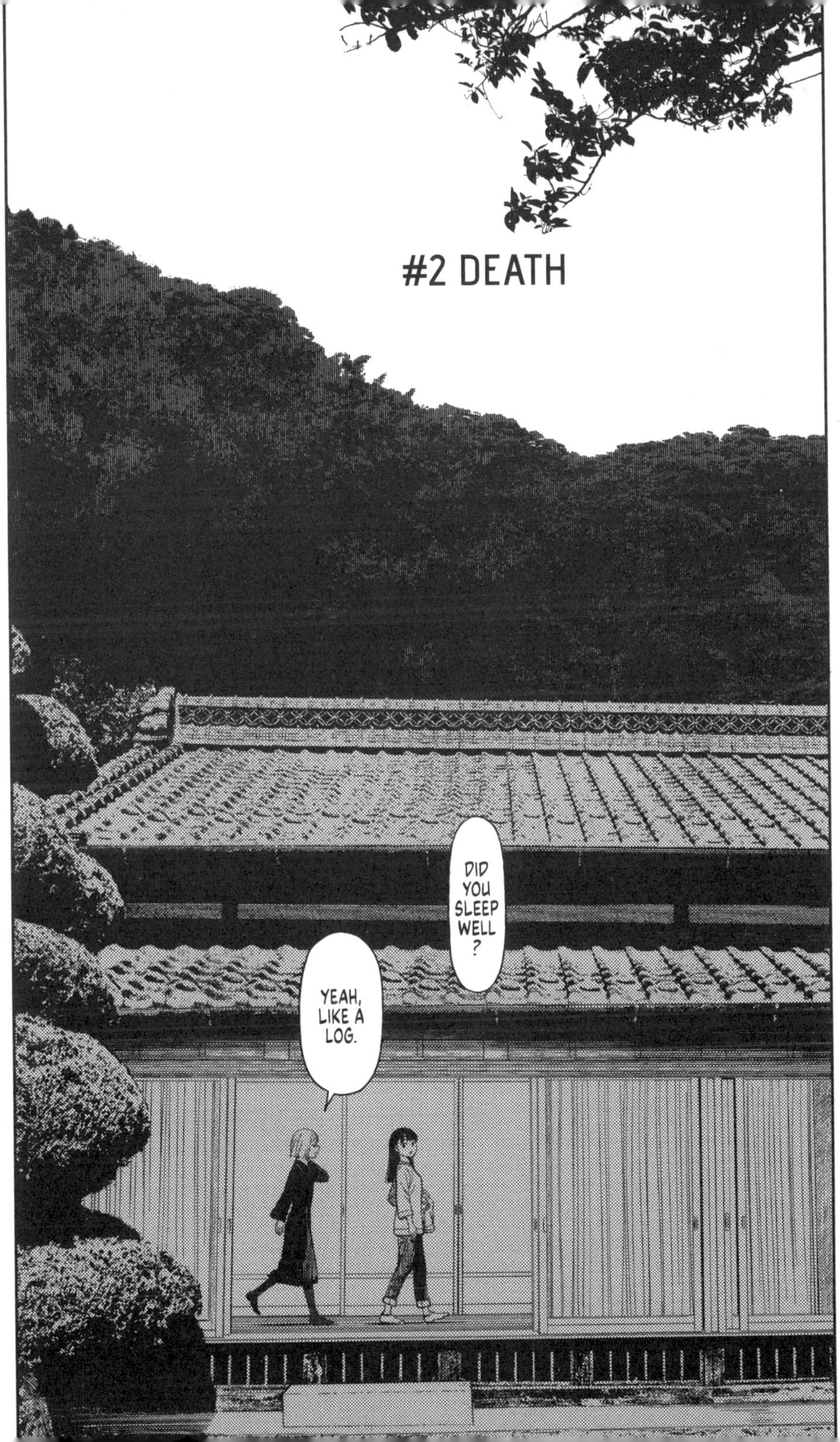
#2 DEATH
DID YOU SLEEP WELL?
YEAH, LIKE A LOG.

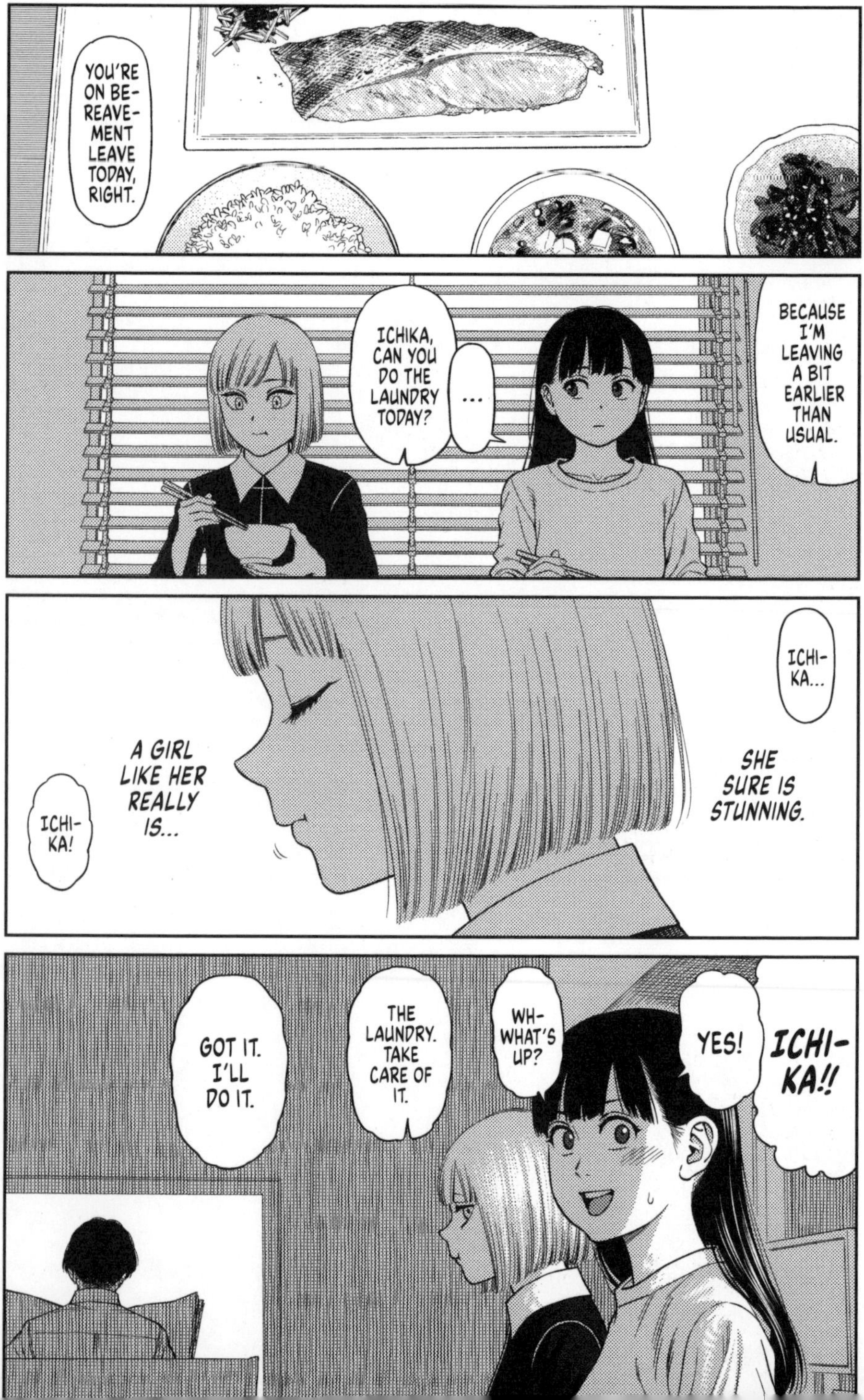
YOU'RE ON BEREAVEMENT LEAVE TODAY, RIGHT.
BECAUSE I'M LEAVING A BIT EARLIER THAN USUAL.
...
ICHIKA, CAN YOU DO THE LAUNDRY TODAY?
ICHIKA...
SHE SURE IS STUNNING.
A GIRL LIKE HER REALLY IS...
ICHIKA!
ICHIKA!!
YES!
WH-WHAT'S UP?
THE LAUNDRY. TAKE CARE OF IT.
GOT IT. I'LL DO IT.

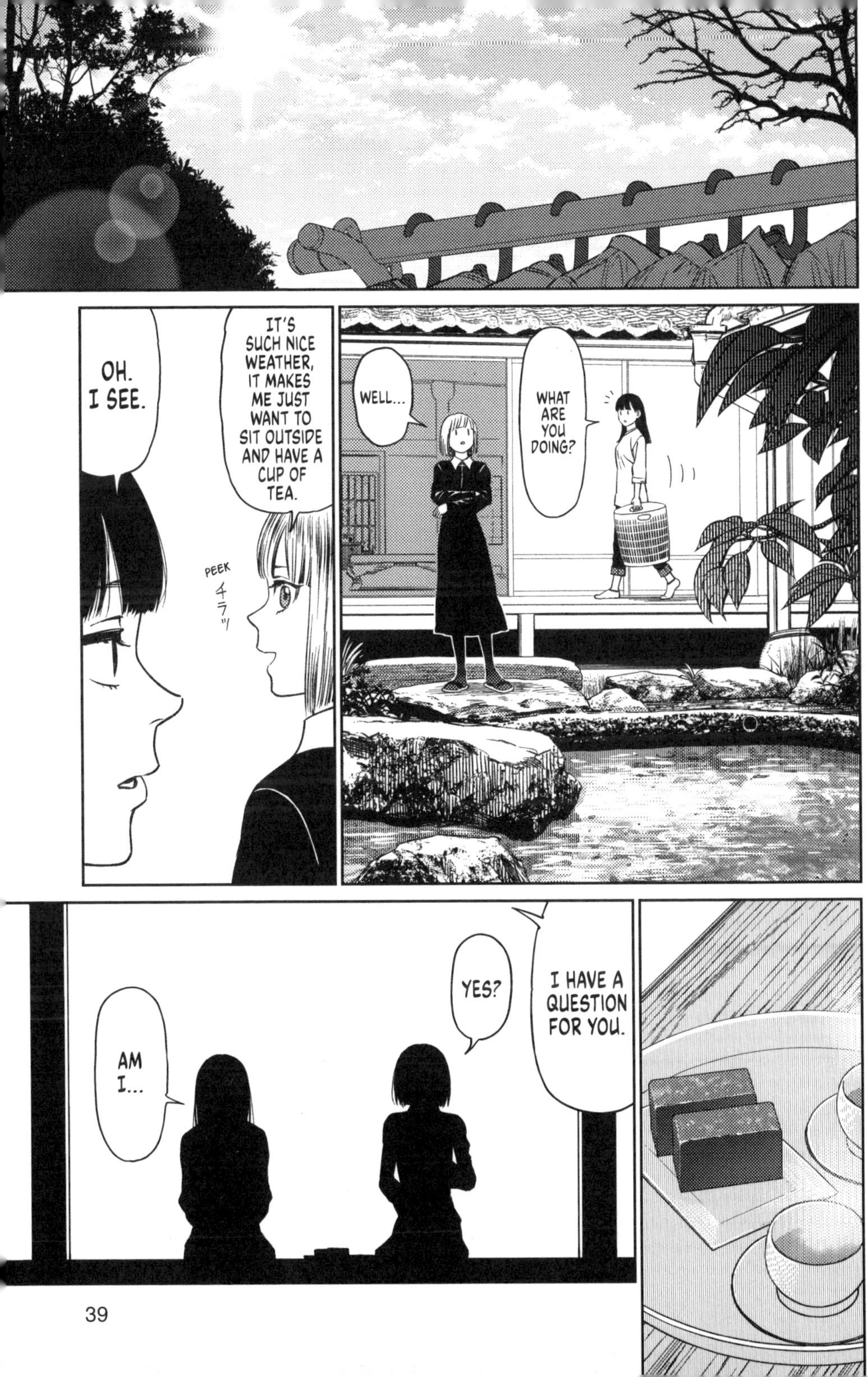
WHAT ARE YOU DOING?
WELL...
IT'S SUCH NICE WEATHER, IT MAKES ME JUST WANT TO SIT OUTSIDE AND HAVE A CUP OF TEA.
PEEK
チラッ
OH. I SEE.
I HAVE A QUESTION FOR YOU.
YES?
AM I...

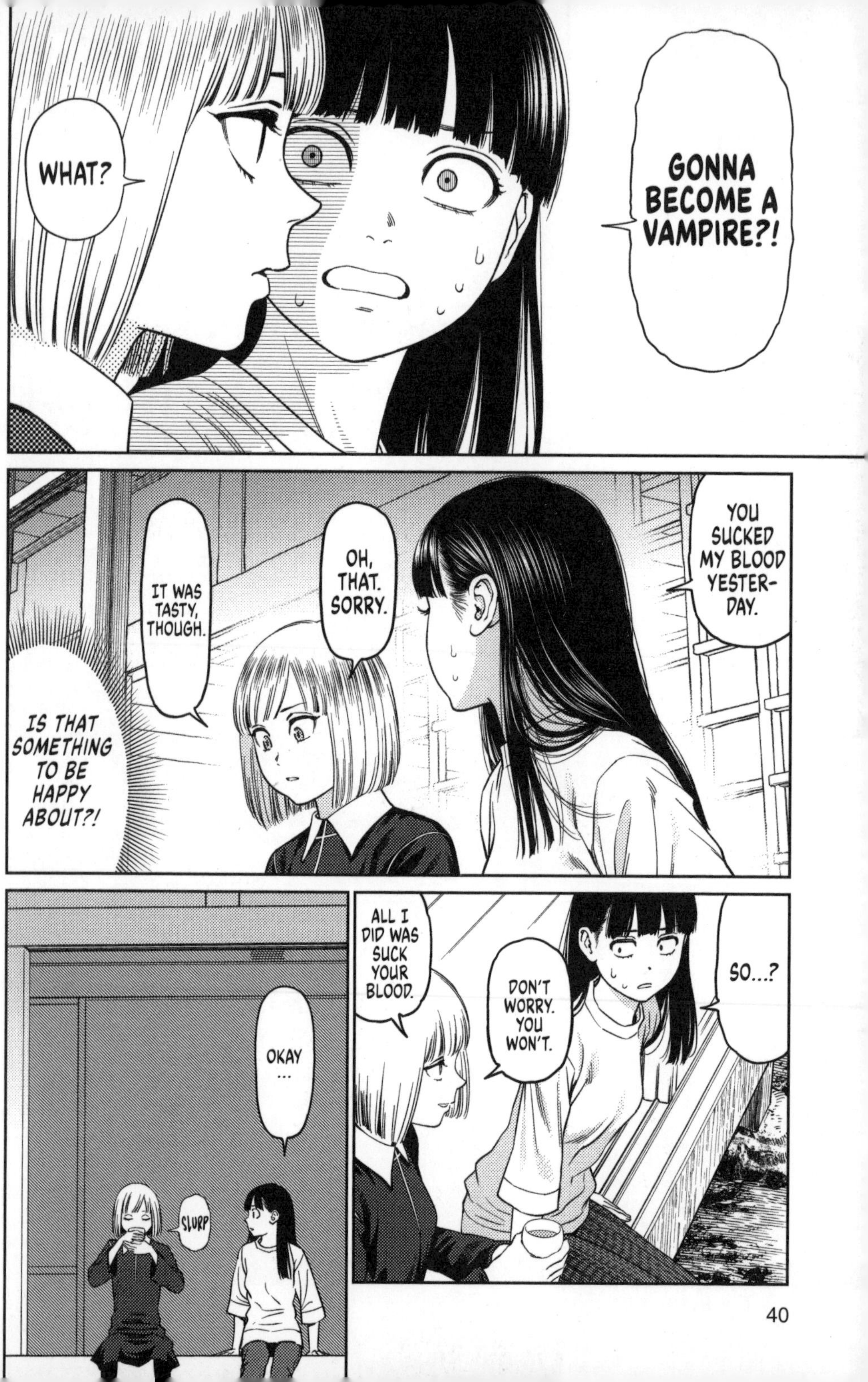
GONNA BECOME A VAMPIRE?!
WHAT?
YOU SUCKED MY BLOOD YESTER-DAY.
OH, THAT. SORRY.
IT WAS TASTY, THOUGH.
IS THAT SOMETHING TO BE HAPPY ABOUT?!
SO...?
DON'T WORRY. YOU WON'T.
ALL I DID WAS SUCK YOUR BLOOD.
OKAY ...
SLURP

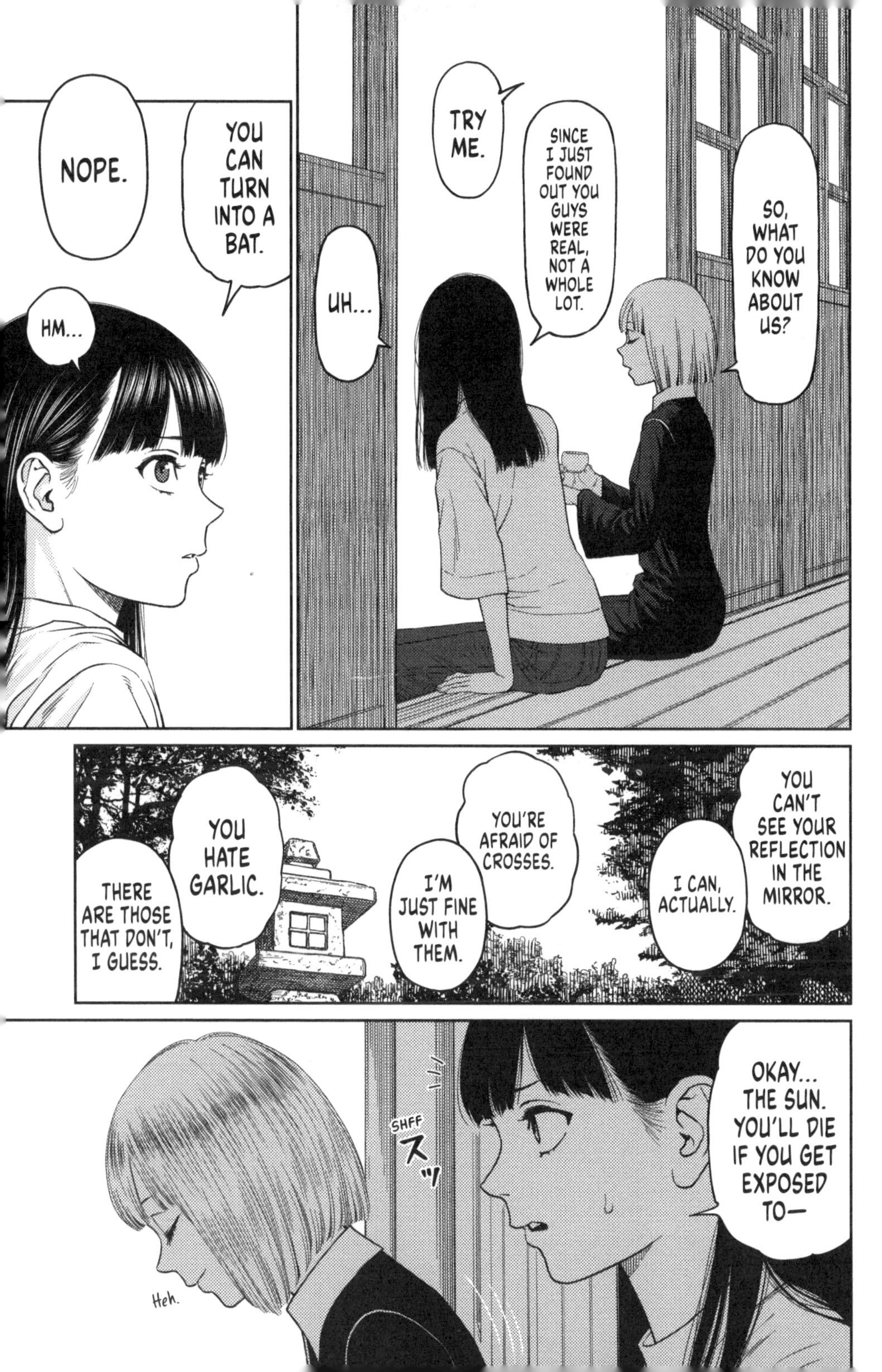
SO, WHAT DO YOU KNOW ABOUT US?
SINCE I JUST FOUND OUT YOU GUYS WERE REAL, NOT A WHOLE LOT.
TRY ME.
UH...
YOU CAN TURN INTO A BAT.
NOPE.
HM...
YOU CAN'T SEE YOUR REFLECTION IN THE MIRROR.
I CAN, ACTUALLY.
YOU'RE AFRAID OF CROSSES.
I'M JUST FINE WITH THEM.
YOU HATE GARLIC.
THERE ARE THOSE THAT DON'T, I GUESS.
OKAY... THE SUN. YOU'LL DIE IF YOU GET EXPOSED TO—
SHFF
スッ
Heh.

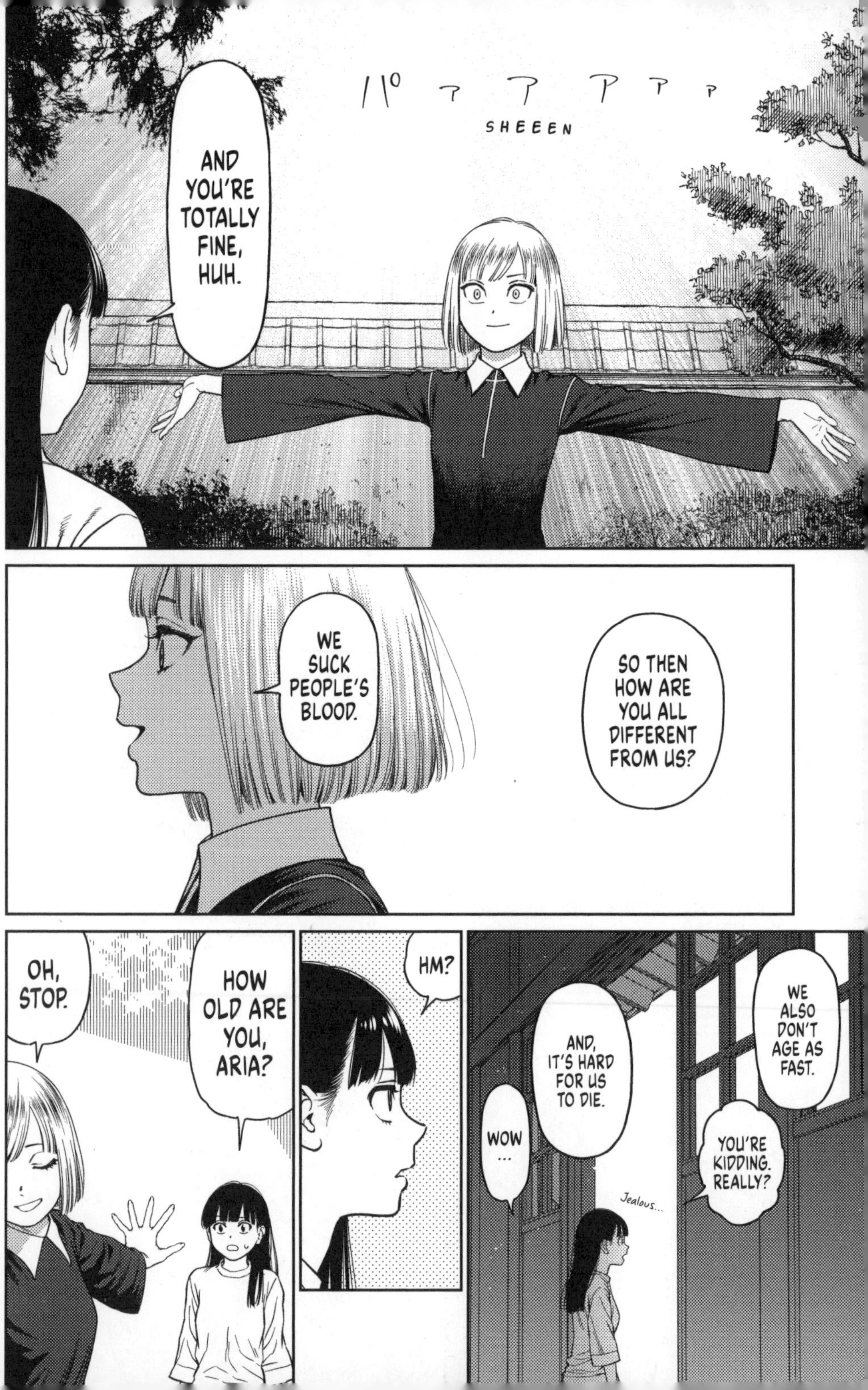
パァアアァァ
SHEEEN
AND YOU'RE TOTALLY FINE, HUH.
SO THEN HOW ARE YOU ALL DIFFERENT FROM US?
WE SUCK PEOPLE'S BLOOD.
WE ALSO DON'T AGE AS FAST.
AND, IT'S HARD FOR US TO DIE.
YOU'RE KIDDING. REALLY?
WOW...
Jealous...
HM?
HOW OLD ARE YOU, ARIA?
OH, STOP.

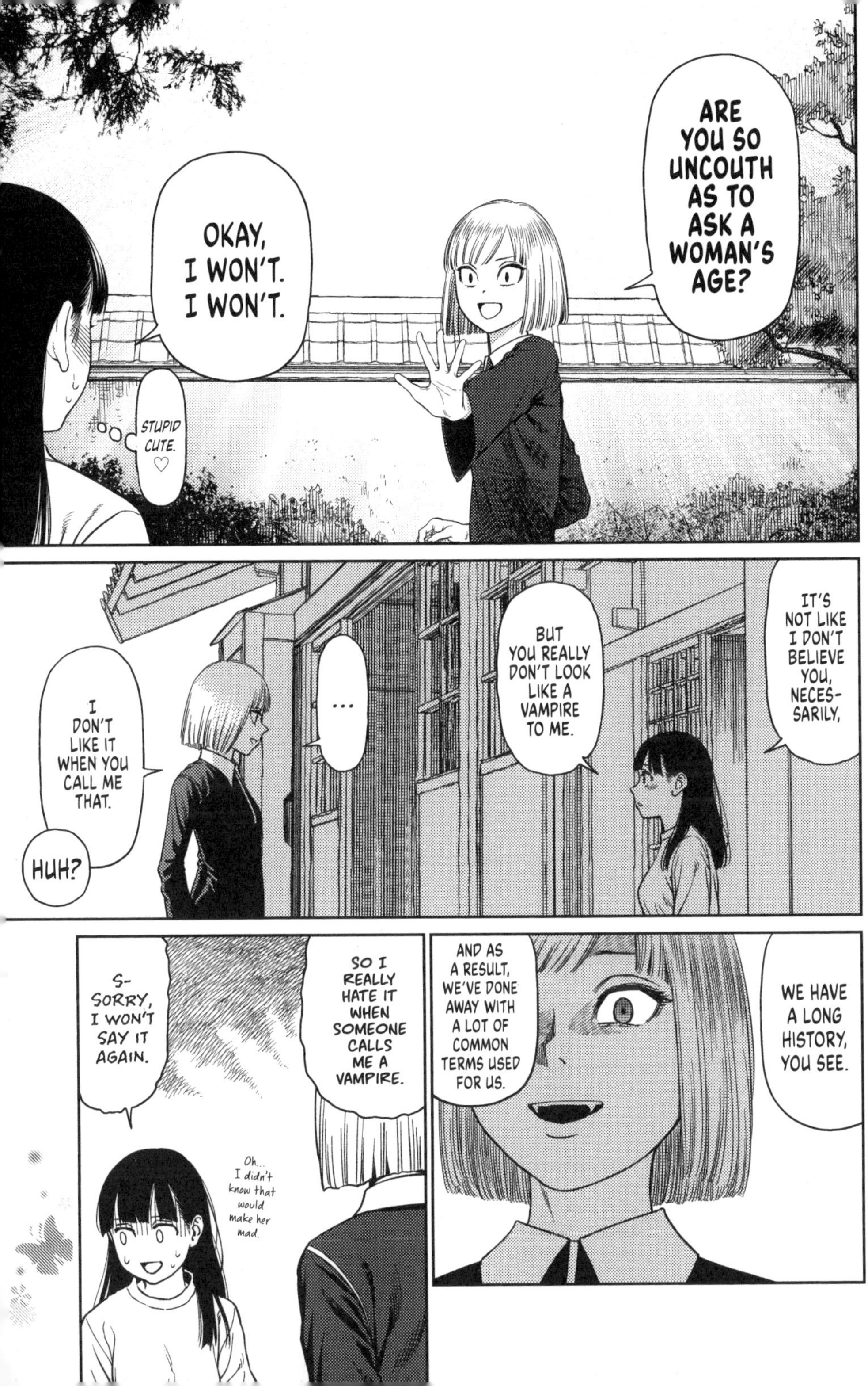
ARE YOU SO UNCOUTH AS TO ASK A WOMAN'S AGE?
OKAY, I WON'T. I WON'T.
STUPID CUTE. ♡
IT'S NOT LIKE I DON'T BELIEVE YOU, NECES-SARILY,
BUT YOU REALLY DON'T LOOK LIKE A VAMPIRE TO ME.
...
I DON'T LIKE IT WHEN YOU CALL ME THAT.
HUH?
WE HAVE A LONG HISTORY, YOU SEE.
AND AS A RESULT, WE'VE DONE AWAY WITH A LOT OF COMMON TERMS USED FOR US.
SO I REALLY HATE IT WHEN SOMEONE CALLS ME A VAMPIRE.
S-SORRY, I WON'T SAY IT AGAIN.
Oh... I didn't know that would make her mad.

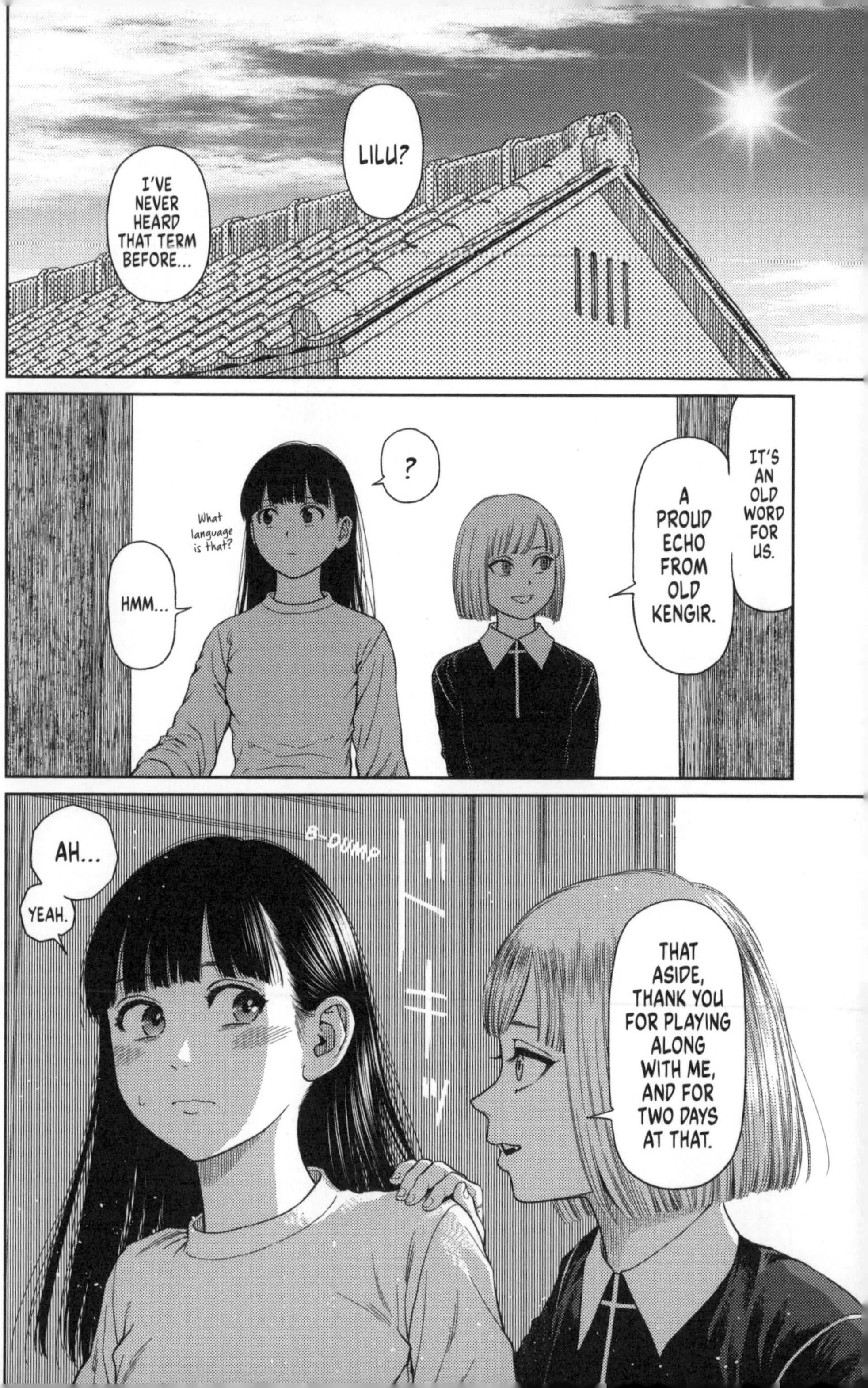
LILU?
I'VE NEVER HEARD THAT TERM BEFORE...
IT'S AN OLD WORD FOR US.
A PROUD ECHO FROM OLD KENGIR.
?
What language is that?
HMM...
THAT ASIDE, THANK YOU FOR PLAYING ALONG WITH ME, AND FOR TWO DAYS AT THAT.
B-DUMP
AH...
YEAH.

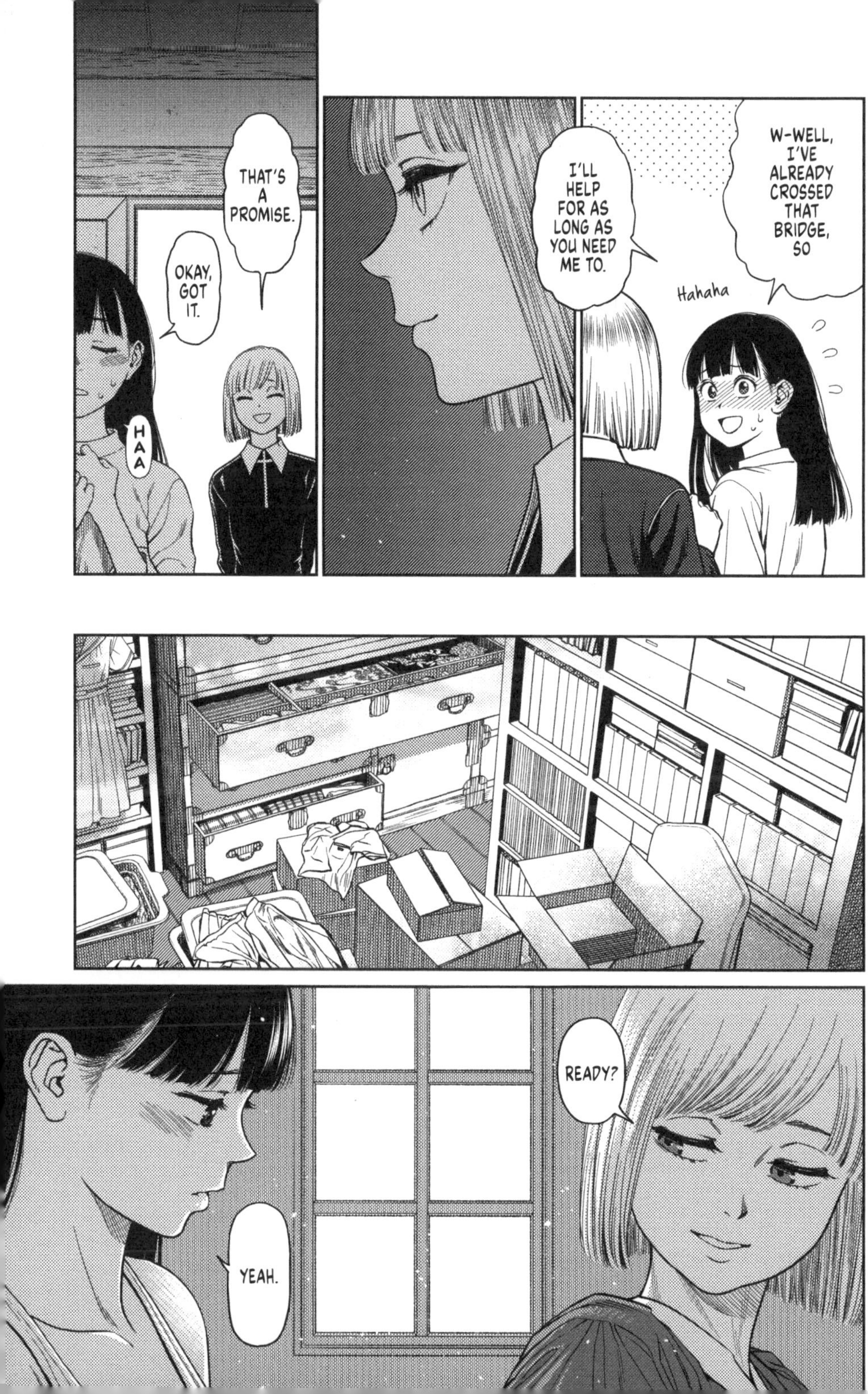
W-WELL, I'VE ALREADY CROSSED THAT BRIDGE, SO
Hahaha
I'LL HELP FOR AS LONG AS YOU NEED ME TO.
THAT'S A PROMISE.
OKAY, GOT IT.
HAA
READY?
YEAH.

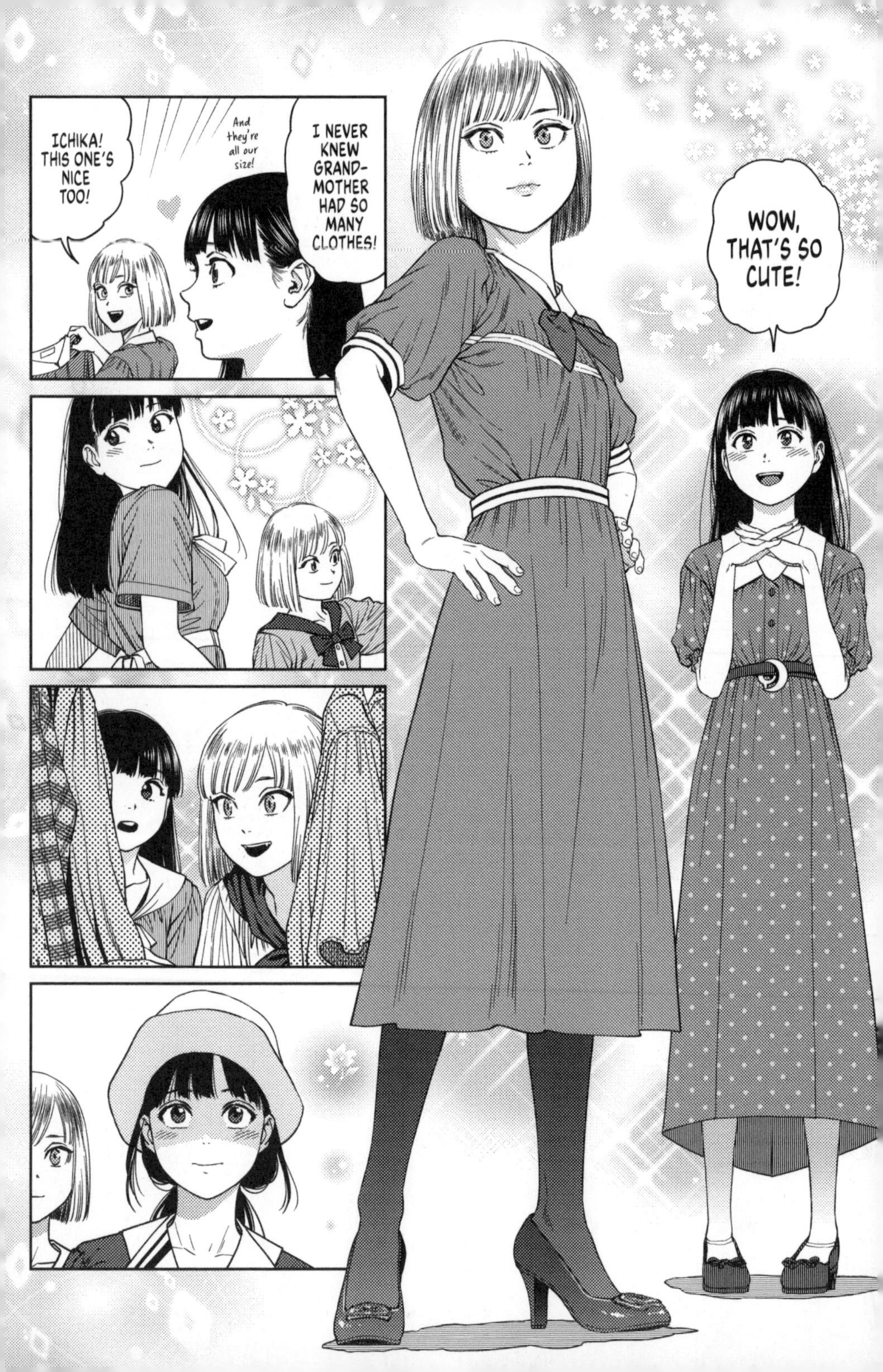
WOW, THAT'S SO CUTE!
I NEVER KNEW GRANDMOTHER HAD SO MANY CLOTHES!
And they're all our size!
ICHIKA! THIS ONE'S NICE TOO!

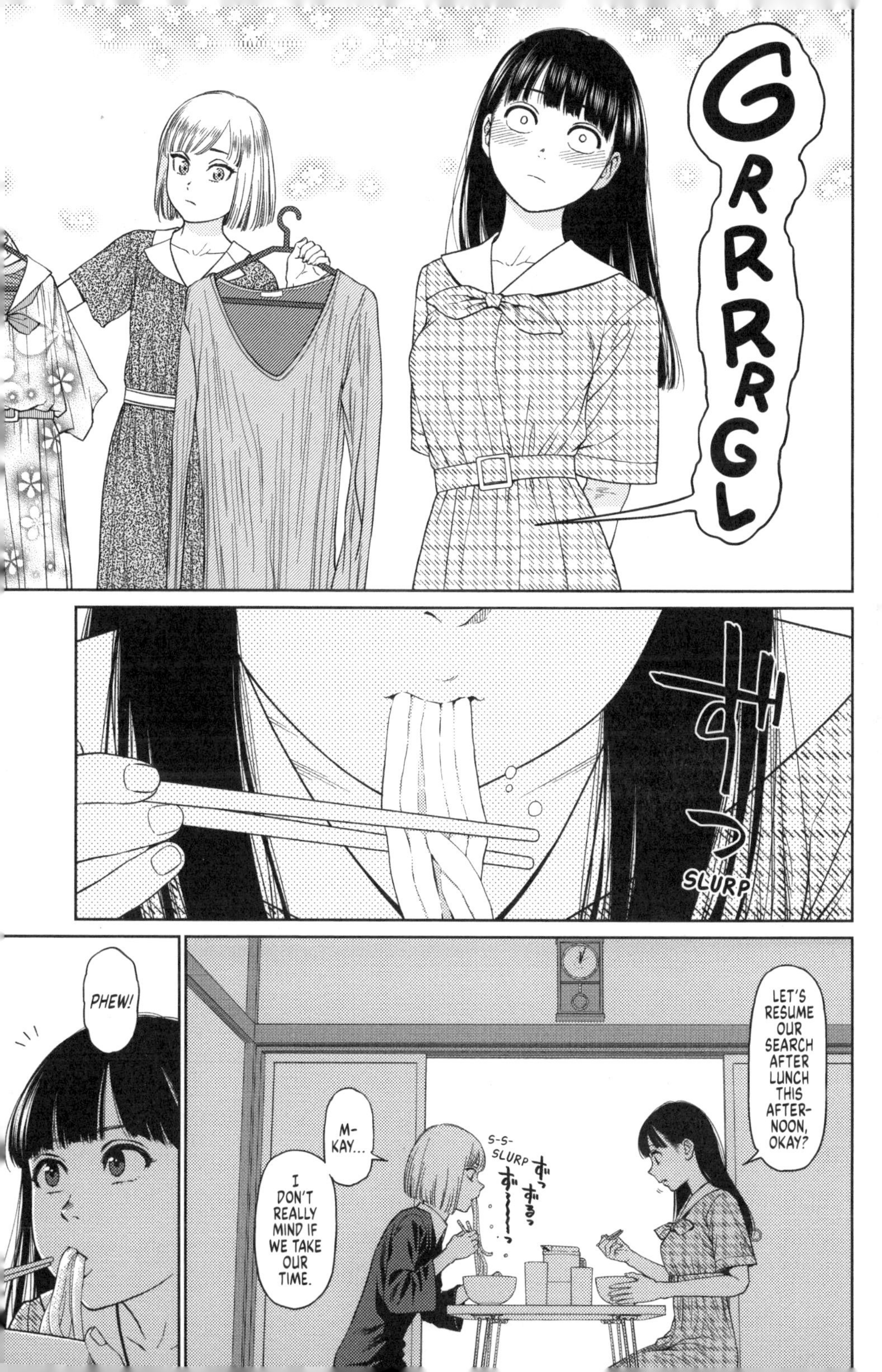
GRRRRGL
ずっ
SLURP
LET'S RESUME OUR SEARCH AFTER LUNCH THIS AFTERNOON, OKAY?
M-KAY...
I DON'T REALLY MIND IF WE TAKE OUR TIME.
S-S-SLURP
ずっずるっ ず～～～っ
PHEW!

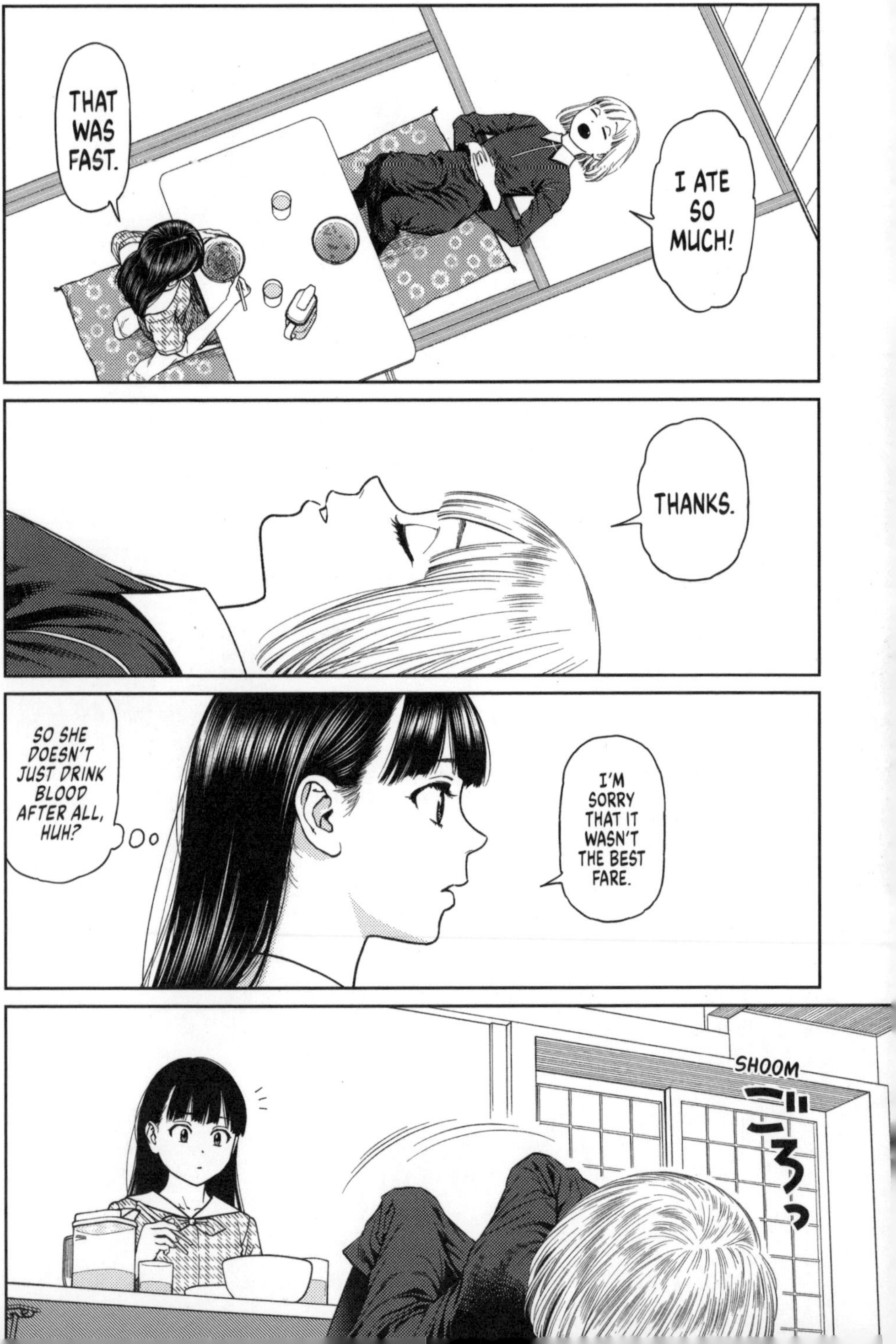
I ATE SO MUCH!
THAT WAS FAST.
THANKS.
I'M SORRY THAT IT WASN'T THE BEST FARE.
SO SHE DOESN'T JUST DRINK BLOOD AFTER ALL, HUH?
SHOOM
ごろっ

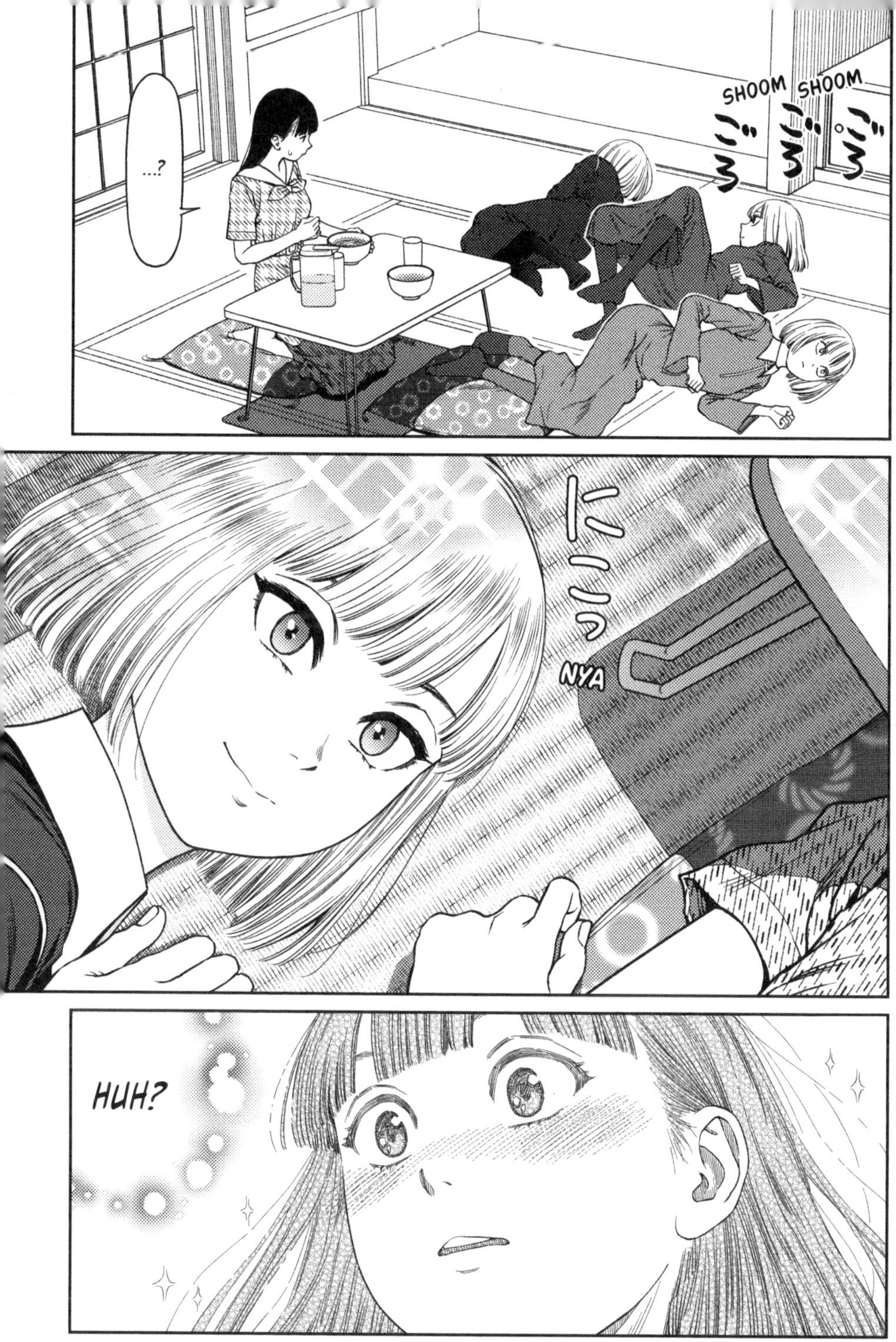
SHOOM SHOOM
...?
NYA
HUH?

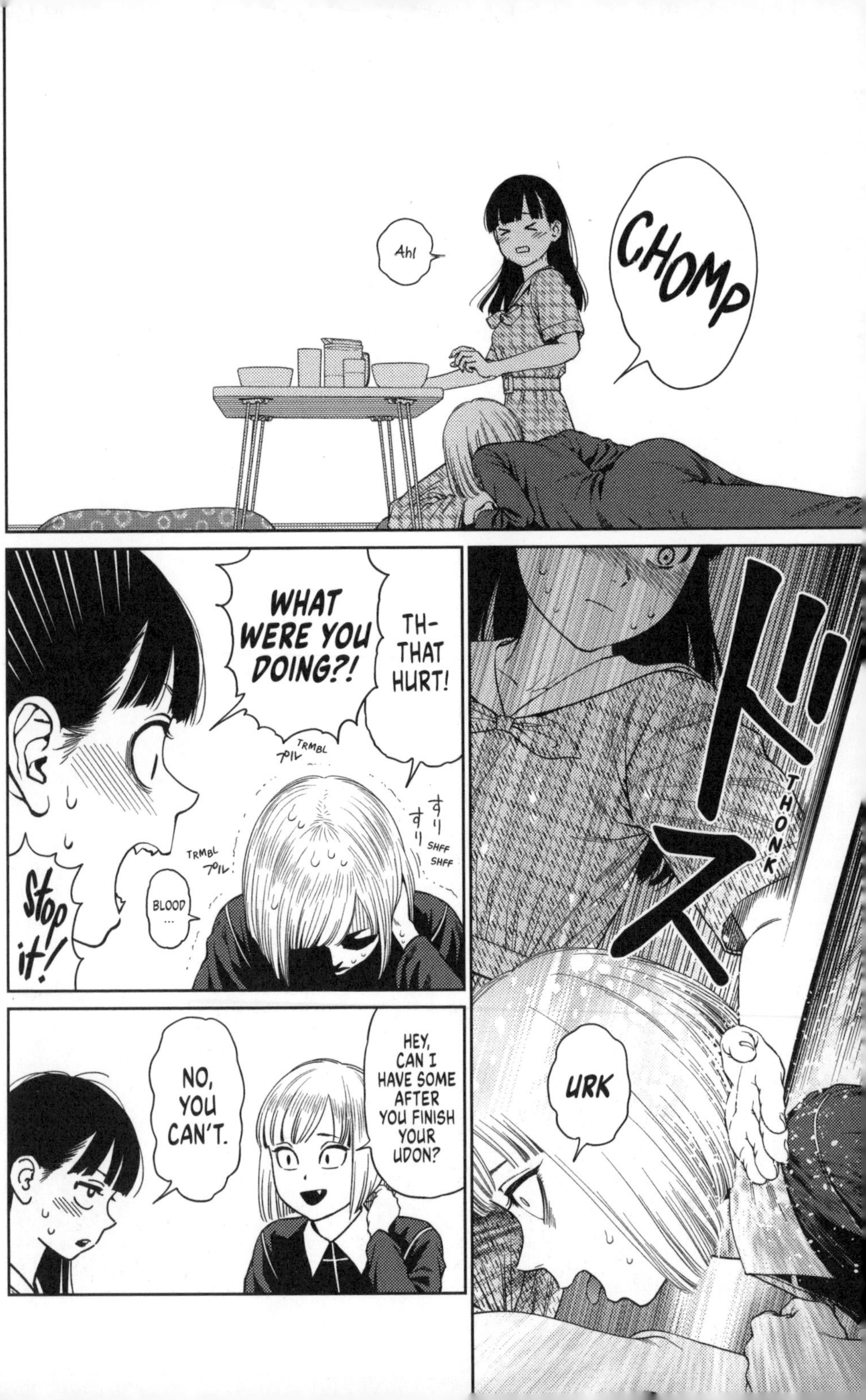
CHOMP
Ah!
ドス
THONK
URK
TH- THAT HURT!
WHAT WERE YOU DOING?!
TRMBL プル
すり すり
SHFF SHFF
TRMBL プル
BLOOD ...
Stop it!
HEY, CAN I HAVE SOME AFTER YOU FINISH YOUR UDON?
NO, YOU CAN'T.

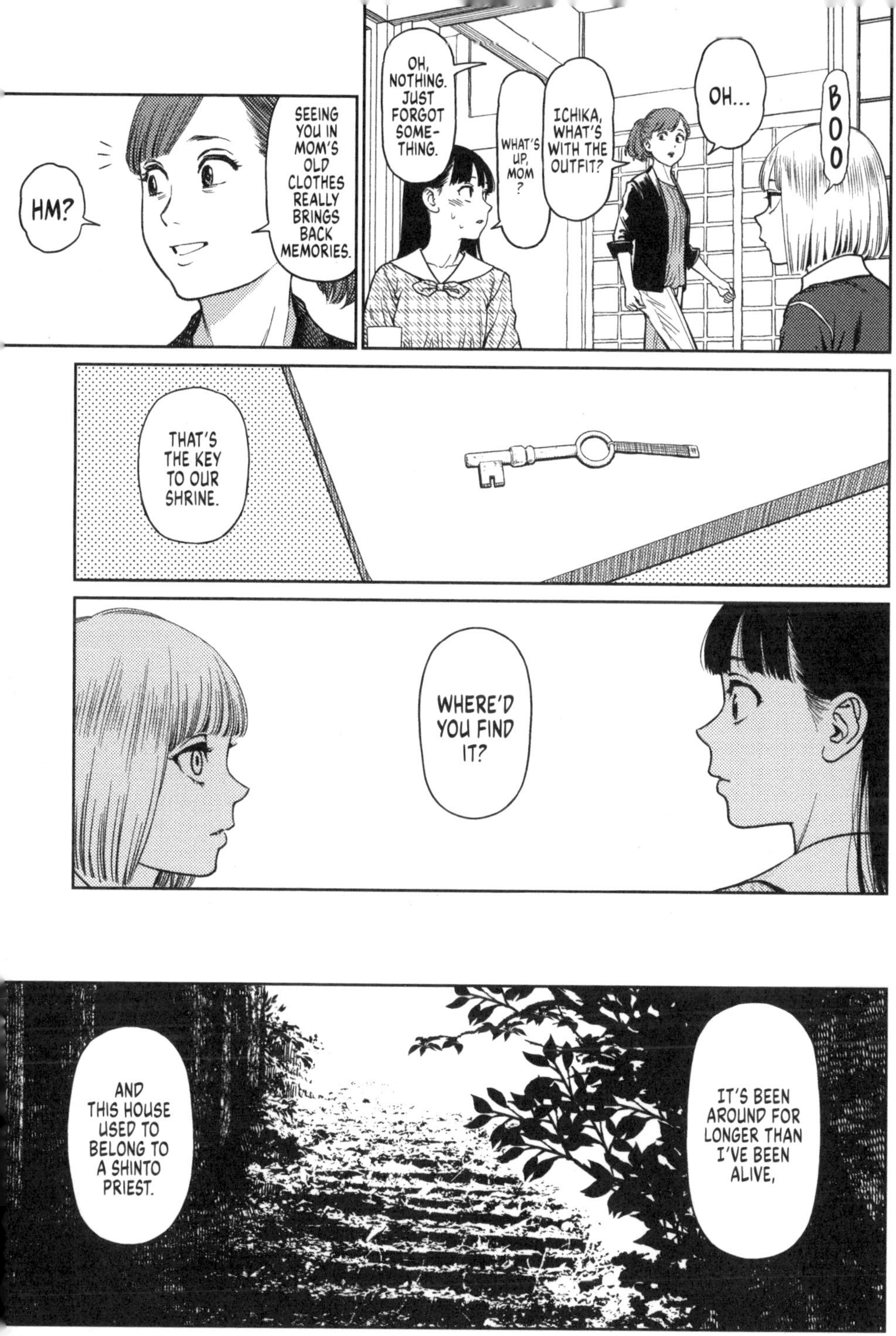
BOO
OH...
ICHIKA, WHAT'S WITH THE OUTFIT?
WHAT'S UP, MOM?
OH, NOTHING. JUST FORGOT SOME-THING.
SEEING YOU IN MOM'S OLD CLOTHES REALLY BRINGS BACK MEMORIES.
HM?
THAT'S THE KEY TO OUR SHRINE.
WHERE'D YOU FIND IT?
IT'S BEEN AROUND FOR LONGER THAN I'VE BEEN ALIVE,
AND THIS HOUSE USED TO BELONG TO A SHINTO PRIEST.

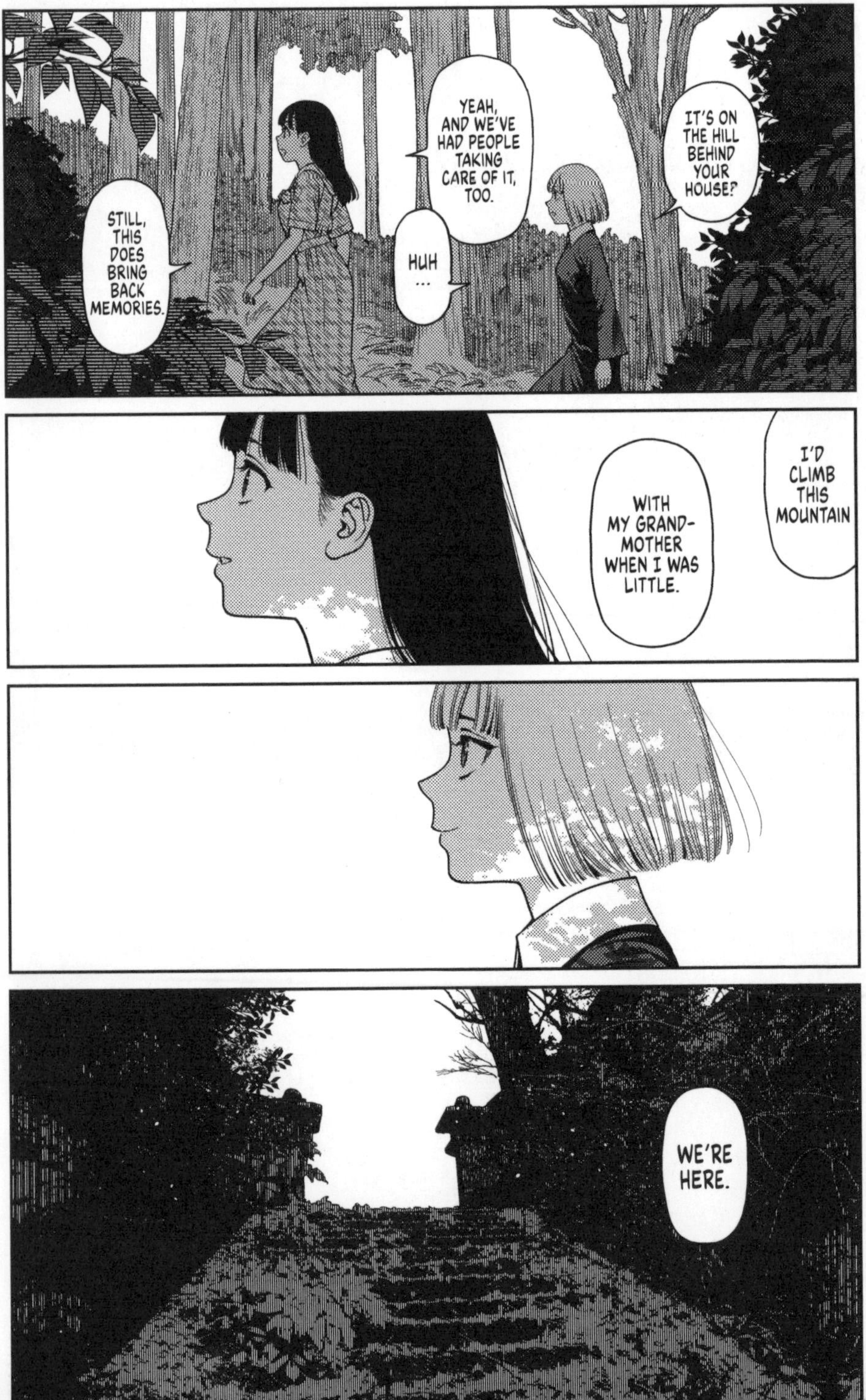
IT'S ON THE HILL BEHIND YOUR HOUSE?
YEAH, AND WE'VE HAD PEOPLE TAKING CARE OF IT, TOO.
HUH ...
STILL, THIS DOES BRING BACK MEMORIES.
I'D CLIMB THIS MOUNTAIN
WITH MY GRAND-MOTHER WHEN I WAS LITTLE.
WE'RE HERE.

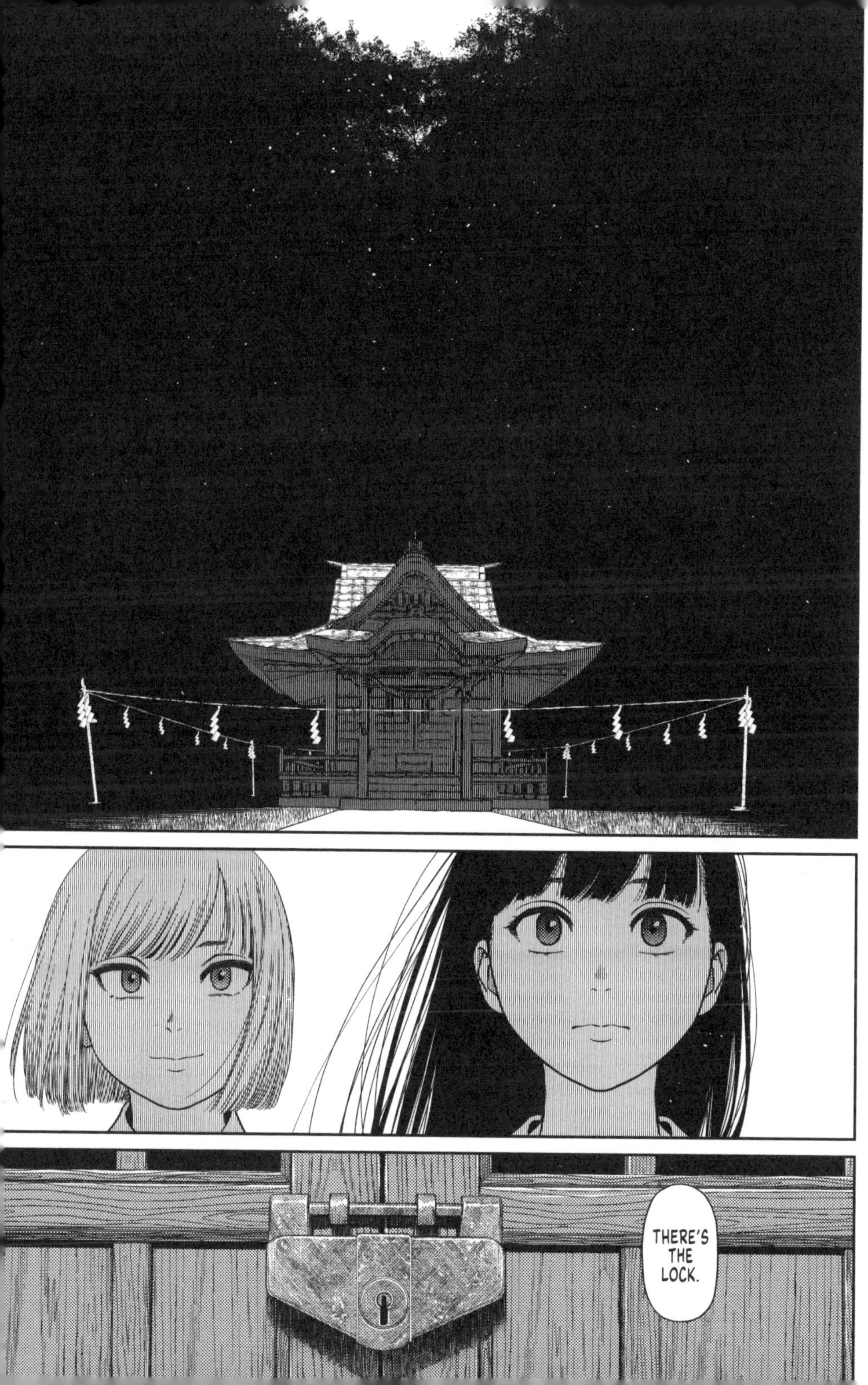
THERE'S THE LOCK.

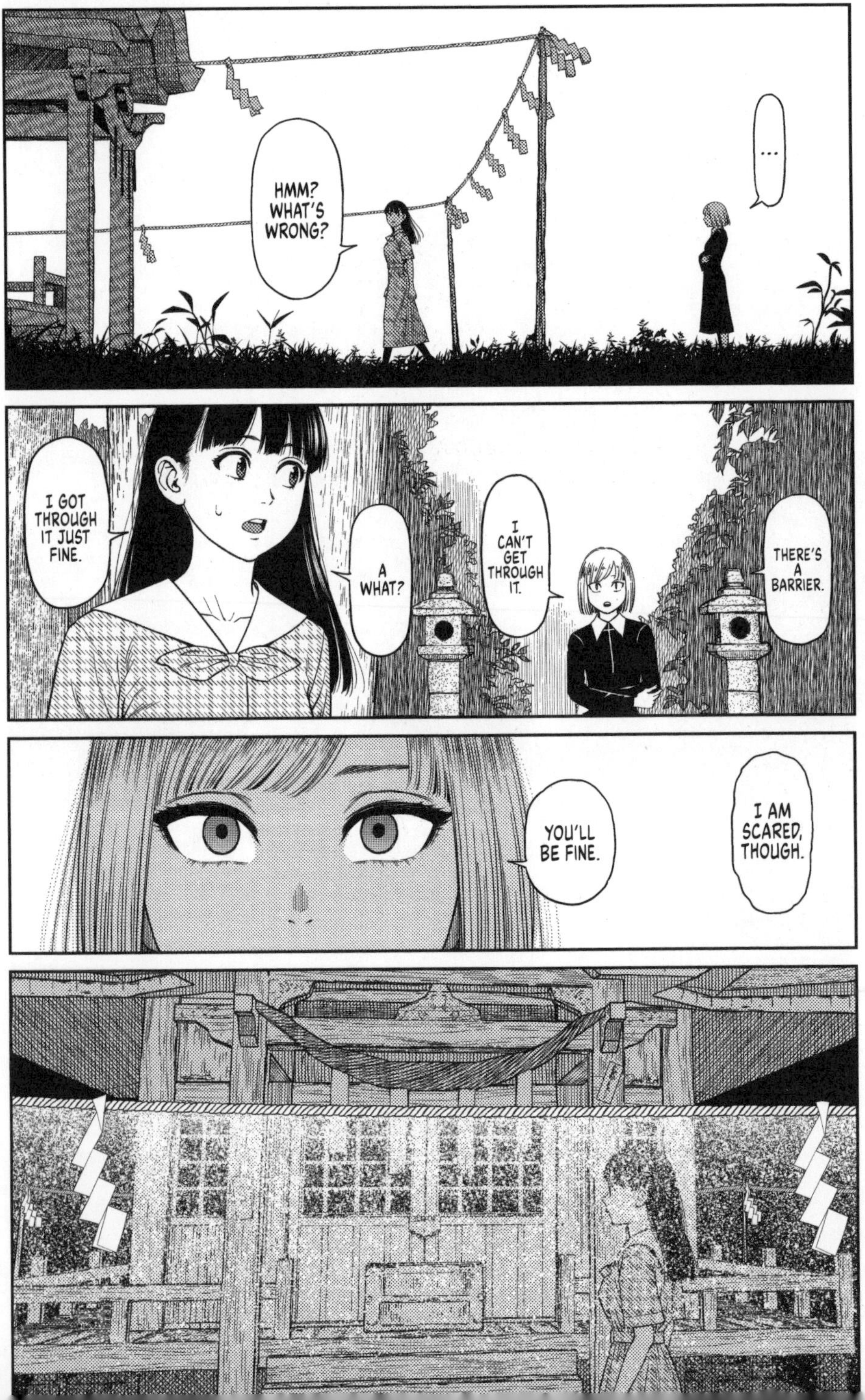

...
HMM? WHAT'S WRONG?
THERE'S A BARRIER.
I CAN'T GET THROUGH IT.
A WHAT?
I GOT THROUGH IT JUST FINE.
I AM SCARED, THOUGH.
YOU'LL BE FINE.

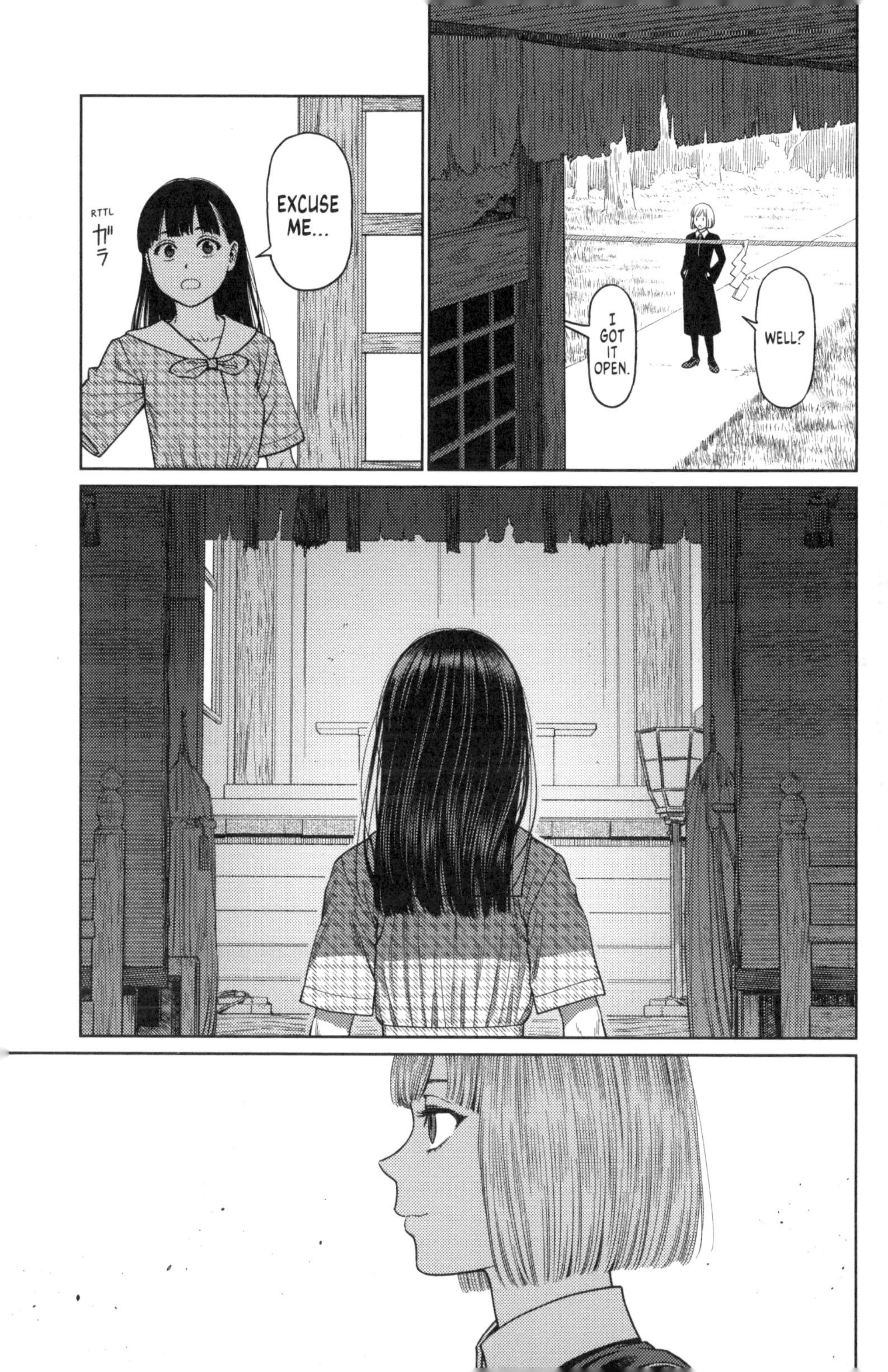
WELL?
I GOT IT OPEN.
EXCUSE ME...
RTTL
ガラ

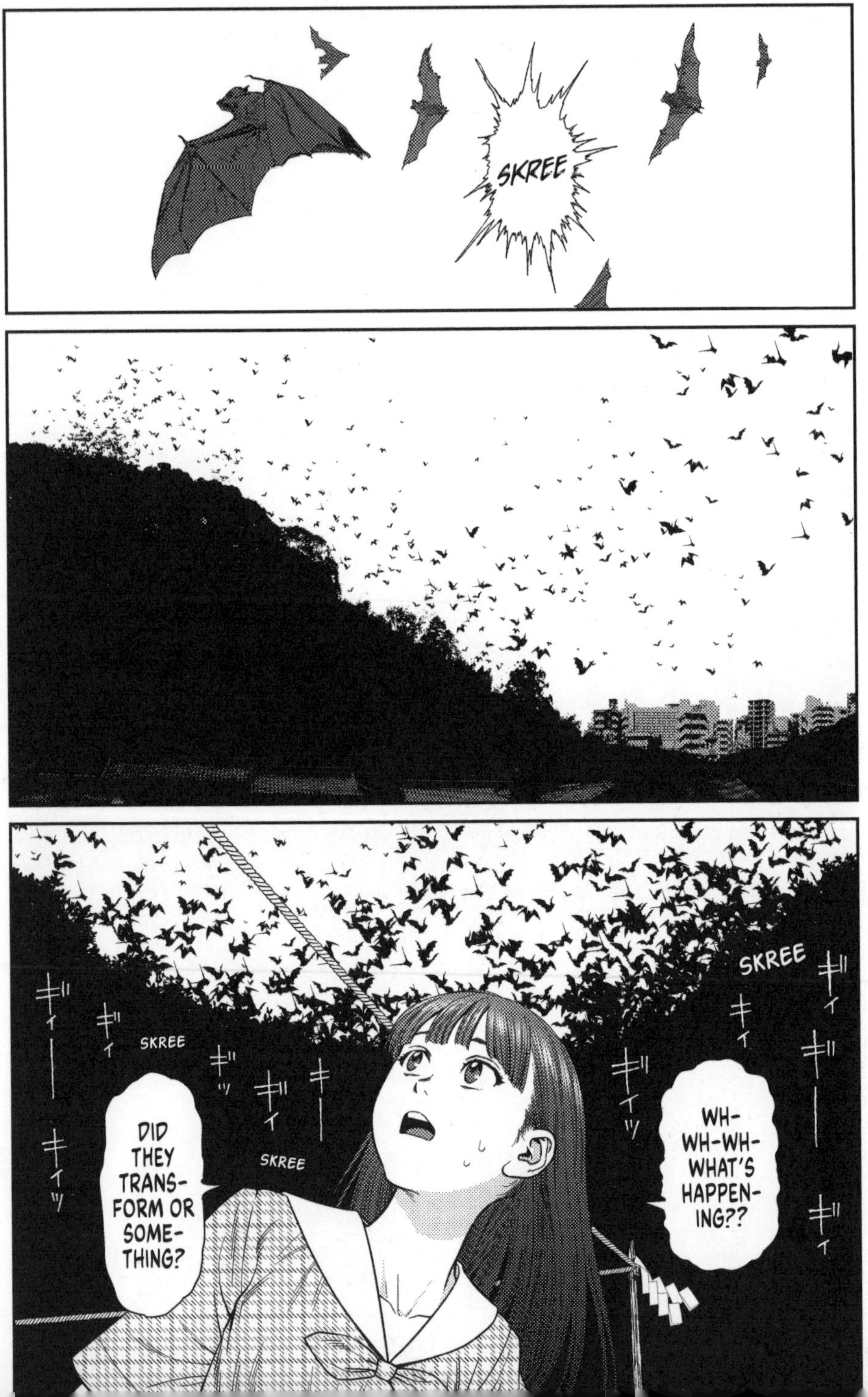
SKREE
SKREE
ギィ
キィ
ギー
ギィ
WH-WH-WH-WHAT'S HAPPEN-ING??
ギィッ
キー
ギィ
SKREE
ギッ
DID THEY TRANS-FORM OR SOME-THING?
SKREE
ギィ
ギィー
キィッ

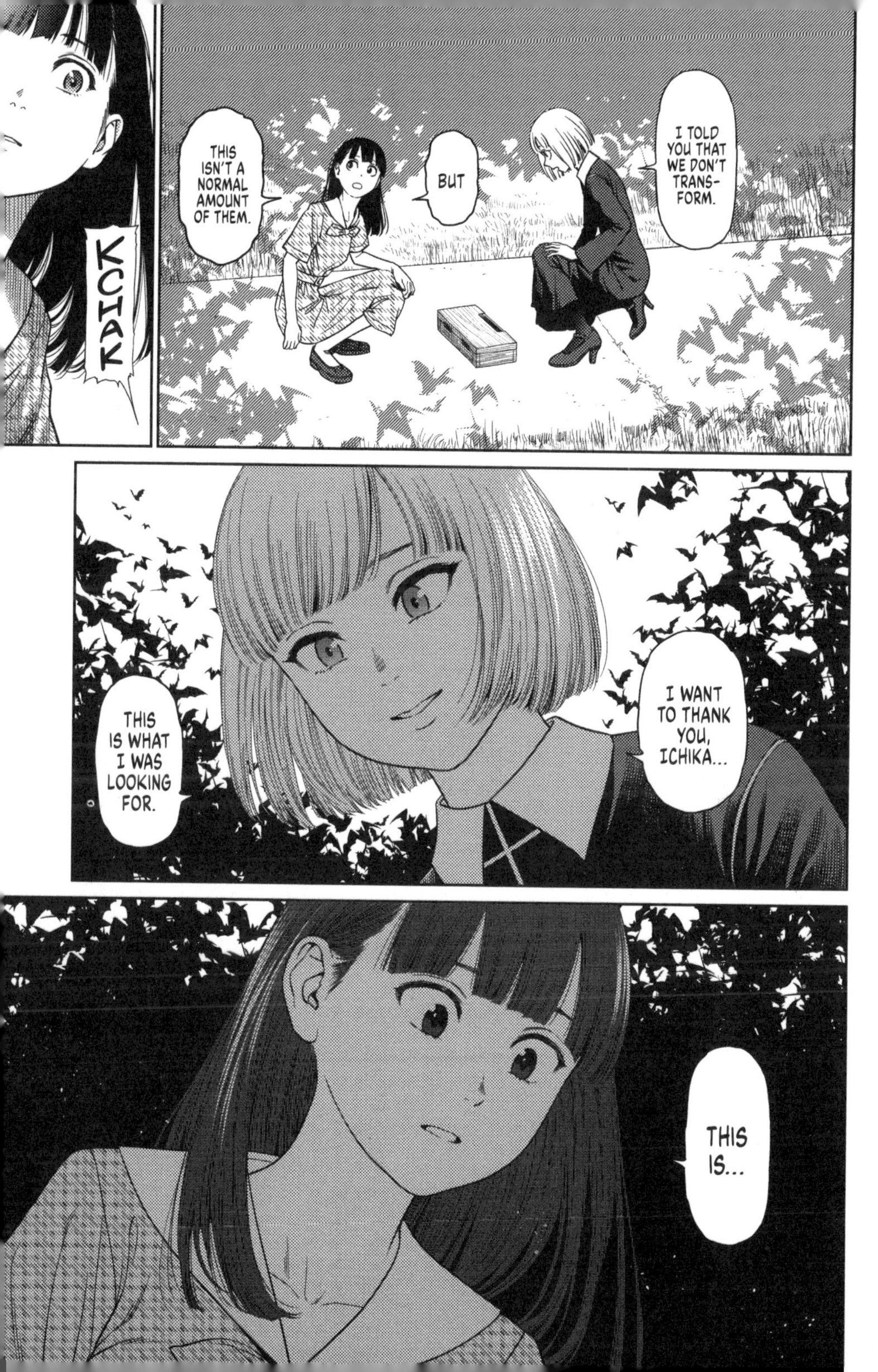
I TOLD YOU THAT WE DON'T TRANS-FORM.
BUT
THIS ISN'T A NORMAL AMOUNT OF THEM.
KCHAK
I WANT TO THANK YOU, ICHIKA...
THIS IS WHAT I WAS LOOKING FOR.
THIS IS...

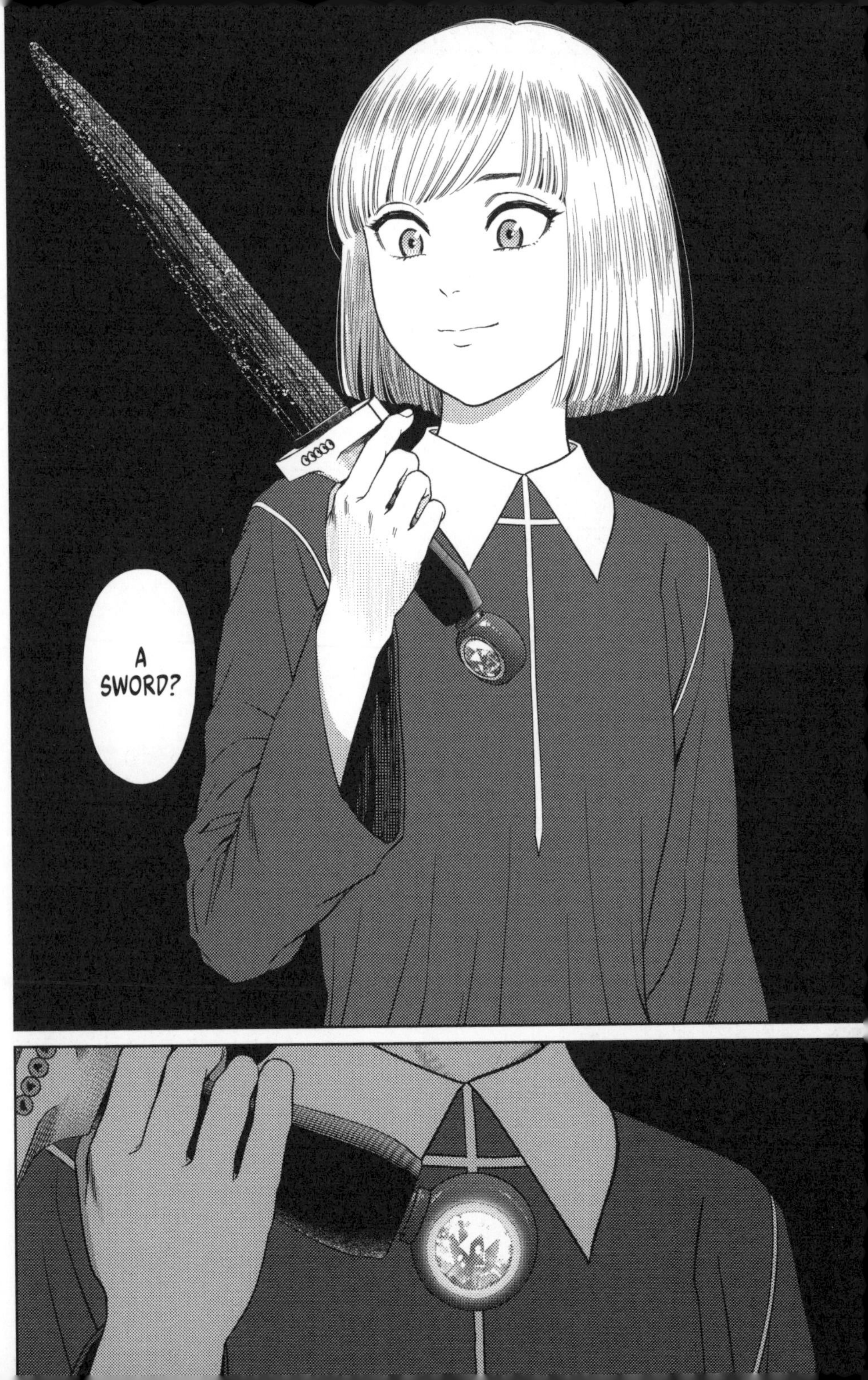
A SWORD?

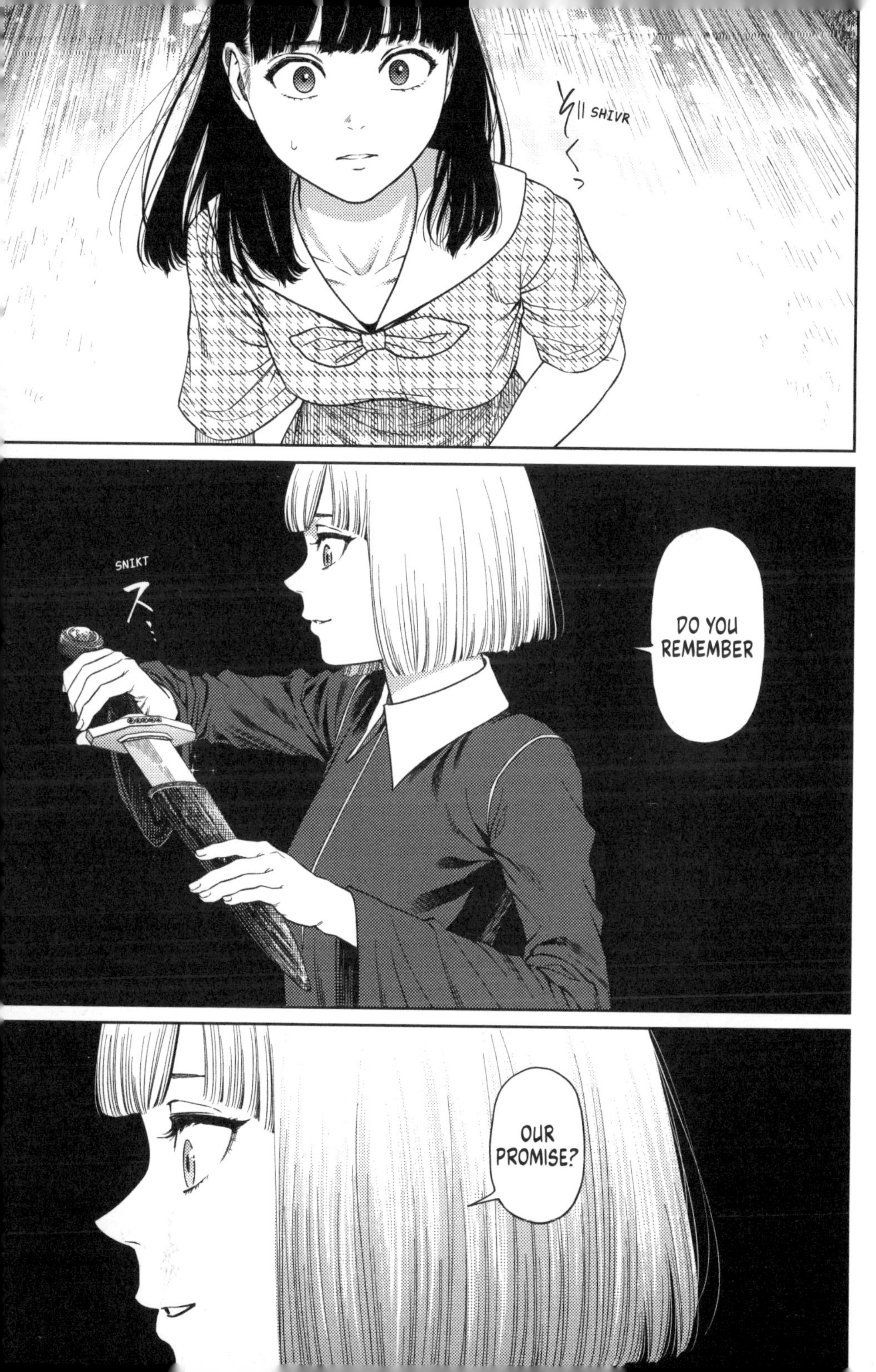
SHIVR
SNIKT
DO YOU REMEMBER
OUR PROMISE?

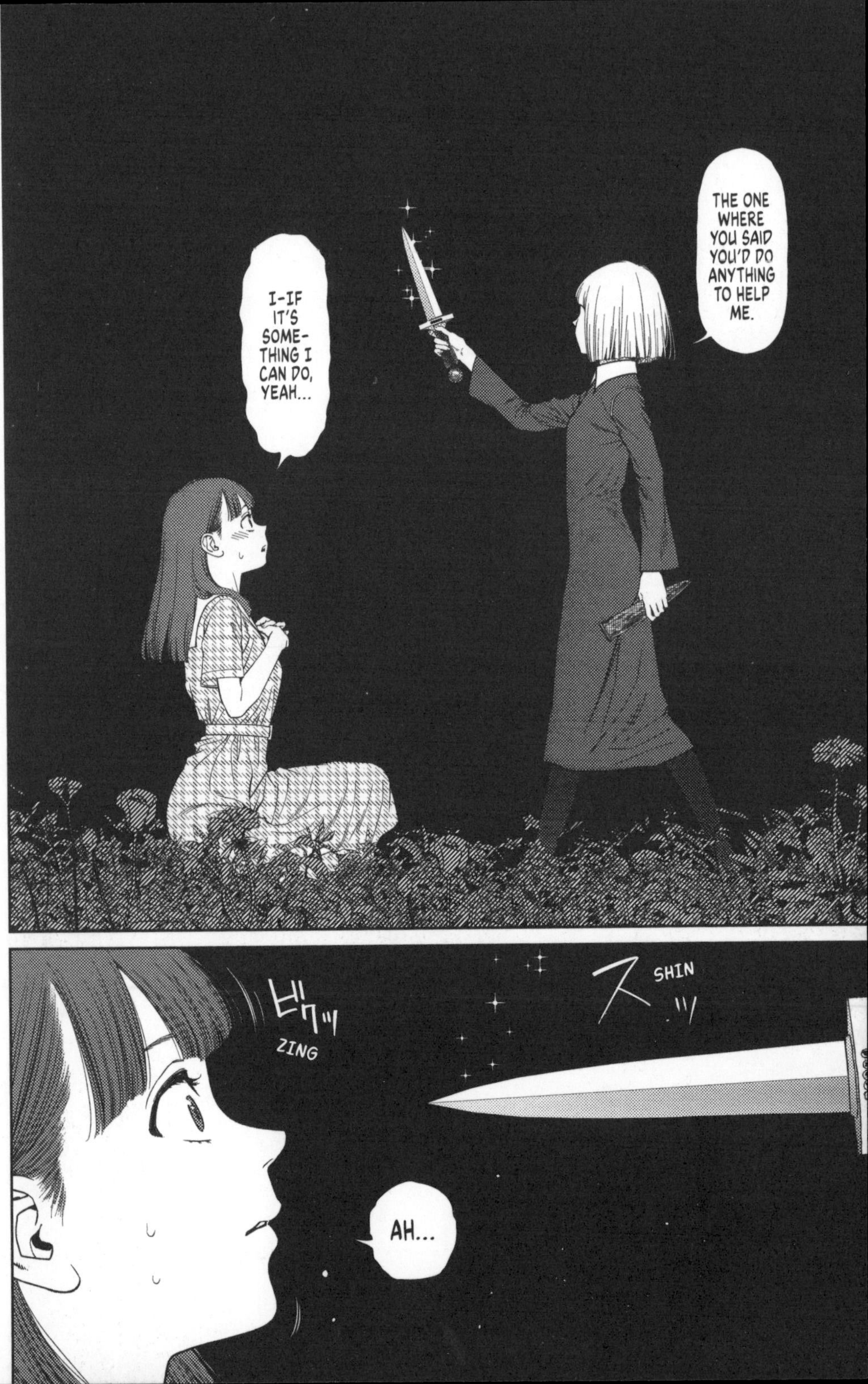
THE ONE WHERE YOU SAID YOU'D DO ANYTHING TO HELP ME.
I-IF IT'S SOME-THING I CAN DO, YEAH...
スッ
SHIN
ビクッ
ZING
AH...

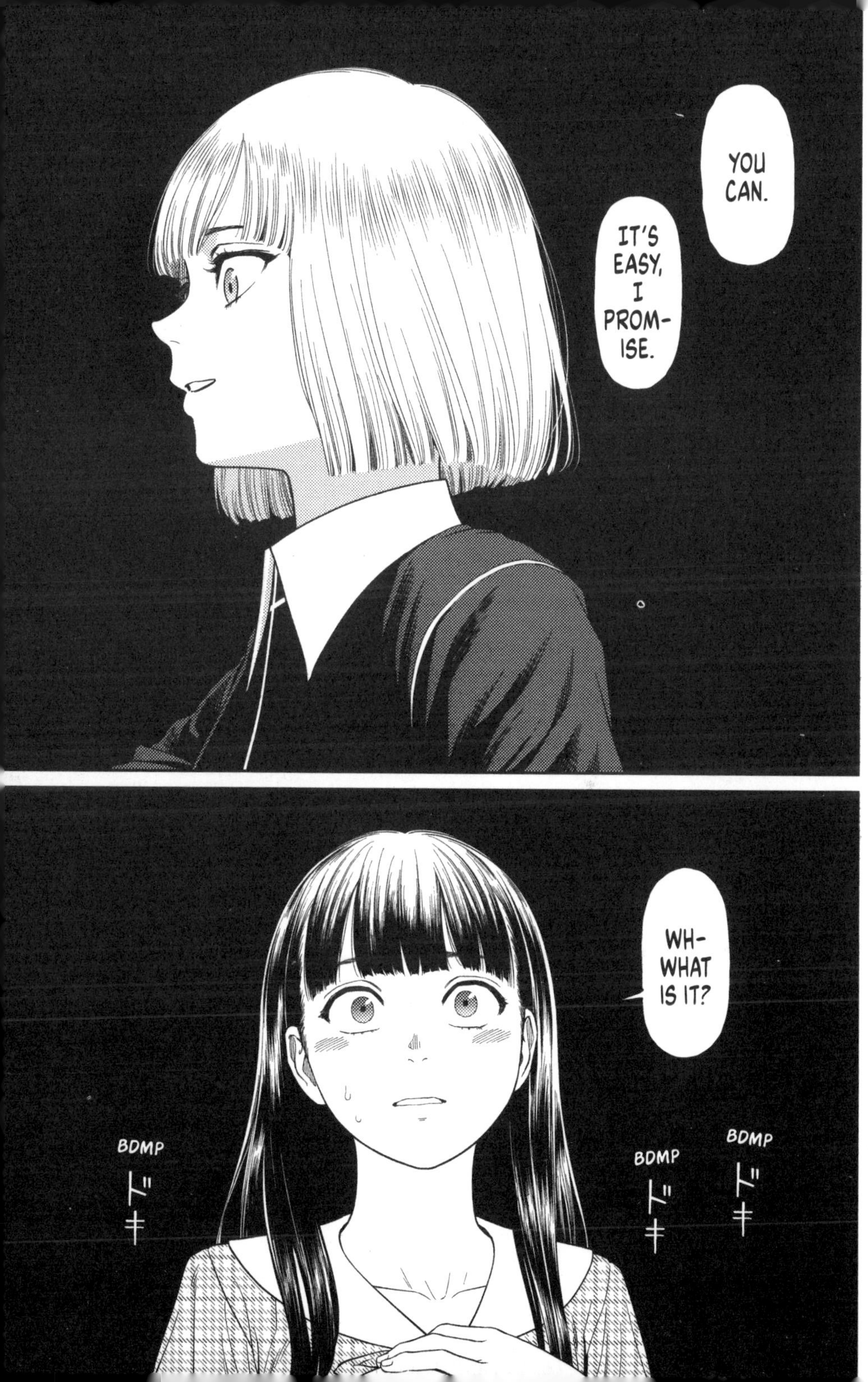
YOU CAN.
IT'S EASY, I PROMISE.
WH-WHAT IS IT?
BDMP
ドキ
BDMP
ドキ
BDMP
ドキ

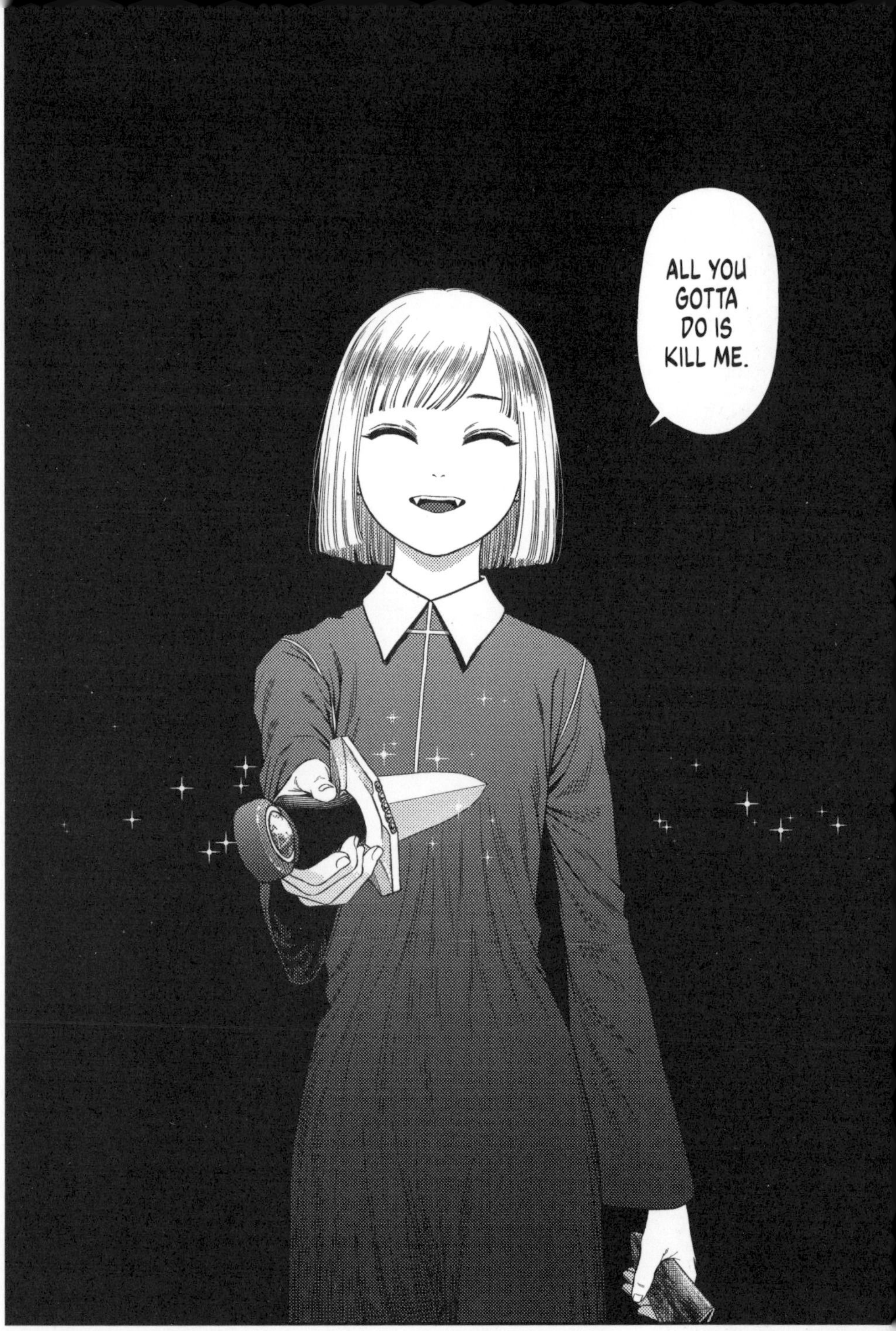
ALL YOU GOTTA DO IS KILL ME.

VAMPEERZ

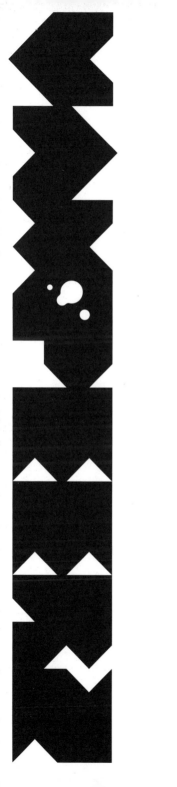

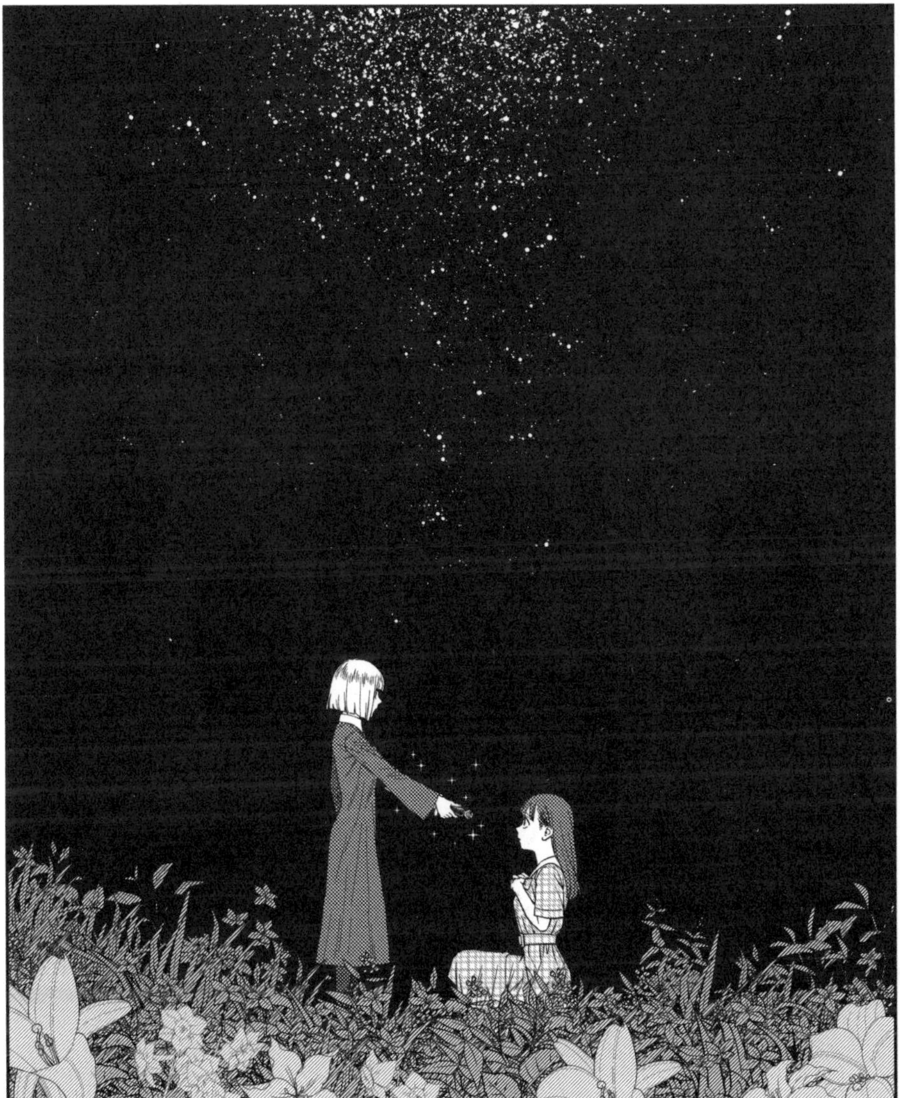

#3 LOVE

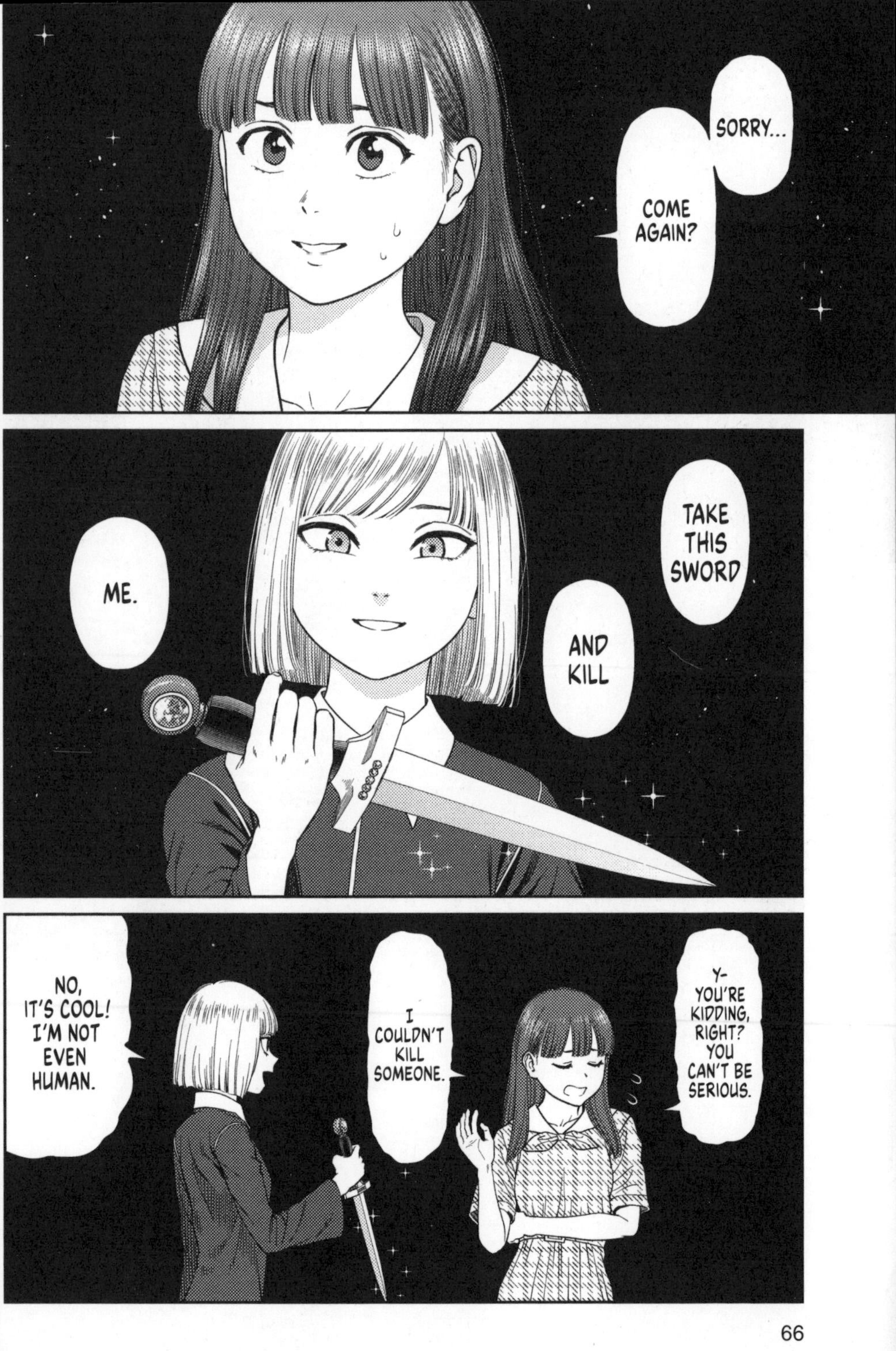
SORRY...
COME AGAIN?
TAKE THIS SWORD
AND KILL
ME.
Y- YOU'RE KIDDING, RIGHT? YOU CAN'T BE SERIOUS.
I COULDN'T KILL SOMEONE.
NO, IT'S COOL! I'M NOT EVEN HUMAN.

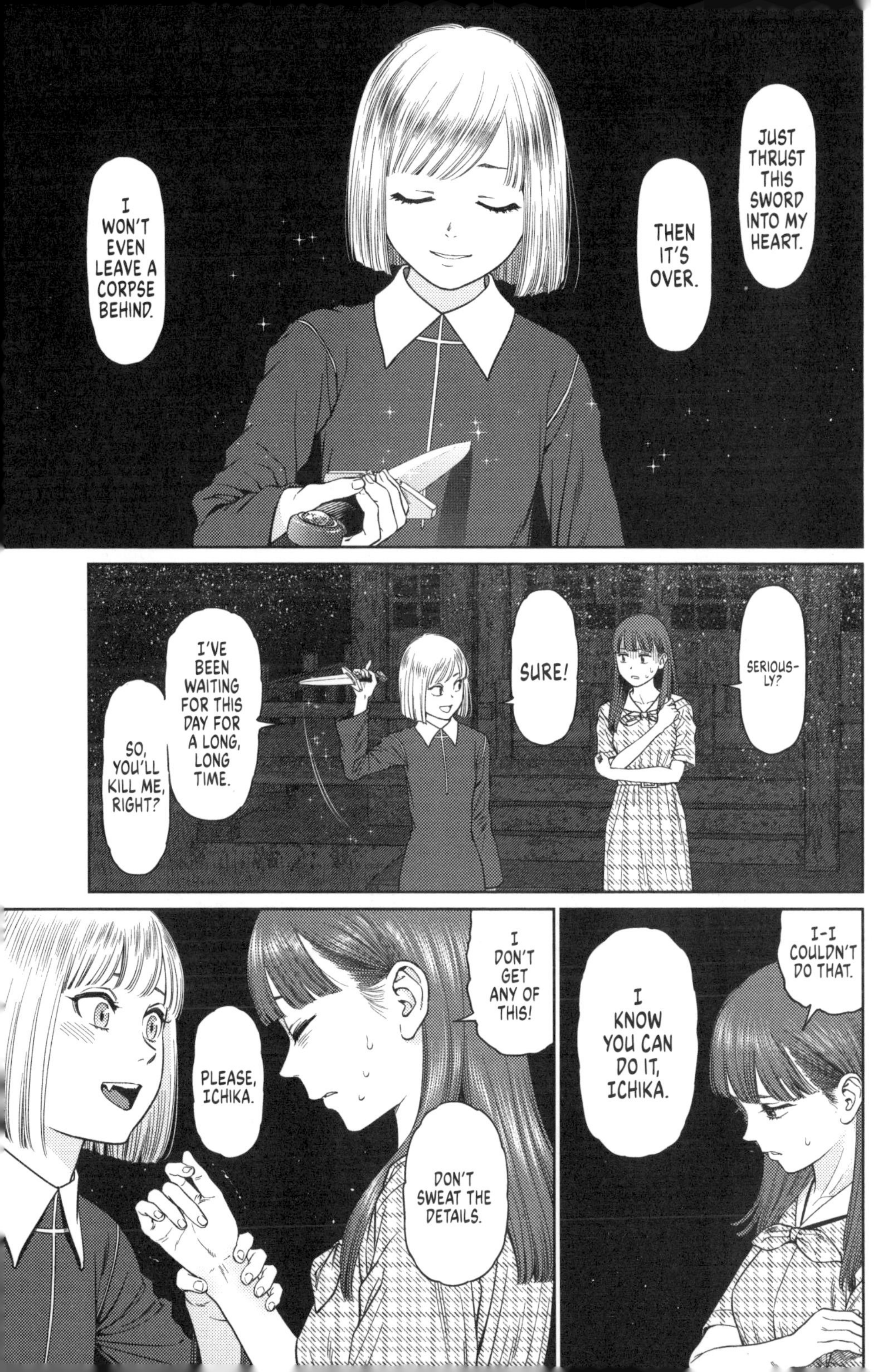
JUST THRUST THIS SWORD INTO MY HEART.
THEN IT'S OVER.
I WON'T EVEN LEAVE A CORPSE BEHIND.
SERIOUSLY?
SURE!
I'VE BEEN WAITING FOR THIS DAY FOR A LONG, LONG TIME.
SO, YOU'LL KILL ME, RIGHT?
I-I COULDN'T DO THAT.
I KNOW YOU CAN DO IT, ICHIKA.
I DON'T GET ANY OF THIS!
PLEASE, ICHIKA.
DON'T SWEAT THE DETAILS.

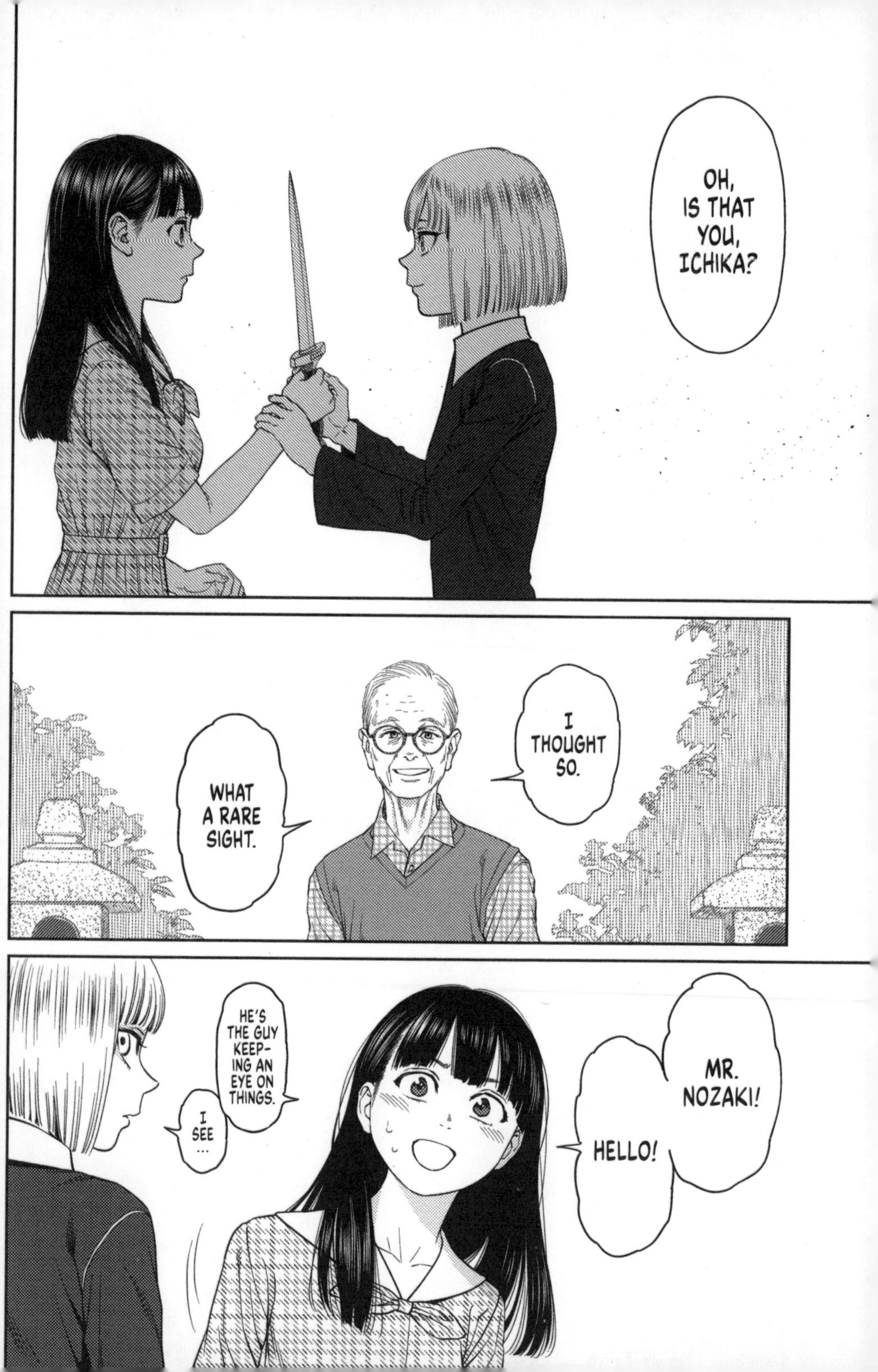
OH, IS THAT YOU, ICHIKA?
I THOUGHT SO.
WHAT A RARE SIGHT.
MR. NOZAKI!
HELLO!
HE'S THE GUY KEEPING AN EYE ON THINGS.
I SEE ...

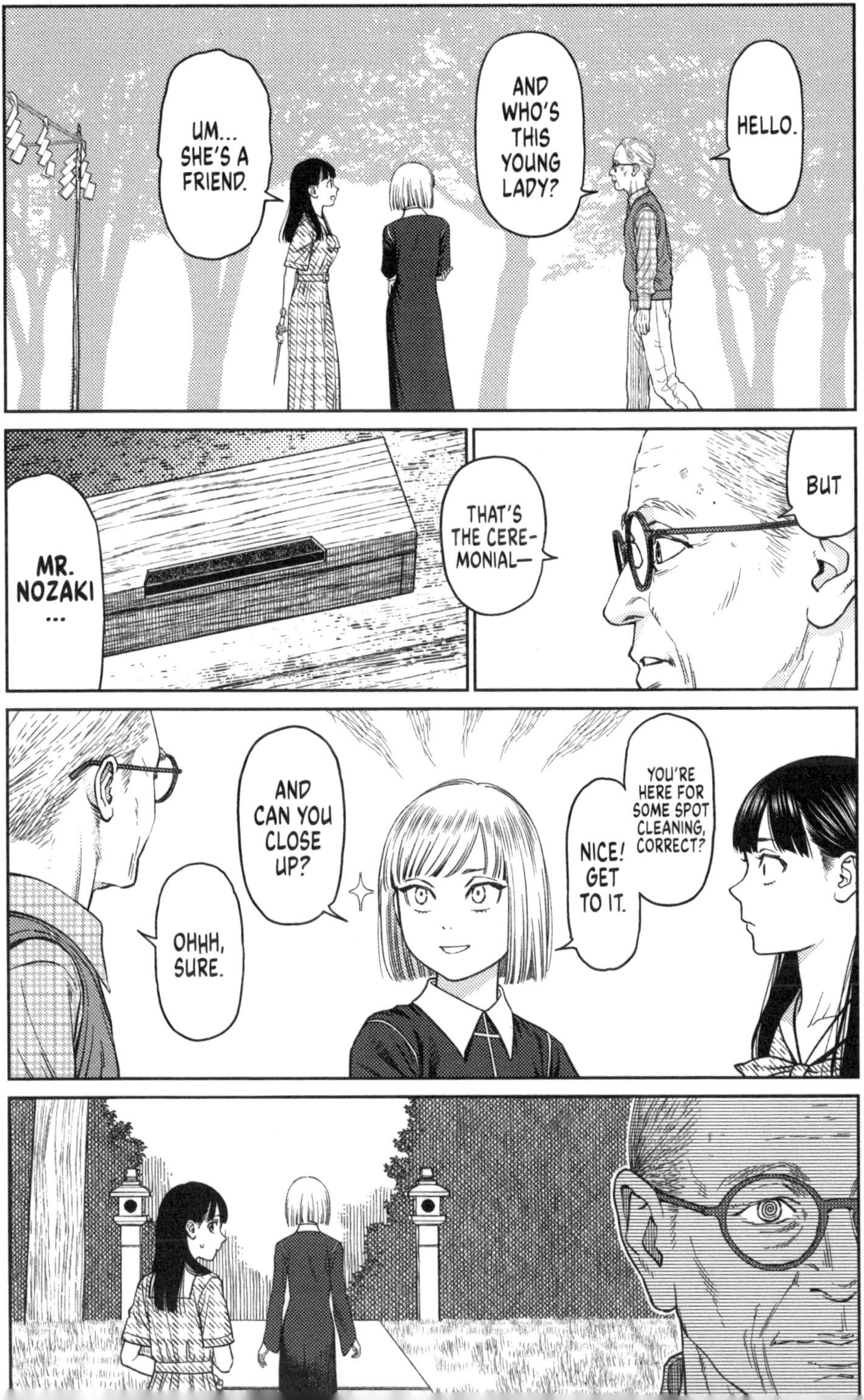
HELLO.
AND WHO'S THIS YOUNG LADY?
UM... SHE'S A FRIEND.
BUT
THAT'S THE CERE-MONIAL—
MR. NOZAKI ...
YOU'RE HERE FOR SOME SPOT CLEANING, CORRECT?
NICE! GET TO IT.
AND CAN YOU CLOSE UP?
OHHH, SURE.

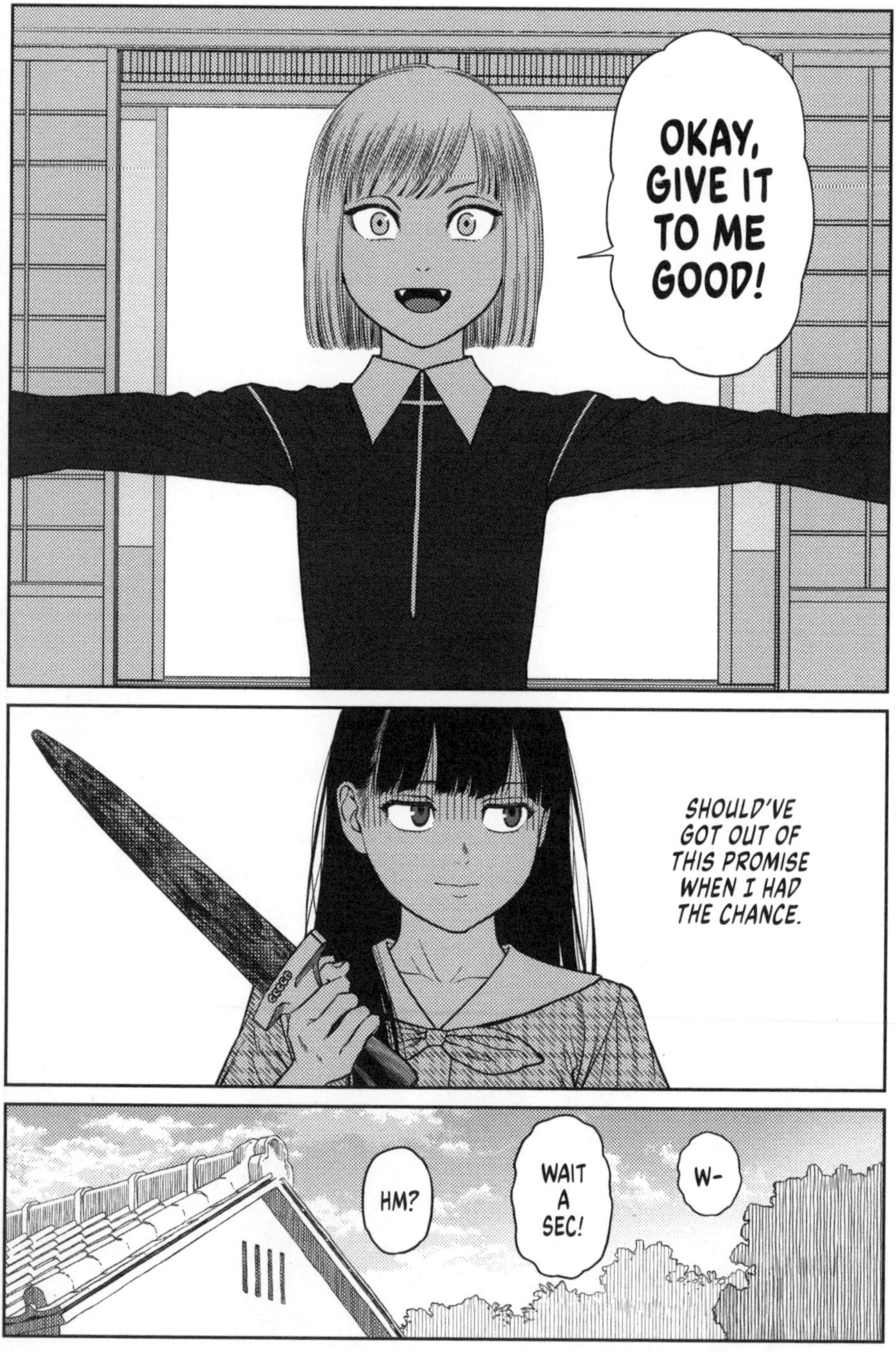
OKAY, GIVE IT TO ME GOOD!
SHOULD'VE GOT OUT OF THIS PROMISE WHEN I HAD THE CHANCE.
W-
WAIT A SEC!
HM?

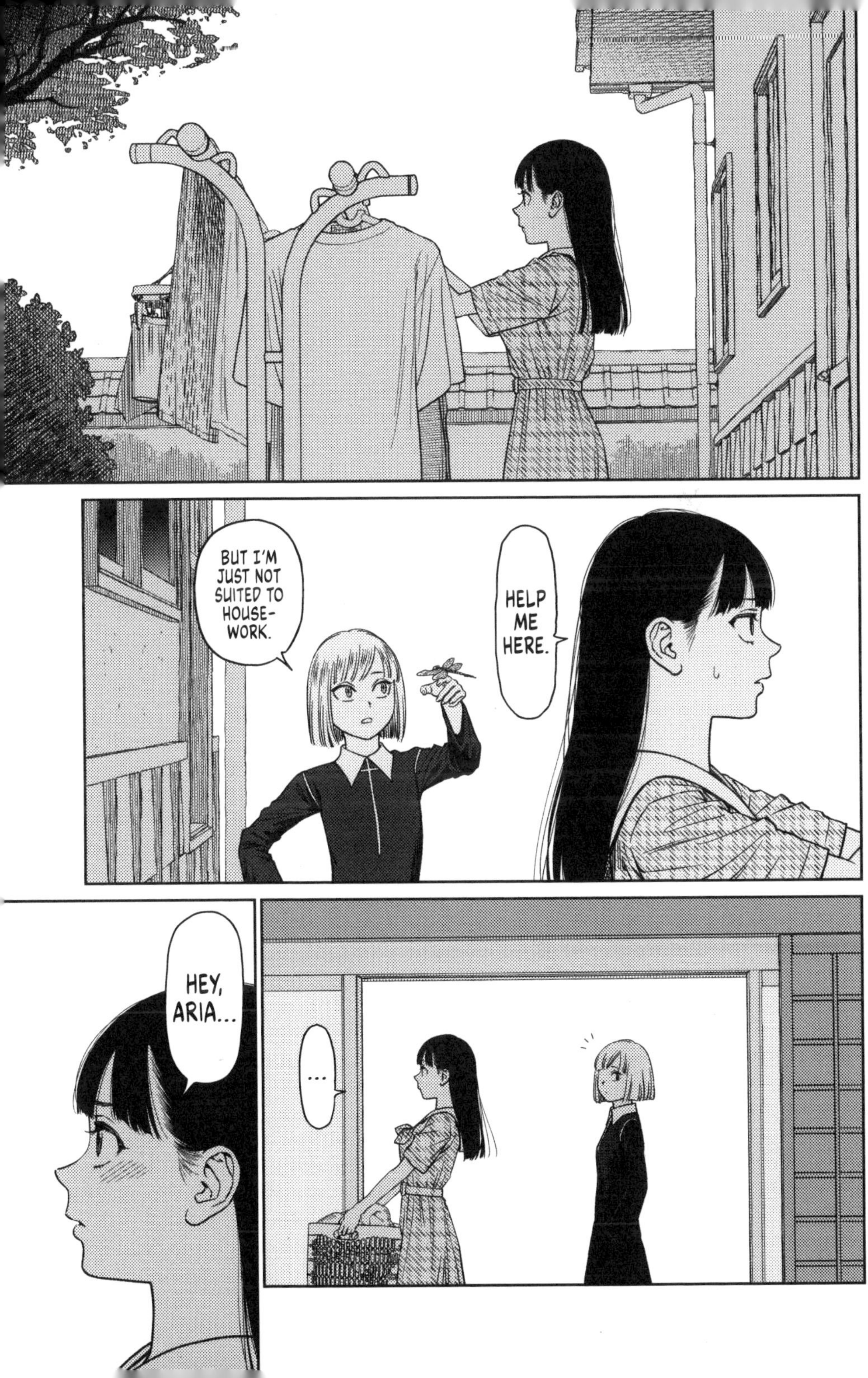
HELP ME HERE.
BUT I'M JUST NOT SUITED TO HOUSE-WORK.
...
HEY, ARIA...

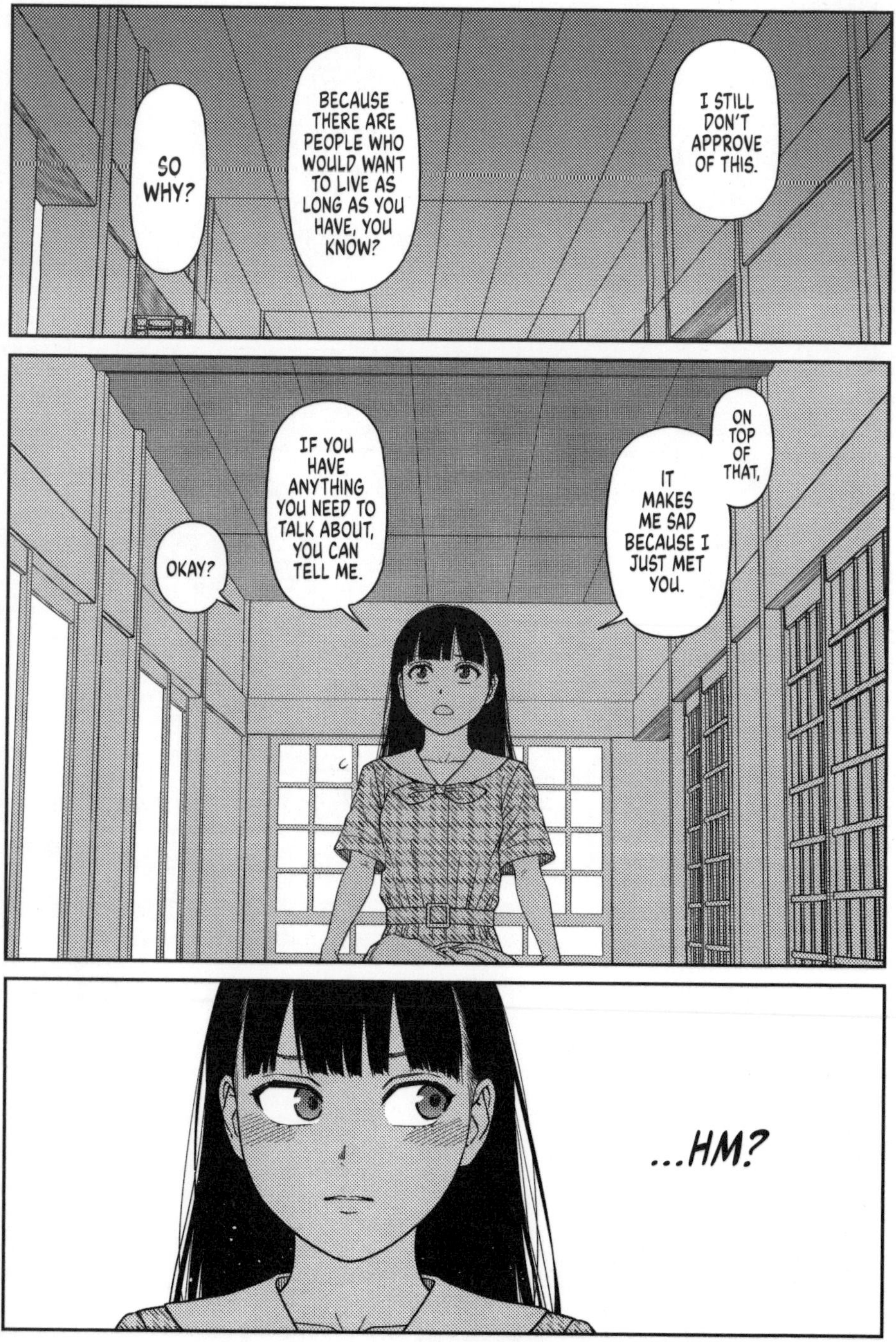
I STILL DON'T APPROVE OF THIS.
BECAUSE THERE ARE PEOPLE WHO WOULD WANT TO LIVE AS LONG AS YOU HAVE, YOU KNOW?
SO WHY?
ON TOP OF THAT,
IT MAKES ME SAD BECAUSE I JUST MET YOU.
IF YOU HAVE ANYTHING YOU NEED TO TALK ABOUT, YOU CAN TELL ME.
OKAY?
...HM?

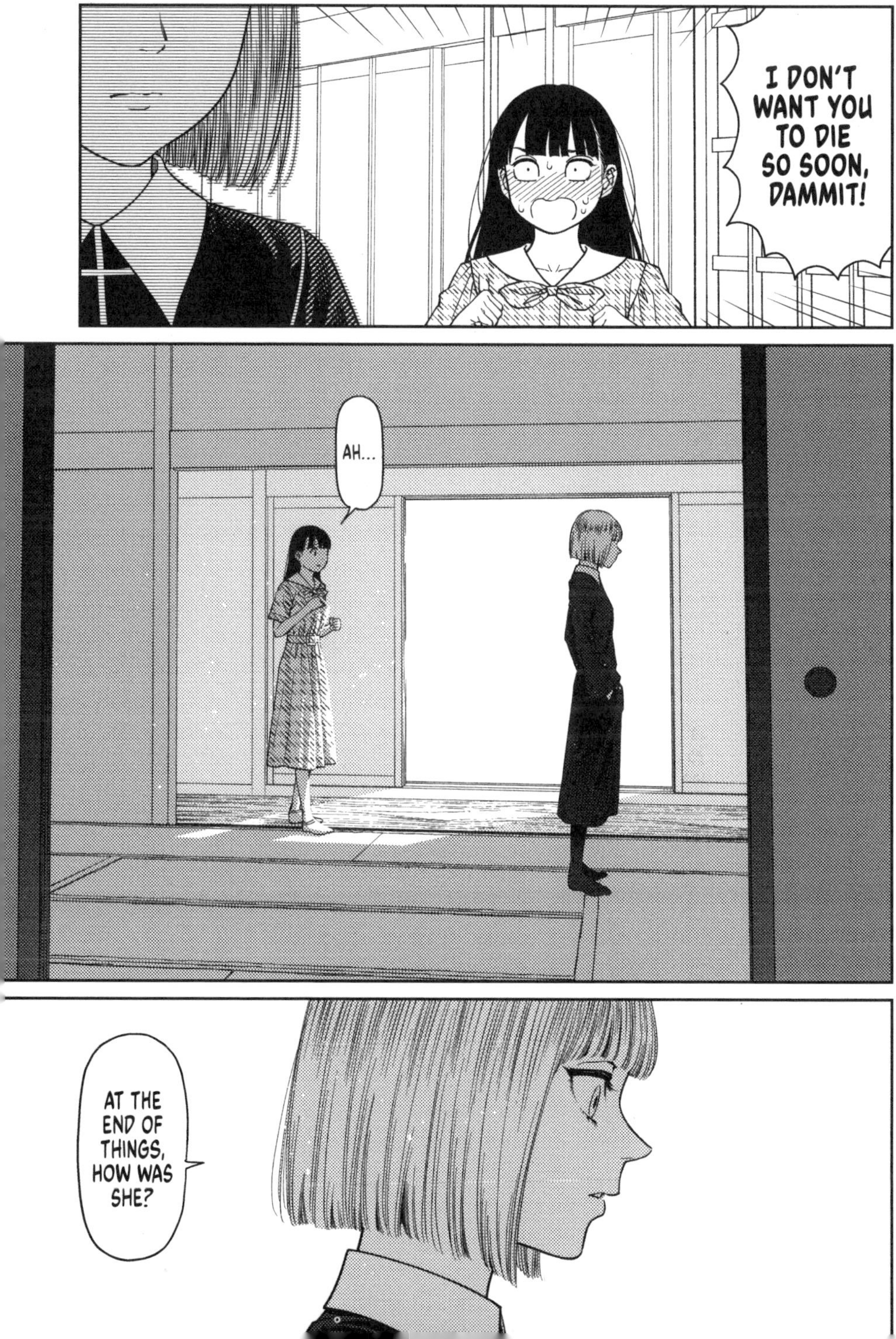
I DON'T WANT YOU TO DIE SO SOON, DAMMIT!
AH...
AT THE END OF THINGS, HOW WAS SHE?

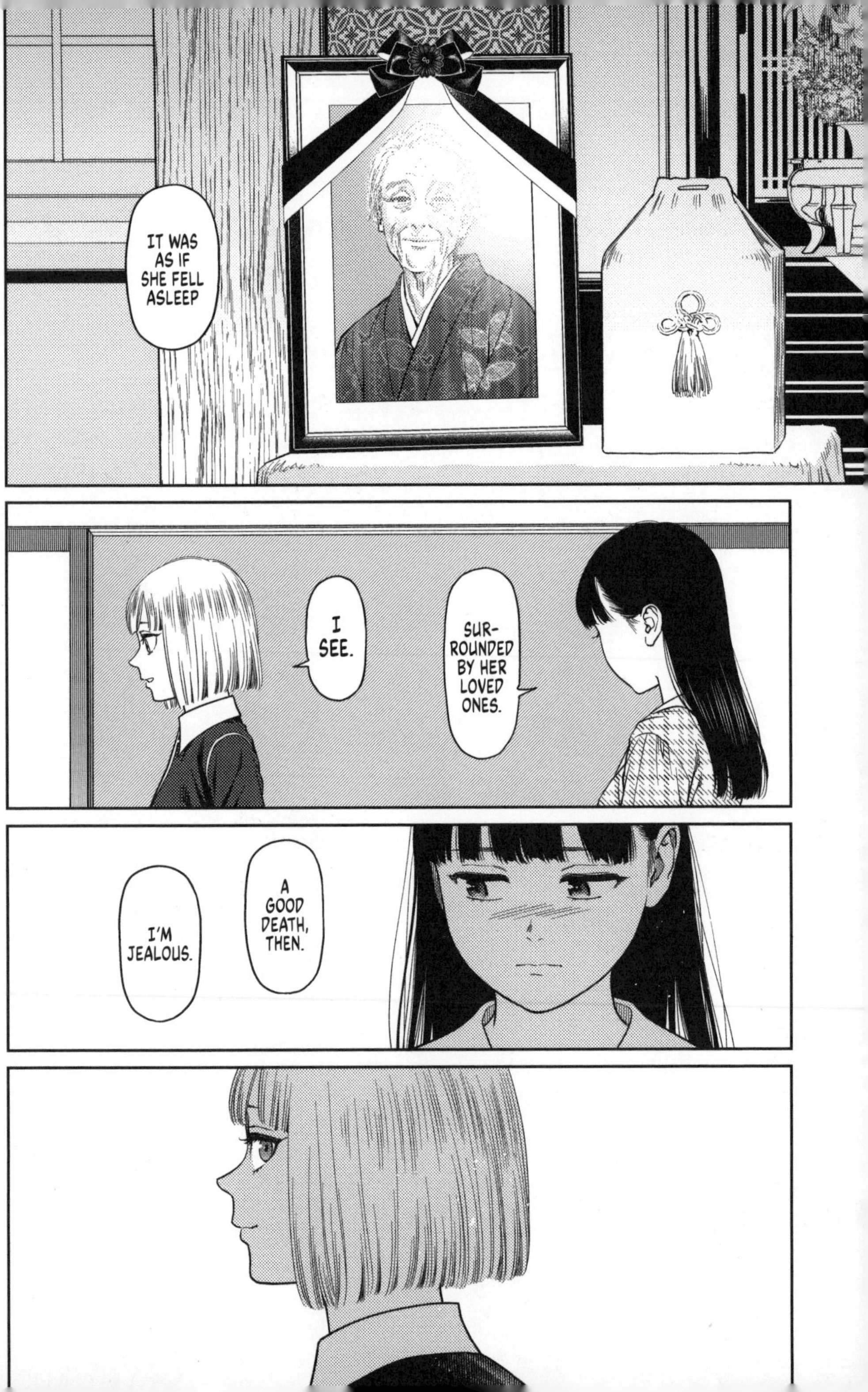

IT WAS AS IF SHE FELL ASLEEP
SUR-ROUNDED BY HER LOVED ONES.
I SEE.
A GOOD DEATH, THEN.
I'M JEALOUS.

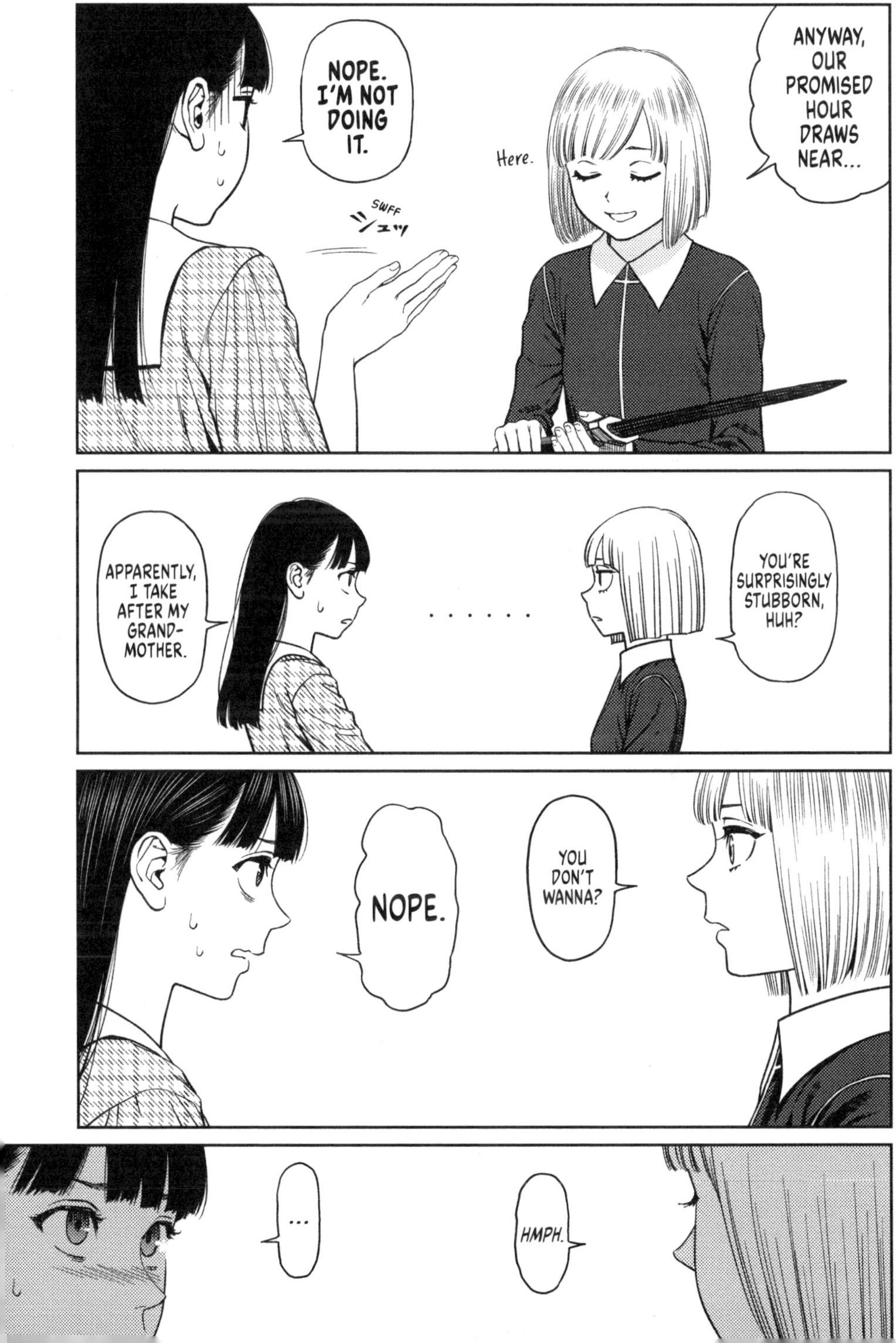
ANYWAY, OUR PROMISED HOUR DRAWS NEAR...
Here.
SWFF
シュッ
NOPE. I'M NOT DOING IT.
YOU'RE SURPRISINGLY STUBBORN, HUH?
....
APPARENTLY, I TAKE AFTER MY GRANDMOTHER.
YOU DON'T WANNA?
NOPE.
HMPH.
...

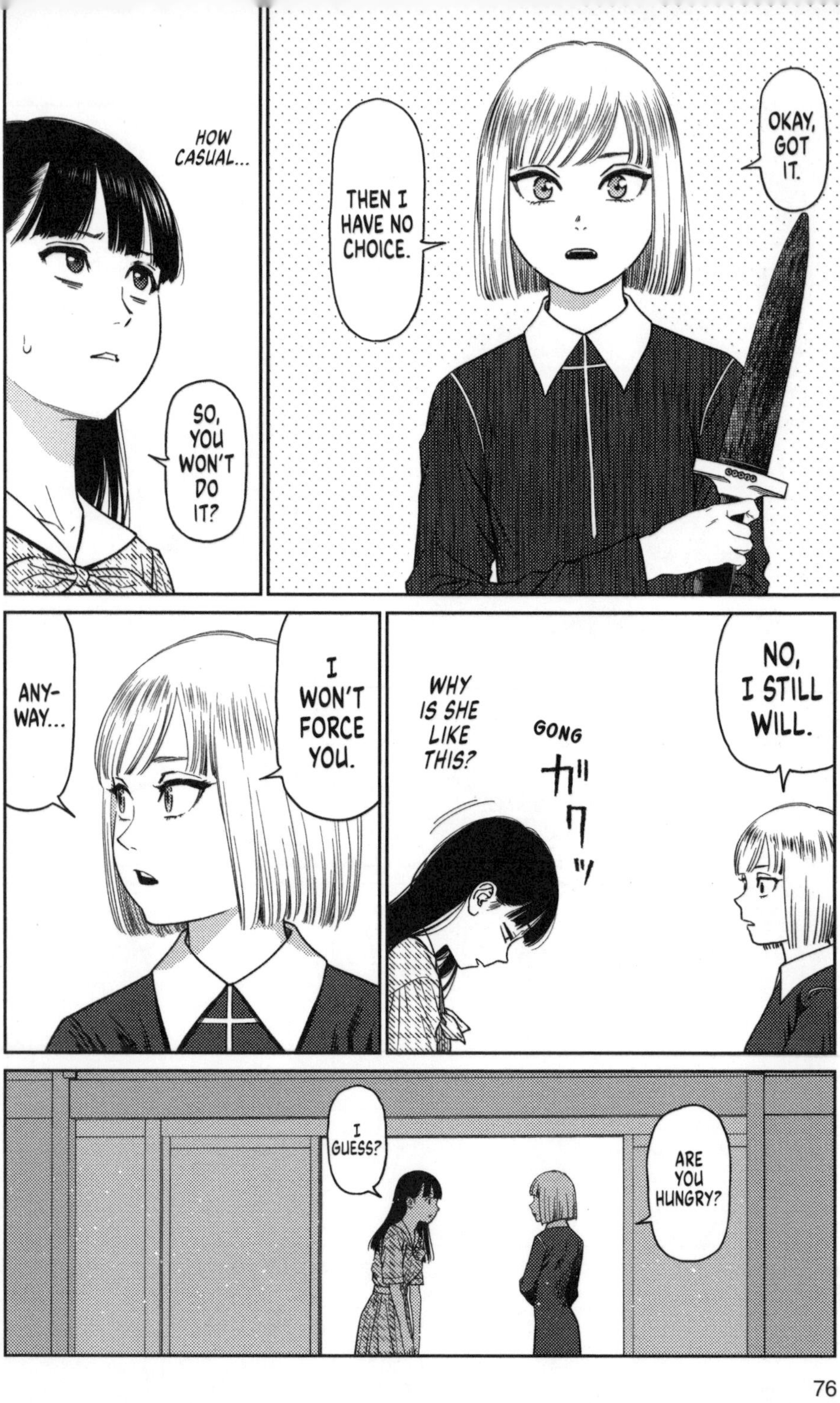
OKAY, GOT IT.
THEN I HAVE NO CHOICE.
HOW CASUAL...
SO, YOU WON'T DO IT?
NO, I STILL WILL.
GONG
ガクッ
WHY IS SHE LIKE THIS?
I WON'T FORCE YOU.
ANY-WAY...
ARE YOU HUNGRY?
I GUESS?

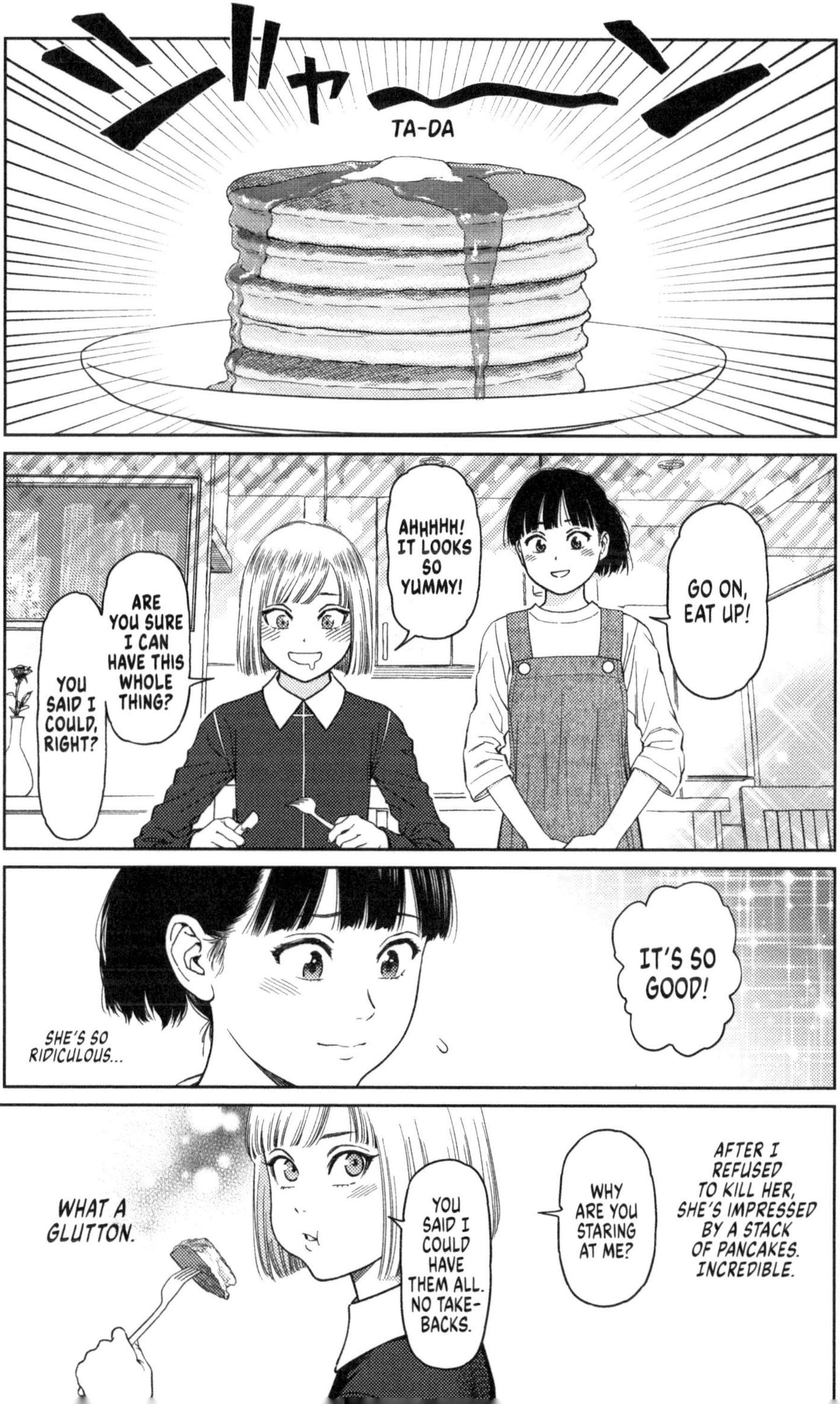
ジャ～～ン
TA-DA
GO ON, EAT UP!
AHHHHH! IT LOOKS SO YUMMY!
ARE YOU SURE I CAN HAVE THIS WHOLE THING?
YOU SAID I COULD, RIGHT?
IT'S SO GOOD!
SHE'S SO RIDICULOUS...
AFTER I REFUSED TO KILL HER, SHE'S IMPRESSED BY A STACK OF PANCAKES. INCREDIBLE.
WHY ARE YOU STARING AT ME?
YOU SAID I COULD HAVE THEM ALL. NO TAKE-BACKS.
WHAT A GLUTTON.

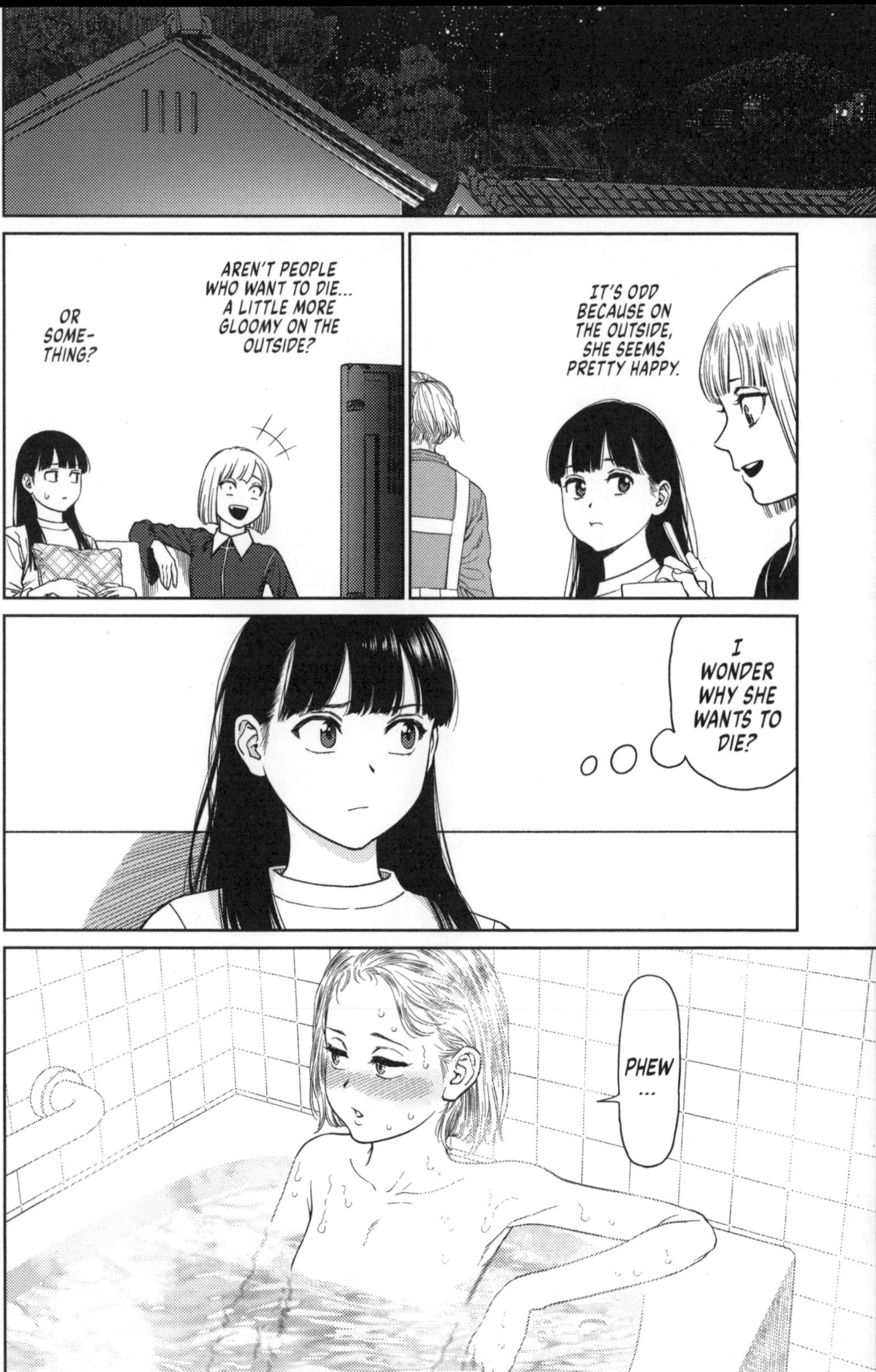
IT'S ODD BECAUSE ON THE OUTSIDE, SHE SEEMS PRETTY HAPPY.
AREN'T PEOPLE WHO WANT TO DIE... A LITTLE MORE GLOOMY ON THE OUTSIDE?
OR SOME-THING?
I WONDER WHY SHE WANTS TO DIE?
PHEW ...

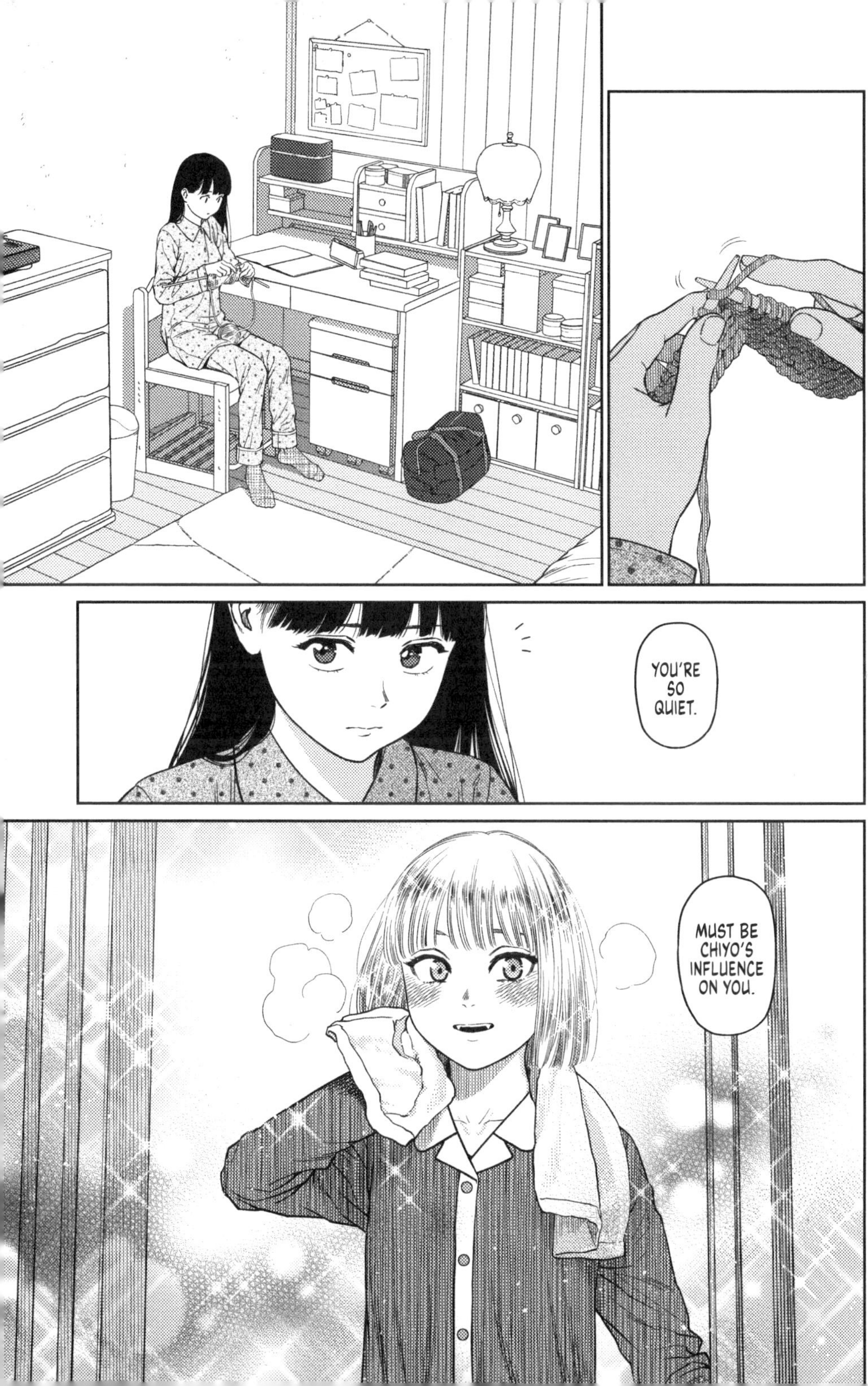
YOU'RE SO QUIET.
MUST BE CHIYO'S INFLUENCE ON YOU.

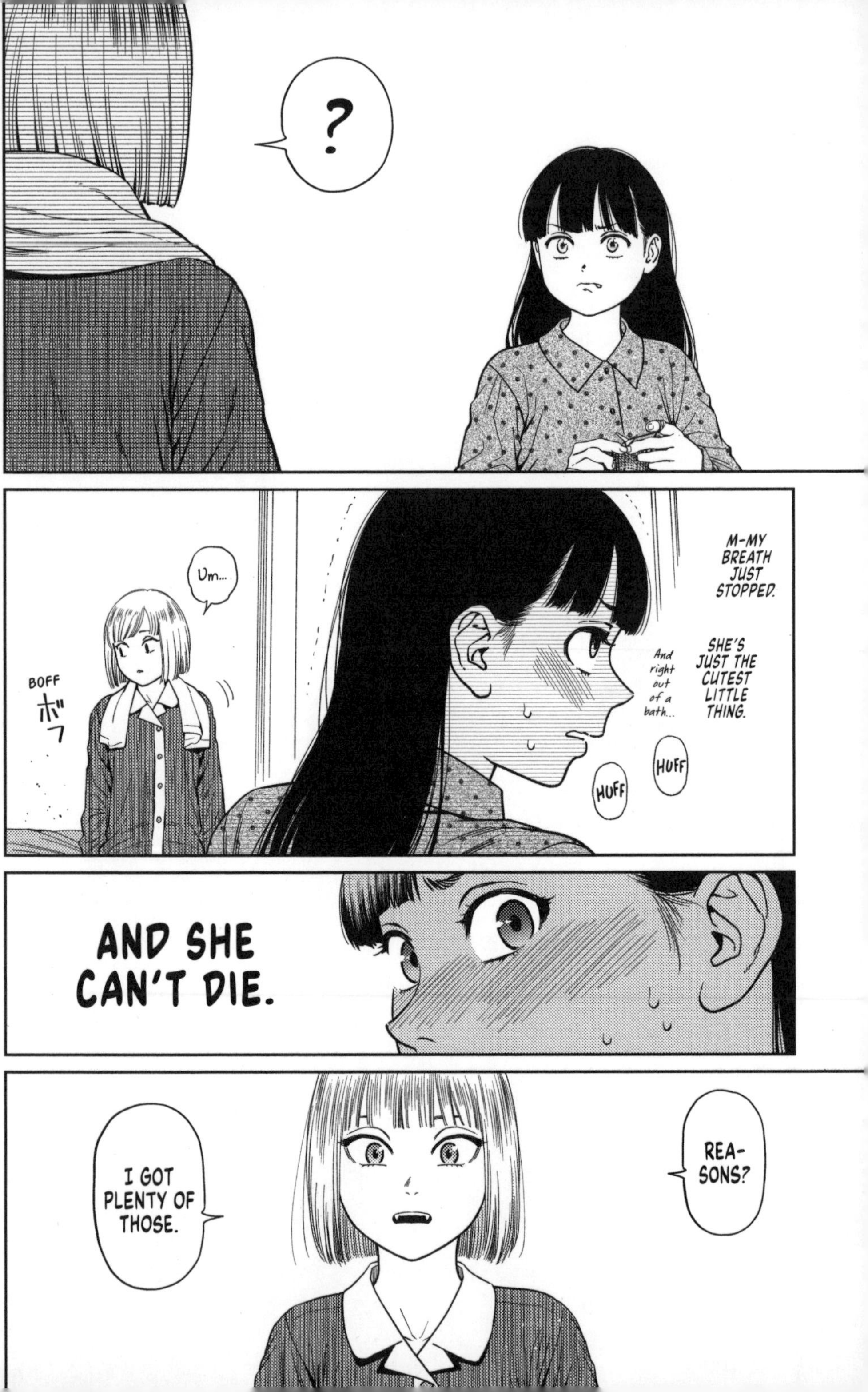
?
M-MY BREATH JUST STOPPED.
SHE'S JUST THE CUTEST LITTLE THING.
And right out of a bath...
HUFF
HUFF
Um...
BOFF
ボフ
AND SHE CAN'T DIE.
REA-SONS?
I GOT PLENTY OF THOSE.

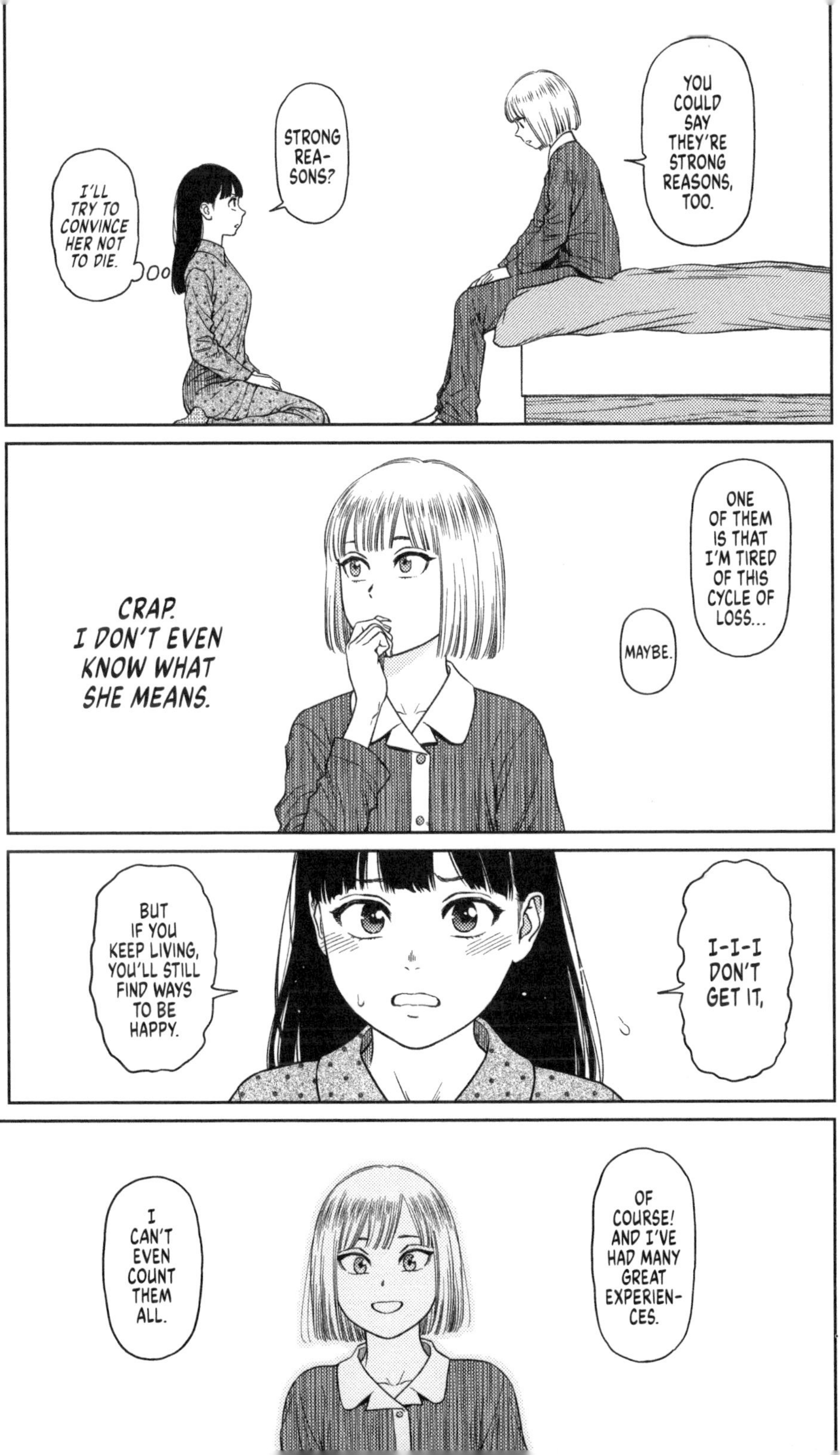
YOU COULD SAY THEY'RE STRONG REASONS, TOO.
STRONG REA-SONS?
I'LL TRY TO CONVINCE HER NOT TO DIE.
ONE OF THEM IS THAT I'M TIRED OF THIS CYCLE OF LOSS...
MAYBE.
CRAP. I DON'T EVEN KNOW WHAT SHE MEANS.
I-I-I DON'T GET IT,
BUT IF YOU KEEP LIVING, YOU'LL STILL FIND WAYS TO BE HAPPY.
OF COURSE! AND I'VE HAD MANY GREAT EXPERIEN-CES.
I CAN'T EVEN COUNT THEM ALL.

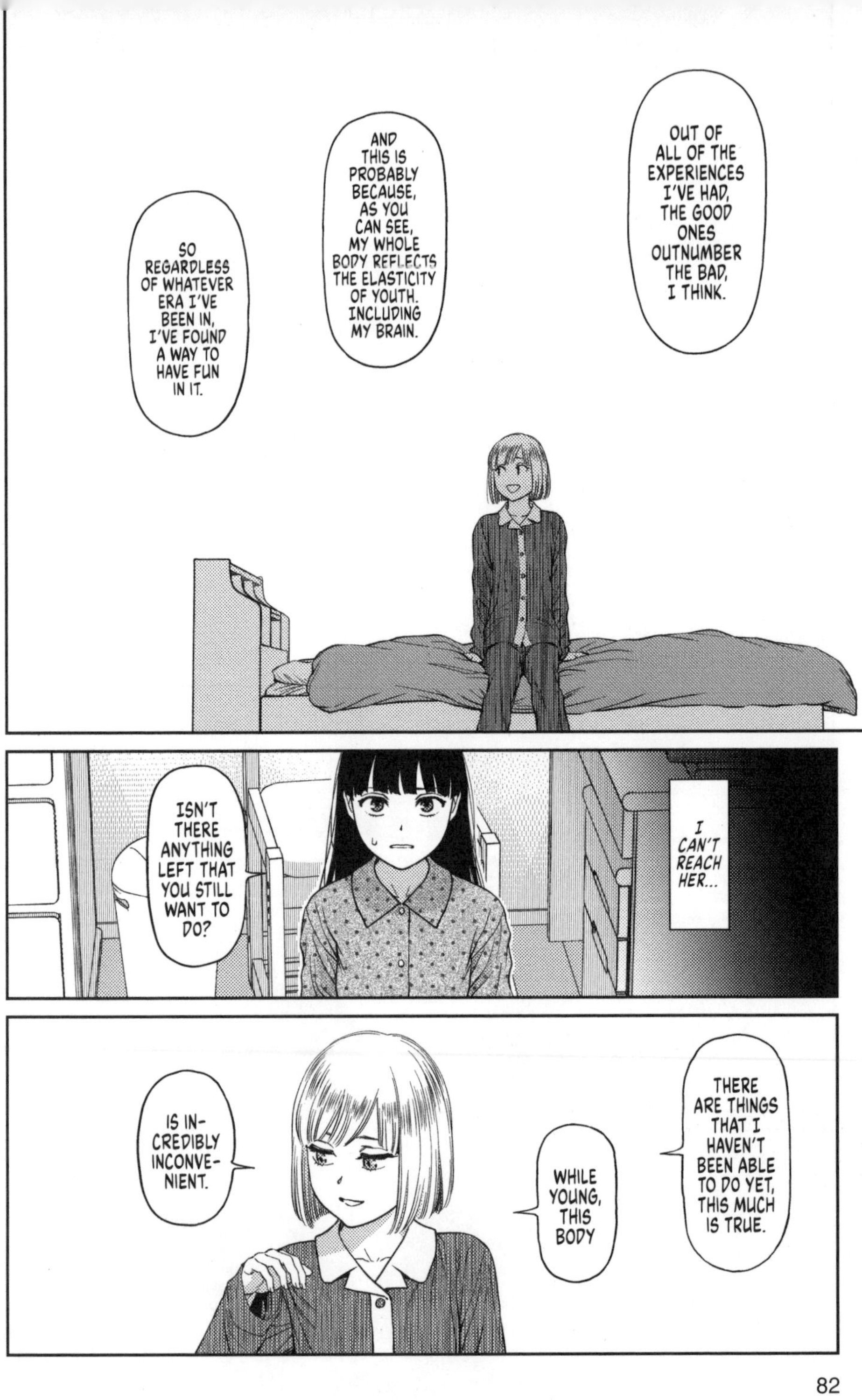
OUT OF ALL OF THE EXPERIENCES I'VE HAD, THE GOOD ONES OUTNUMBER THE BAD, I THINK.
AND THIS IS PROBABLY BECAUSE, AS YOU CAN SEE, MY WHOLE BODY REFLECTS THE ELASTICITY OF YOUTH. INCLUDING MY BRAIN.
SO REGARDLESS OF WHATEVER ERA I'VE BEEN IN, I'VE FOUND A WAY TO HAVE FUN IN IT.
I CAN'T REACH HER...
ISN'T THERE ANYTHING LEFT THAT YOU STILL WANT TO DO?
THERE ARE THINGS THAT I HAVEN'T BEEN ABLE TO DO YET, THIS MUCH IS TRUE.
WHILE YOUNG, THIS BODY
IS IN-CREDIBLY INCONVE-NIENT.

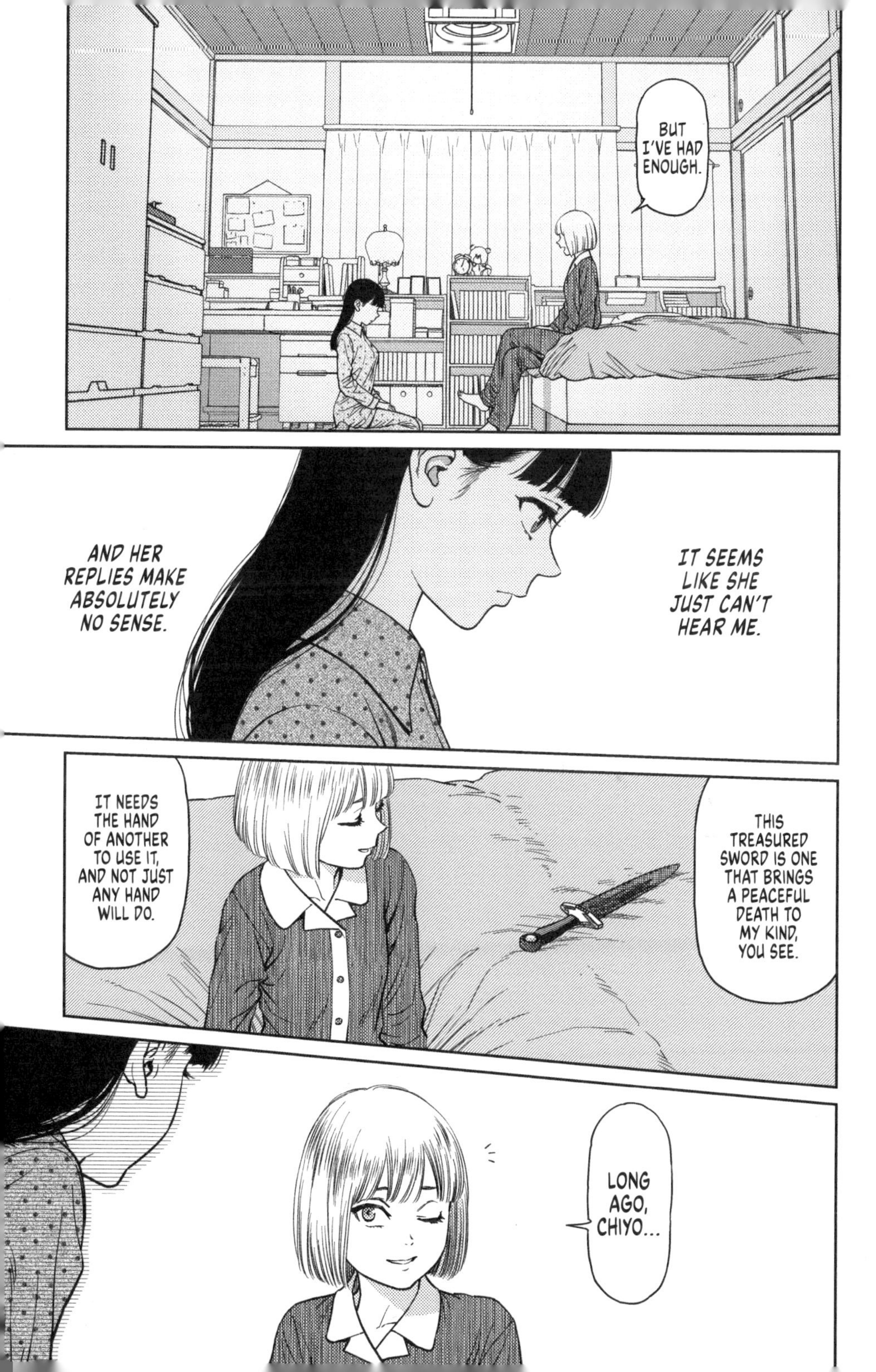
BUT I'VE HAD ENOUGH.
IT SEEMS LIKE SHE JUST CAN'T HEAR ME.
AND HER REPLIES MAKE ABSOLUTELY NO SENSE.
THIS TREASURED SWORD IS ONE THAT BRINGS A PEACEFUL DEATH TO MY KIND, YOU SEE.
IT NEEDS THE HAND OF ANOTHER TO USE IT, AND NOT JUST ANY HAND WILL DO.
LONG AGO, CHIYO...

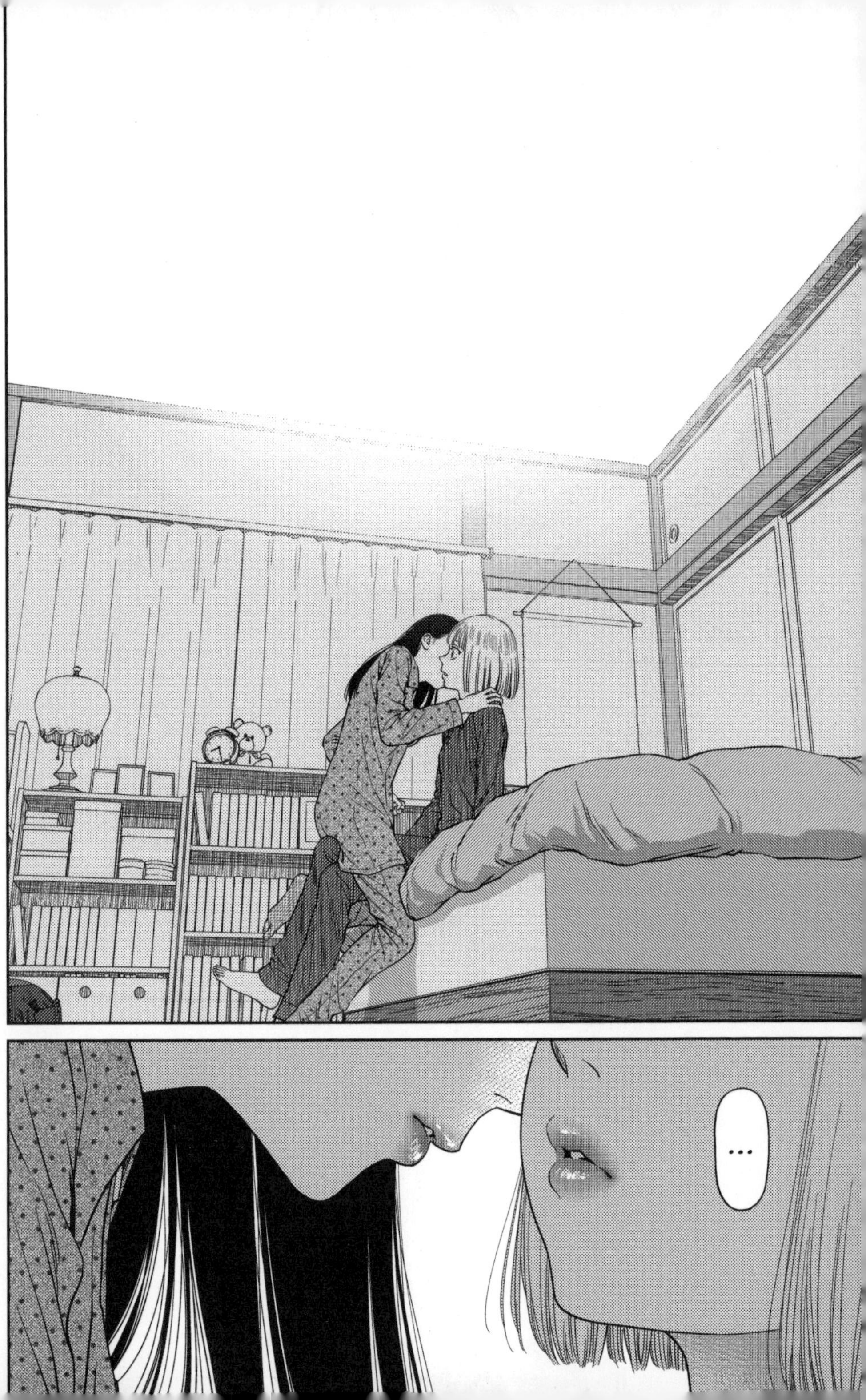
…

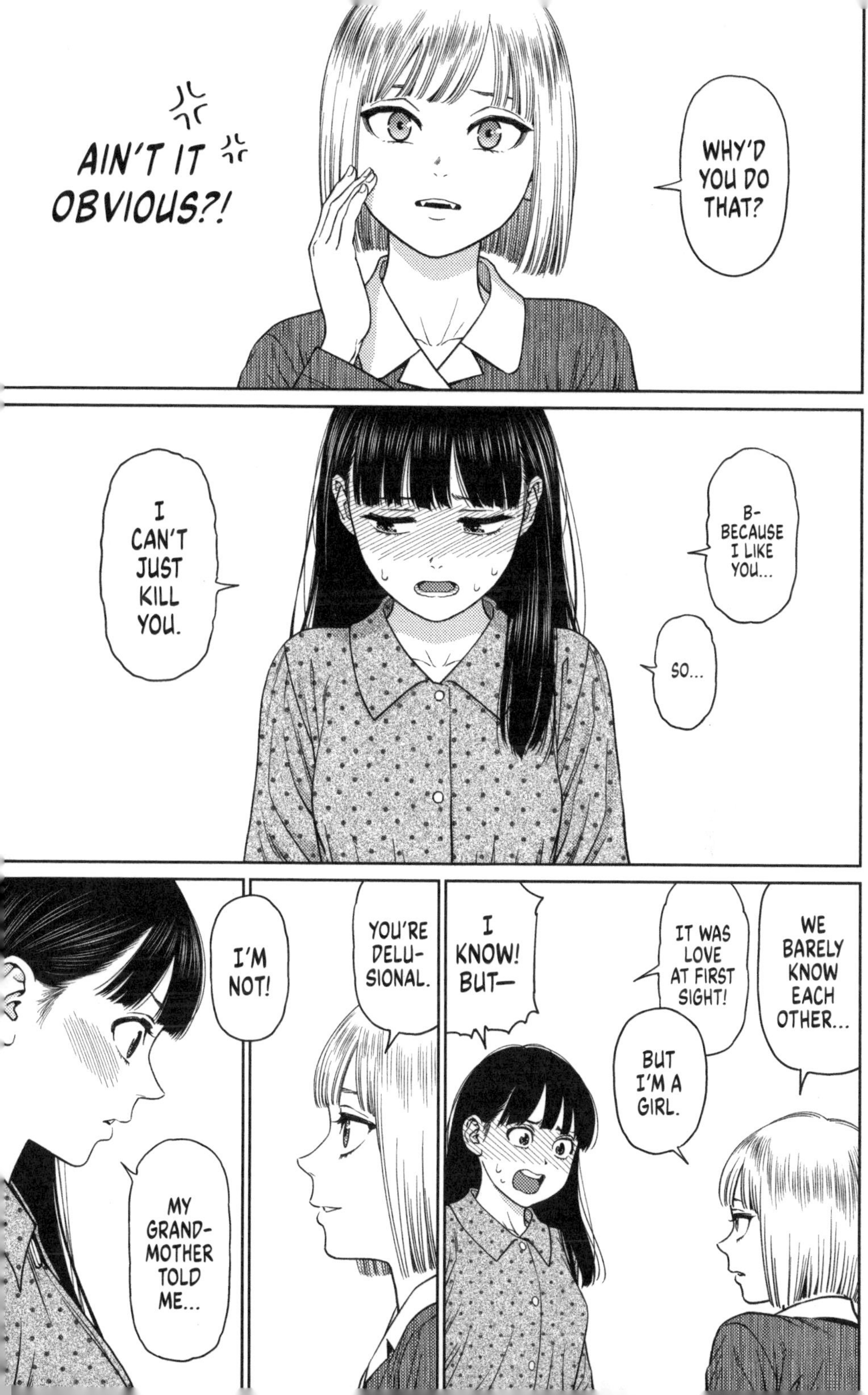
WHY'D YOU DO THAT?
AIN'T IT OBVIOUS?!
B-BECAUSE I LIKE YOU...
SO...
I CAN'T JUST KILL YOU.
WE BARELY KNOW EACH OTHER...
IT WAS LOVE AT FIRST SIGHT!
BUT I'M A GIRL.
I KNOW! BUT—
YOU'RE DELU-SIONAL.
I'M NOT!
MY GRAND-MOTHER TOLD ME...

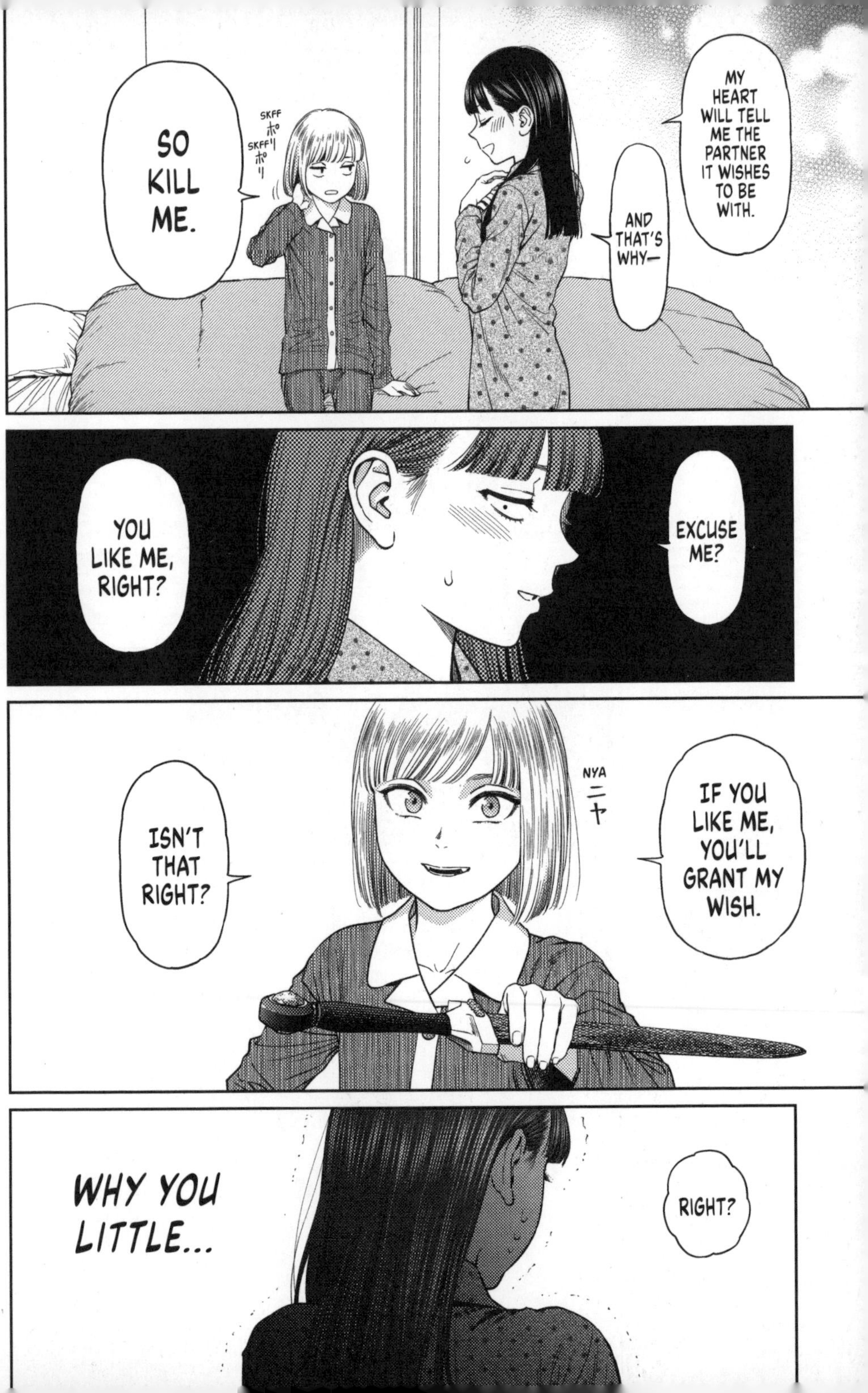
MY HEART WILL TELL ME THE PARTNER IT WISHES TO BE WITH.
AND THAT'S WHY—
SKFF ポリ
SKFF ポリ
SO KILL ME.
EXCUSE ME?
YOU LIKE ME, RIGHT?
NYA ニヤ
IF YOU LIKE ME, YOU'LL GRANT MY WISH.
ISN'T THAT RIGHT?
RIGHT?
WHY YOU LITTLE...

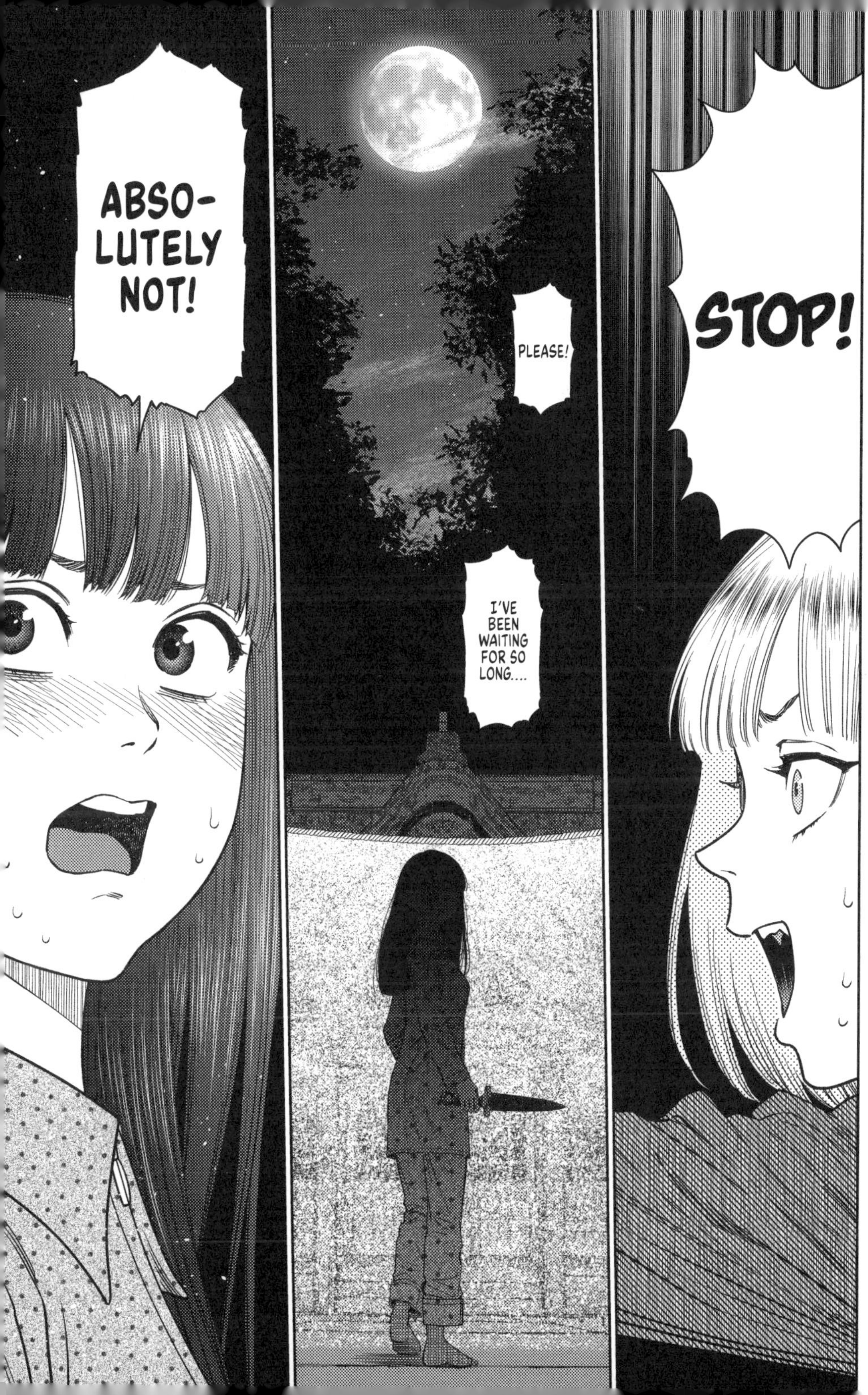
STOP!
PLEASE!
I'VE BEEN WAITING FOR SO LONG....
ABSO-LUTELY NOT!

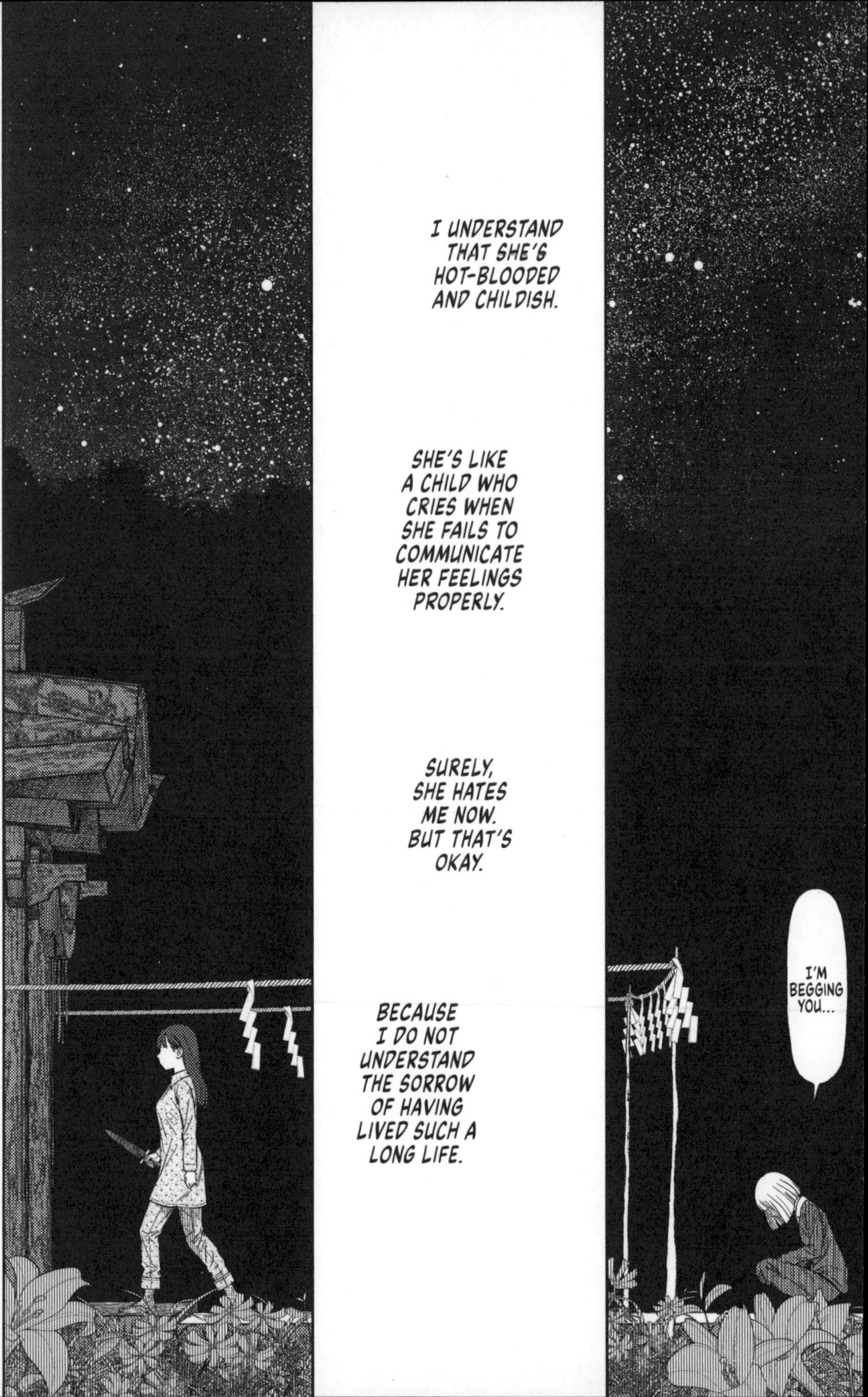
I'M BEGGING YOU...
I UNDERSTAND THAT SHE'S HOT-BLOODED AND CHILDISH.
SHE'S LIKE A CHILD WHO CRIES WHEN SHE FAILS TO COMMUNICATE HER FEELINGS PROPERLY.
SURELY, SHE HATES ME NOW. BUT THAT'S OKAY.
BECAUSE I DO NOT UNDERSTAND THE SORROW OF HAVING LIVED SUCH A LONG LIFE.

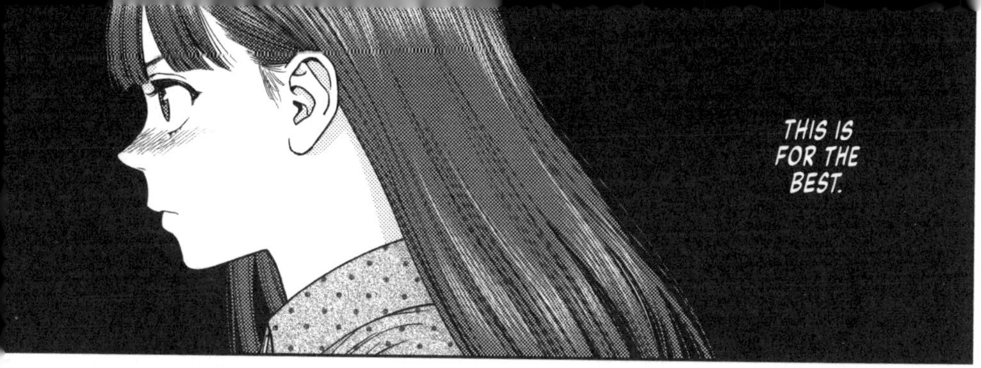
THIS IS FOR THE BEST.

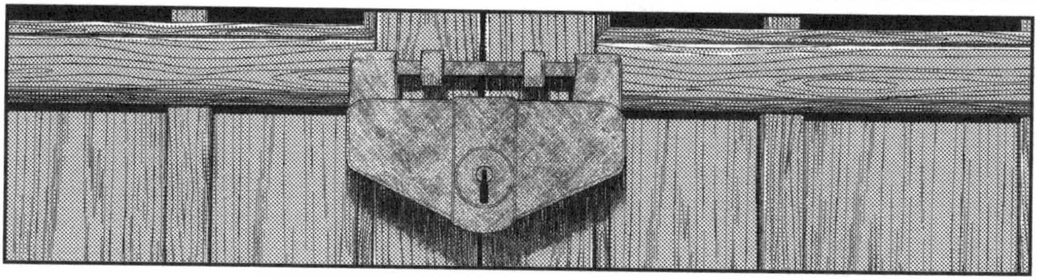

AFTER I CAME BACK OUT OF THE SHRINE, ARIA WAS ALREADY GONE.

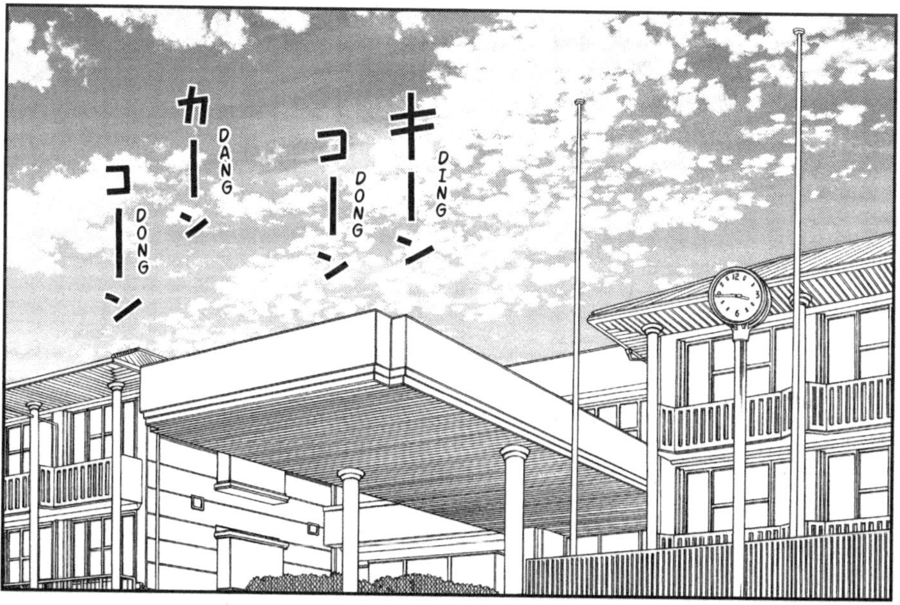
キーン
DING
コーン
DONG
カーン
DANG
コーン
DONG

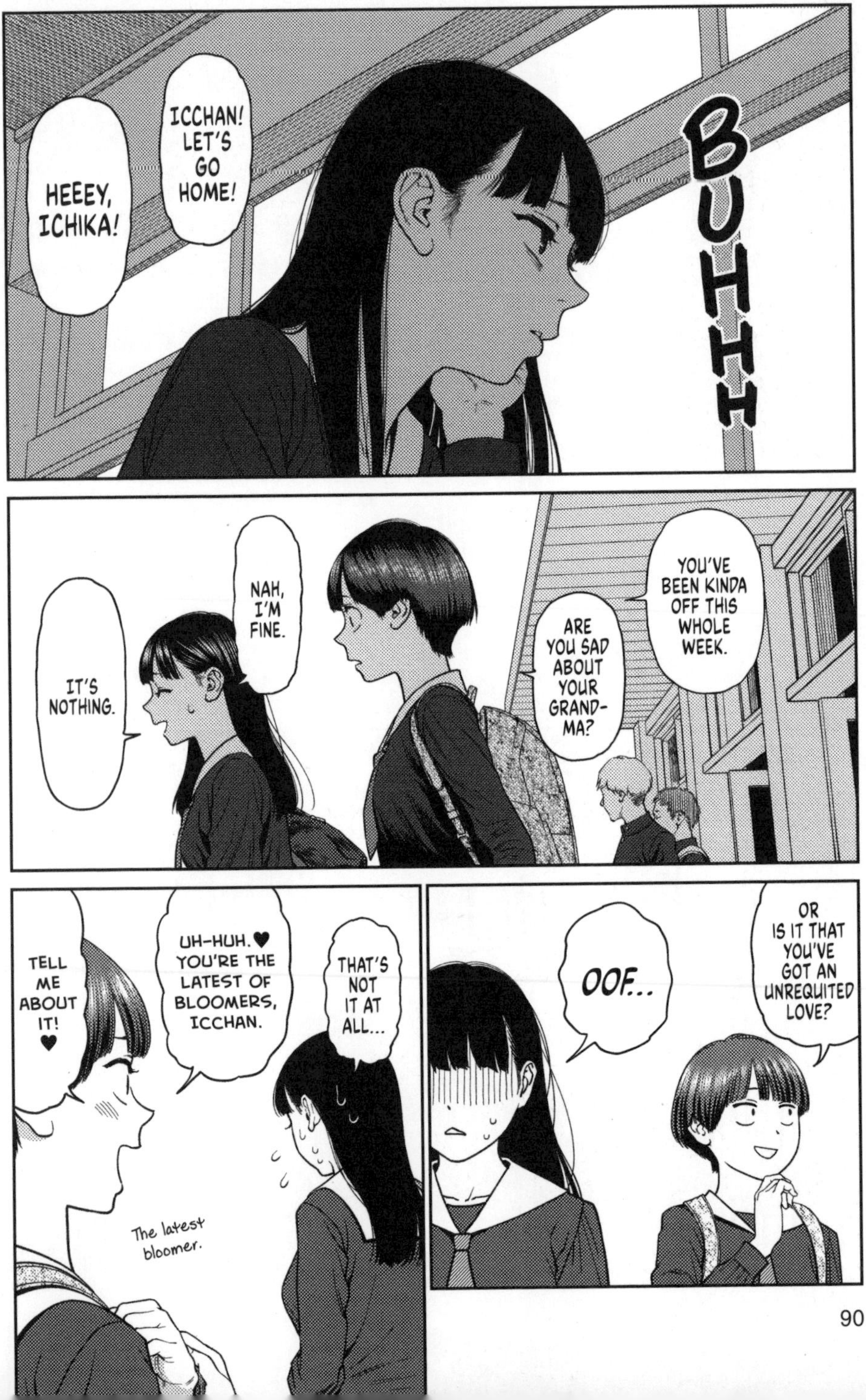
BUHHH
ICCHAN! LET'S GO HOME!
HEEEY, ICHIKA!
YOU'VE BEEN KINDA OFF THIS WHOLE WEEK.
ARE YOU SAD ABOUT YOUR GRAND-MA?
NAH, I'M FINE.
IT'S NOTHING.
OR IS IT THAT YOU'VE GOT AN UNREQUITED LOVE?
OOF...
THAT'S NOT IT AT ALL...
UH-HUH.♥ YOU'RE THE LATEST OF BLOOMERS, ICCHAN.
TELL ME ABOUT IT! ♥
The latest bloomer.

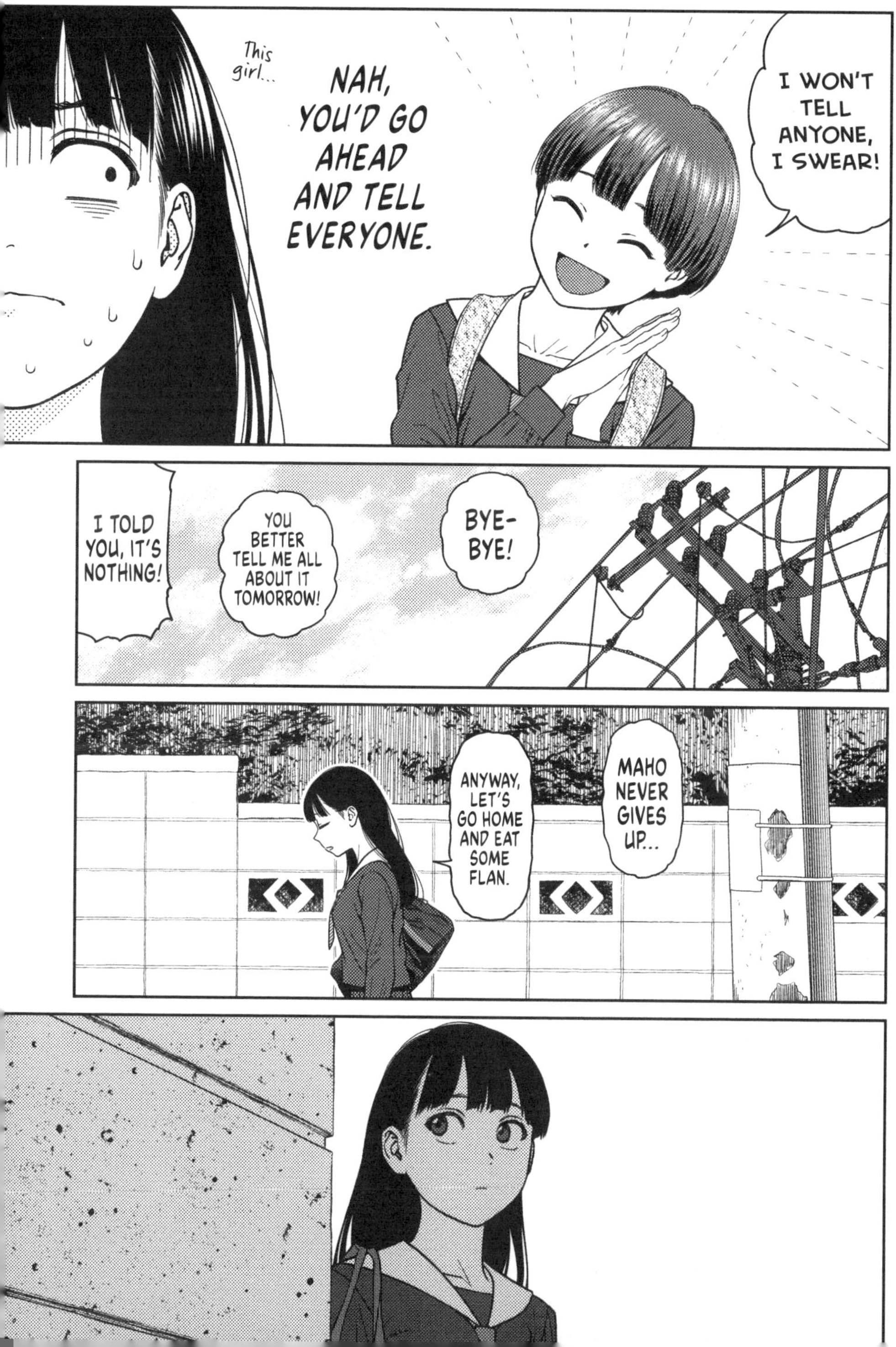
I WON'T TELL ANYONE, I SWEAR!
NAH, YOU'D GO AHEAD AND TELL EVERYONE.
This girl...
BYE-BYE!
YOU BETTER TELL ME ALL ABOUT IT TOMORROW!
I TOLD YOU, IT'S NOTHING!
MAHO NEVER GIVES UP...
ANYWAY, LET'S GO HOME AND EAT SOME FLAN.

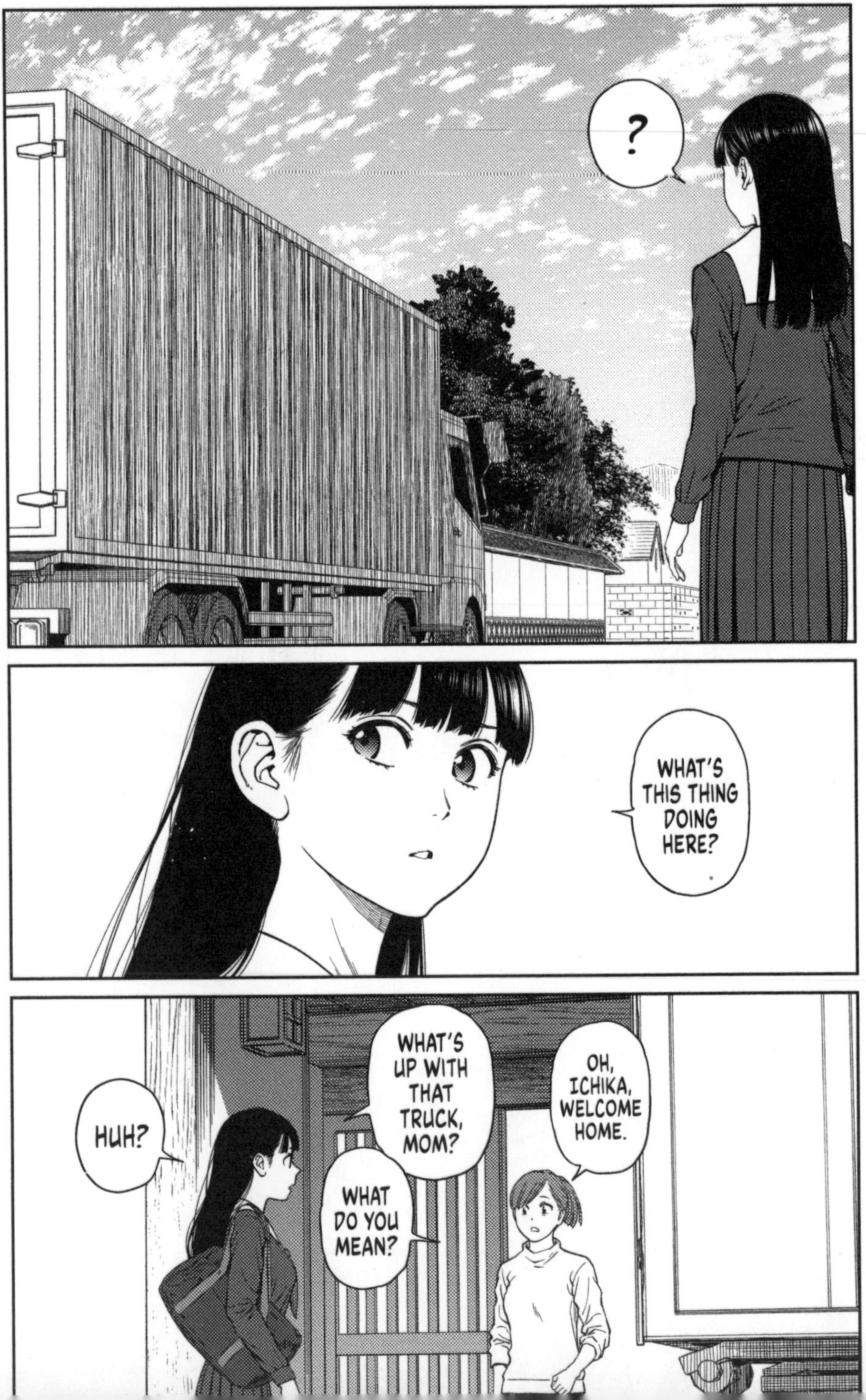
?
WHAT'S THIS THING DOING HERE?
OH, ICHIKA, WELCOME HOME.
WHAT'S UP WITH THAT TRUCK, MOM?
WHAT DO YOU MEAN?
HUH?

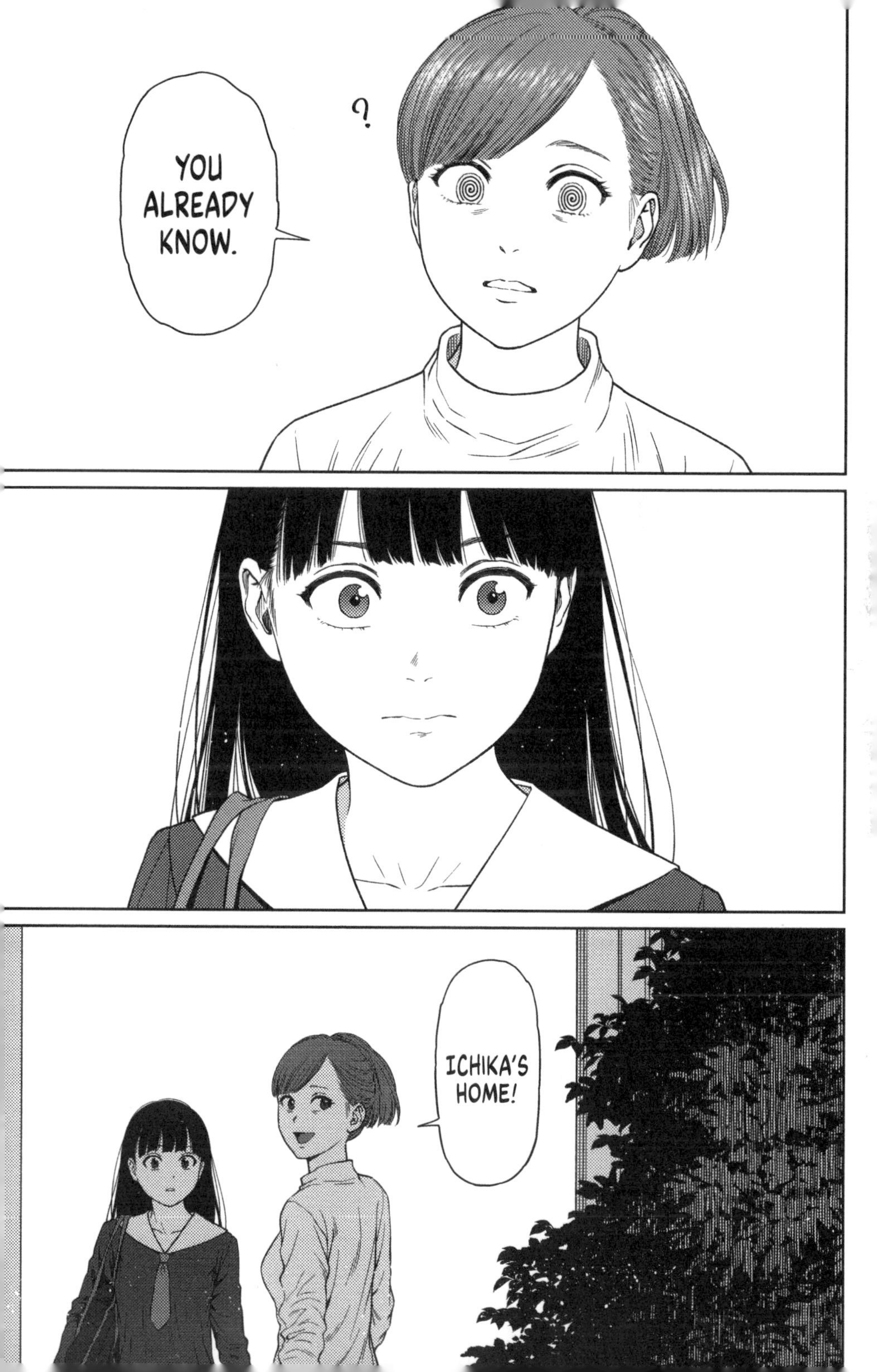
YOU ALREADY KNOW.
?
ICHIKA'S HOME!

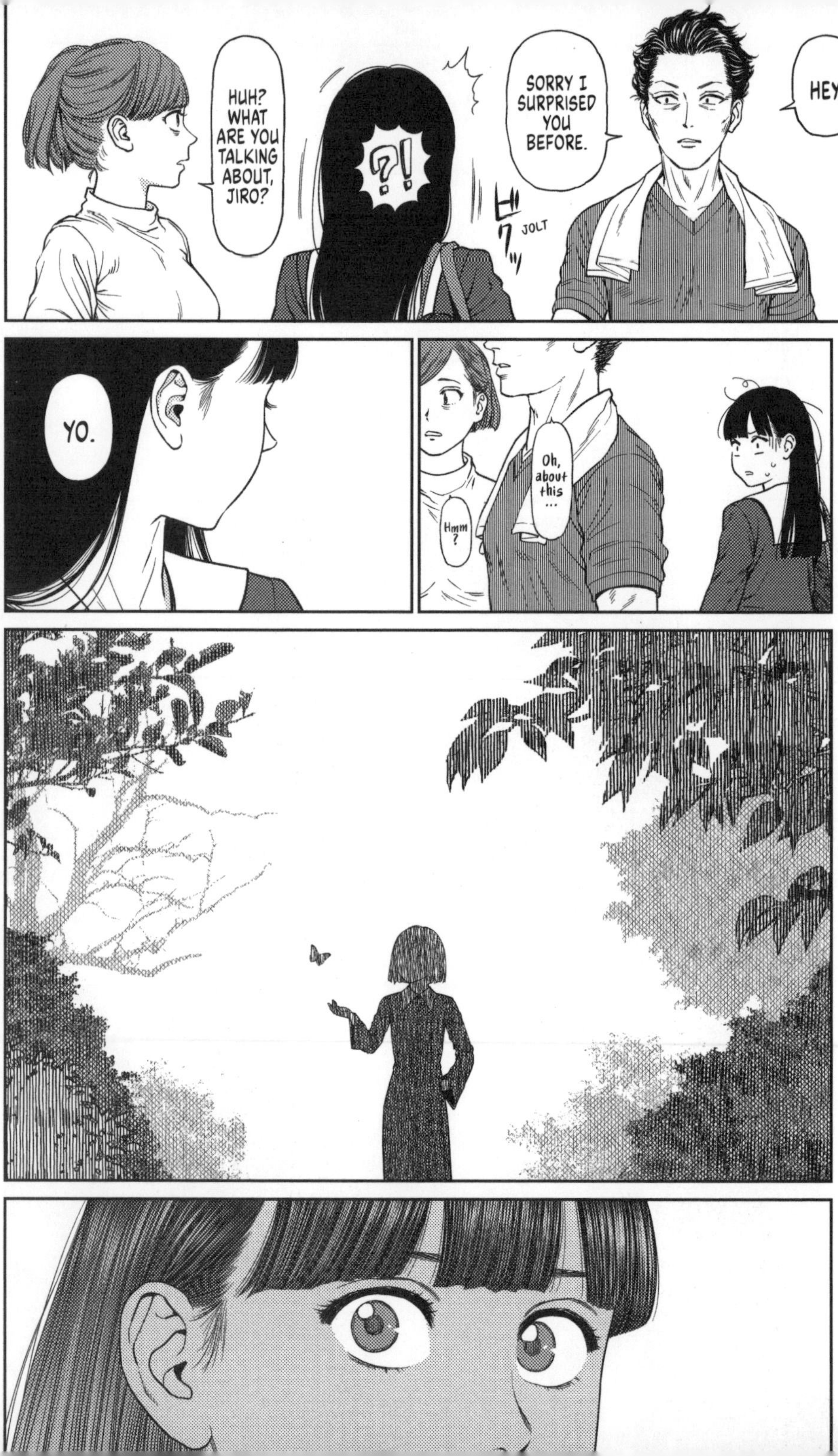
HEY,
SORRY I SURPRISED YOU BEFORE.
?!
ビクッ
JOLT
HUH? WHAT ARE YOU TALKING ABOUT, JIRO?
Oh, about this ...
Hmm?
YO.

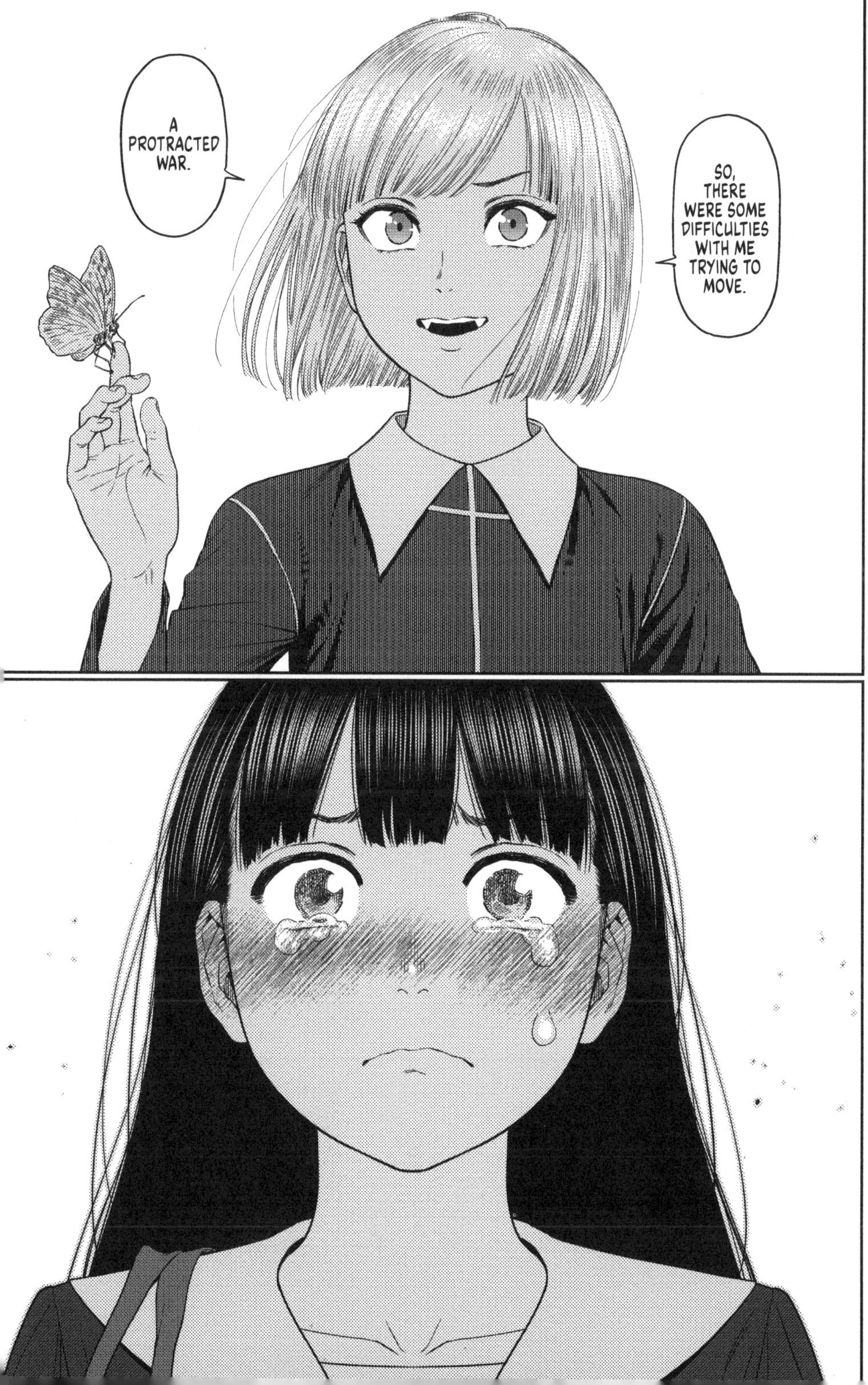
SO, THERE WERE SOME DIFFICULTIES WITH ME TRYING TO MOVE.
A PROTRACTED WAR.

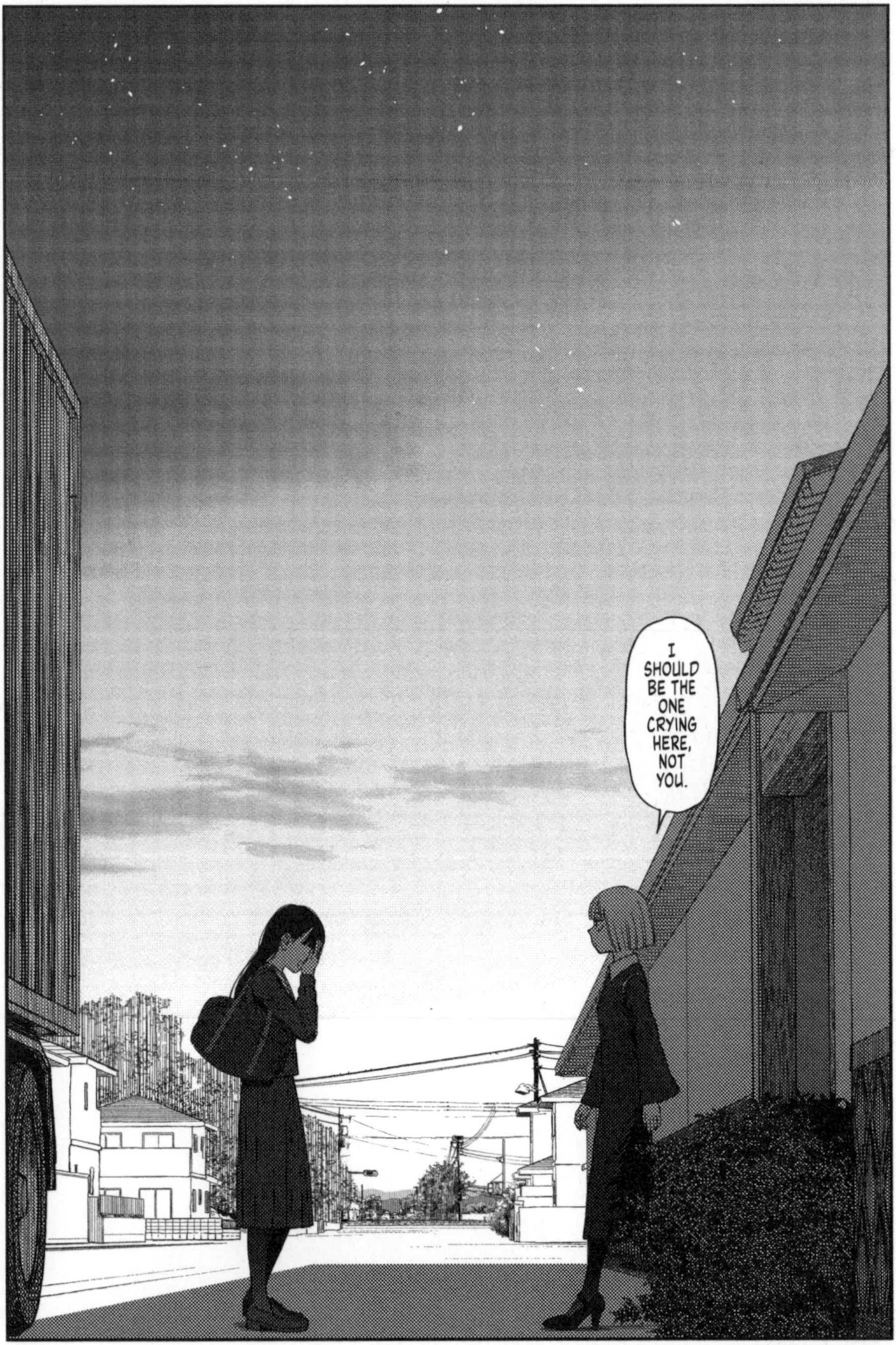
I SHOULD BE THE ONE CRYING HERE, NOT YOU.

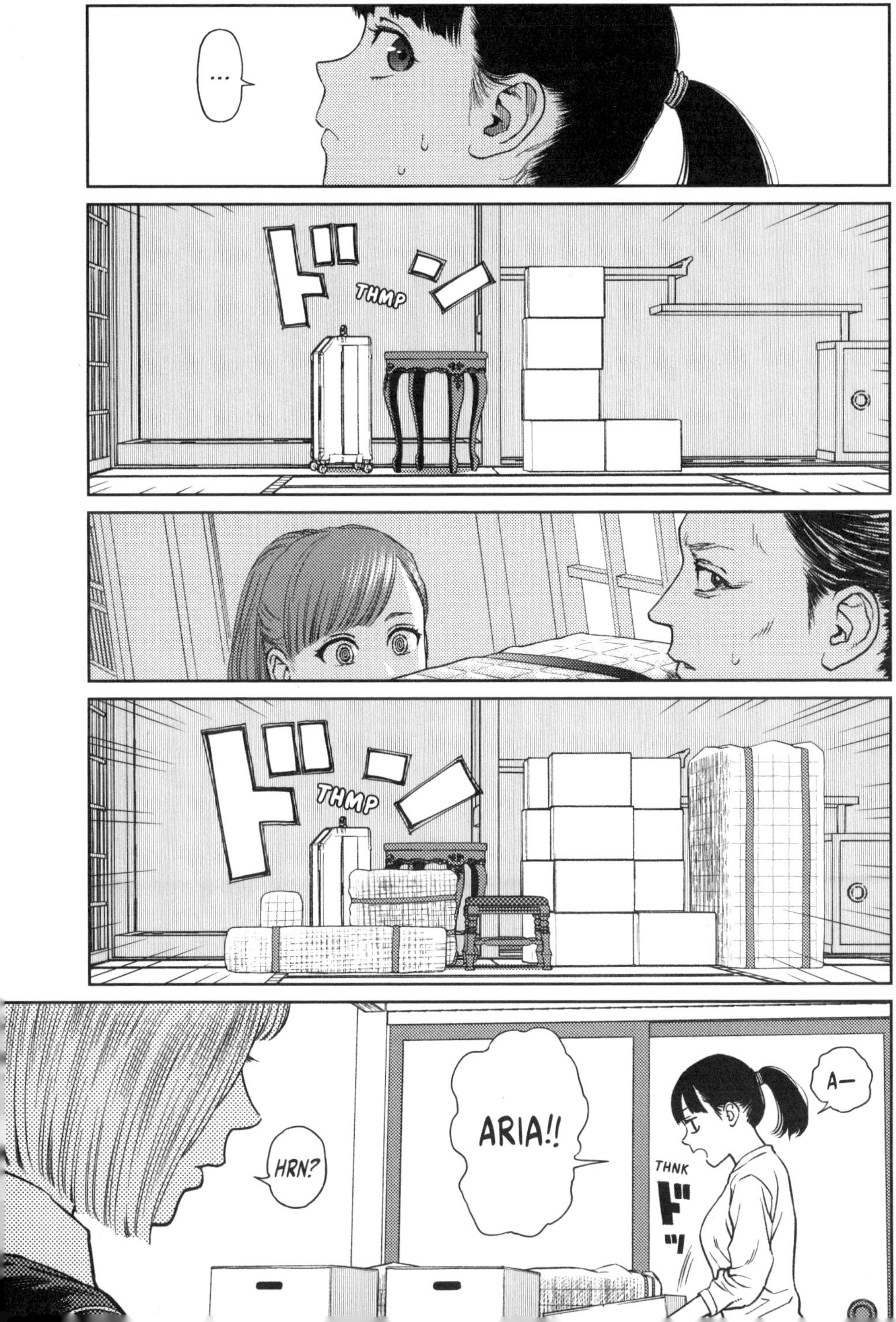
…
ドン
THMP
ドン
THMP
A—
ARIA!!
THNK
ドッ
HRN?

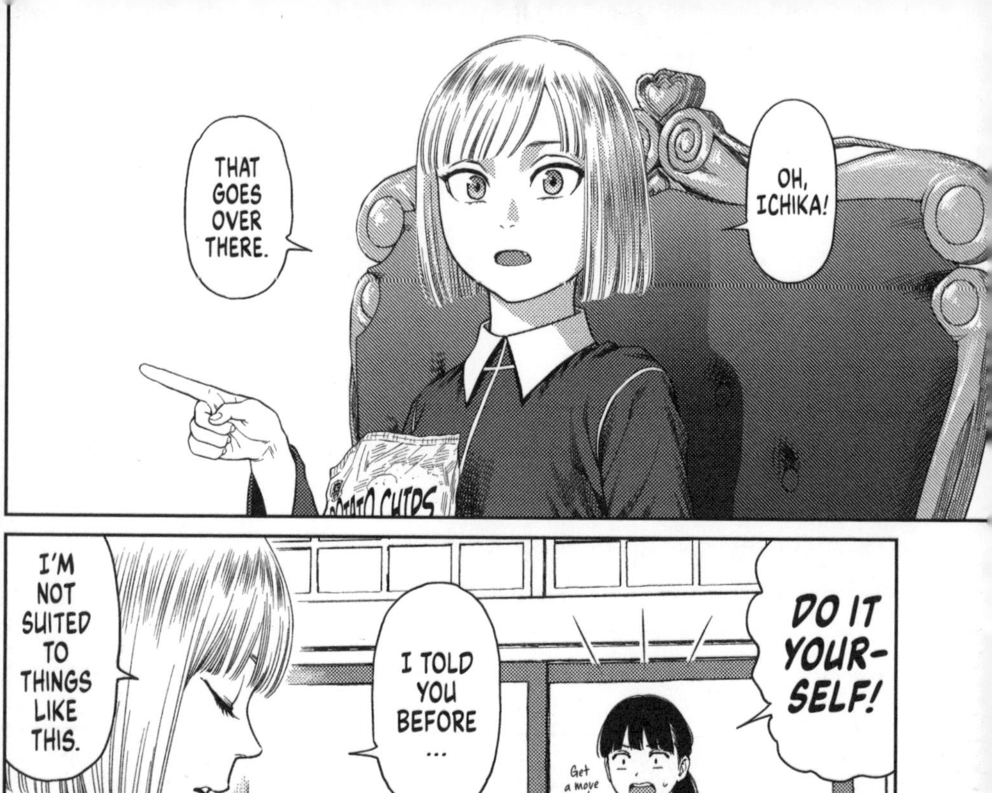
OH, ICHIKA!
THAT GOES OVER THERE.
DO IT YOURSELF!
Get a move on!
I TOLD YOU BEFORE ...
I'M NOT SUITED TO THINGS LIKE THIS.
ポリ
ポリ
KRUNCH
IF I WERE TO DO HARD LABOR LIKE THIS, I'D DIE.
Yum.
IT'S HOPELESS. STOP TRYING.
DRAT!

#4 INTRUDER

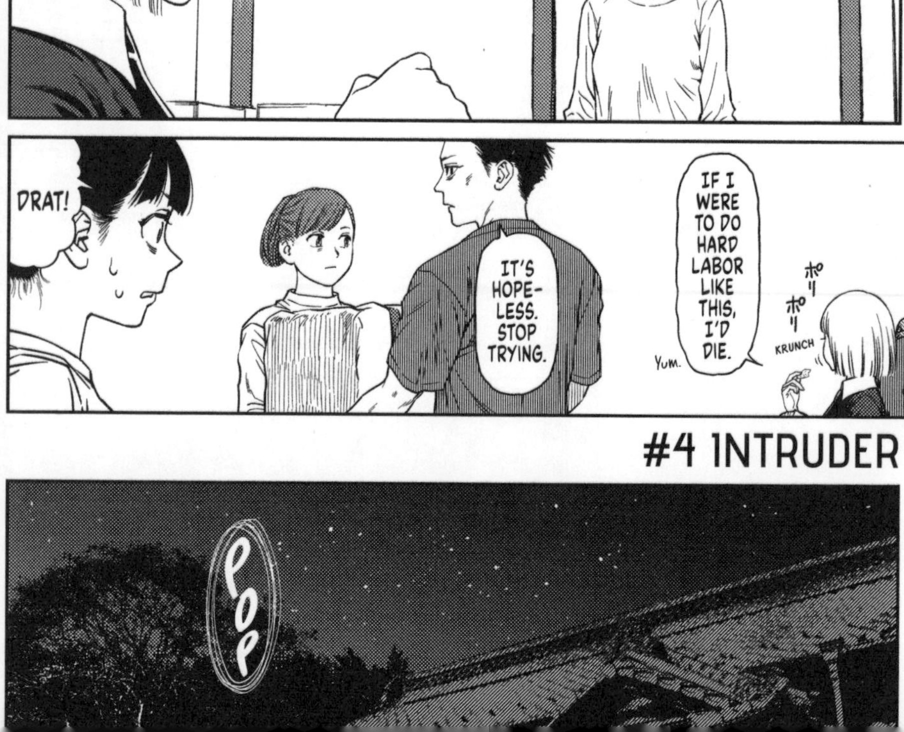
POP

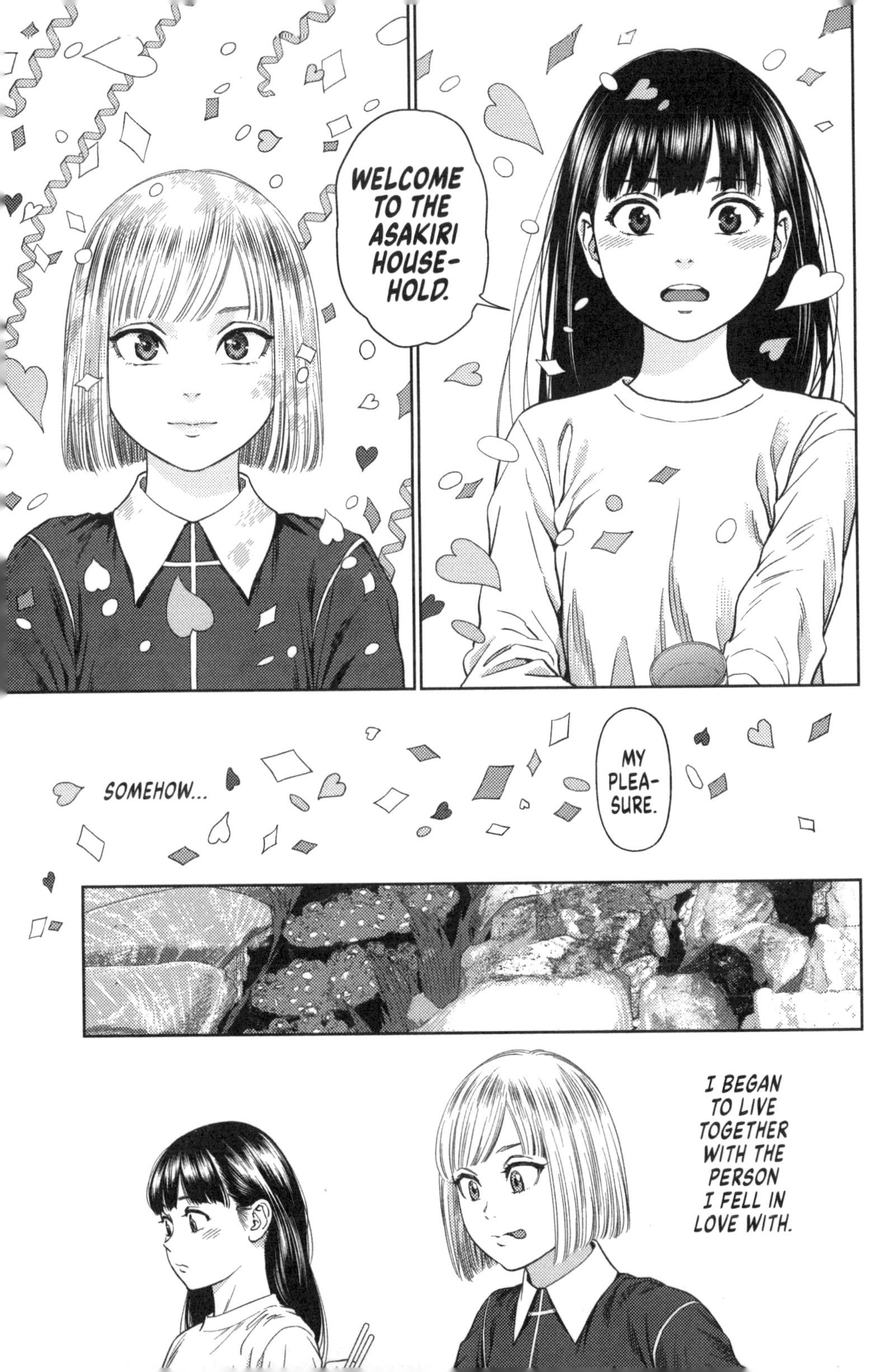
WELCOME TO THE ASAKIRI HOUSEHOLD.
MY PLEASURE.
SOMEHOW...
I BEGAN TO LIVE TOGETHER WITH THE PERSON I FELL IN LOVE WITH.

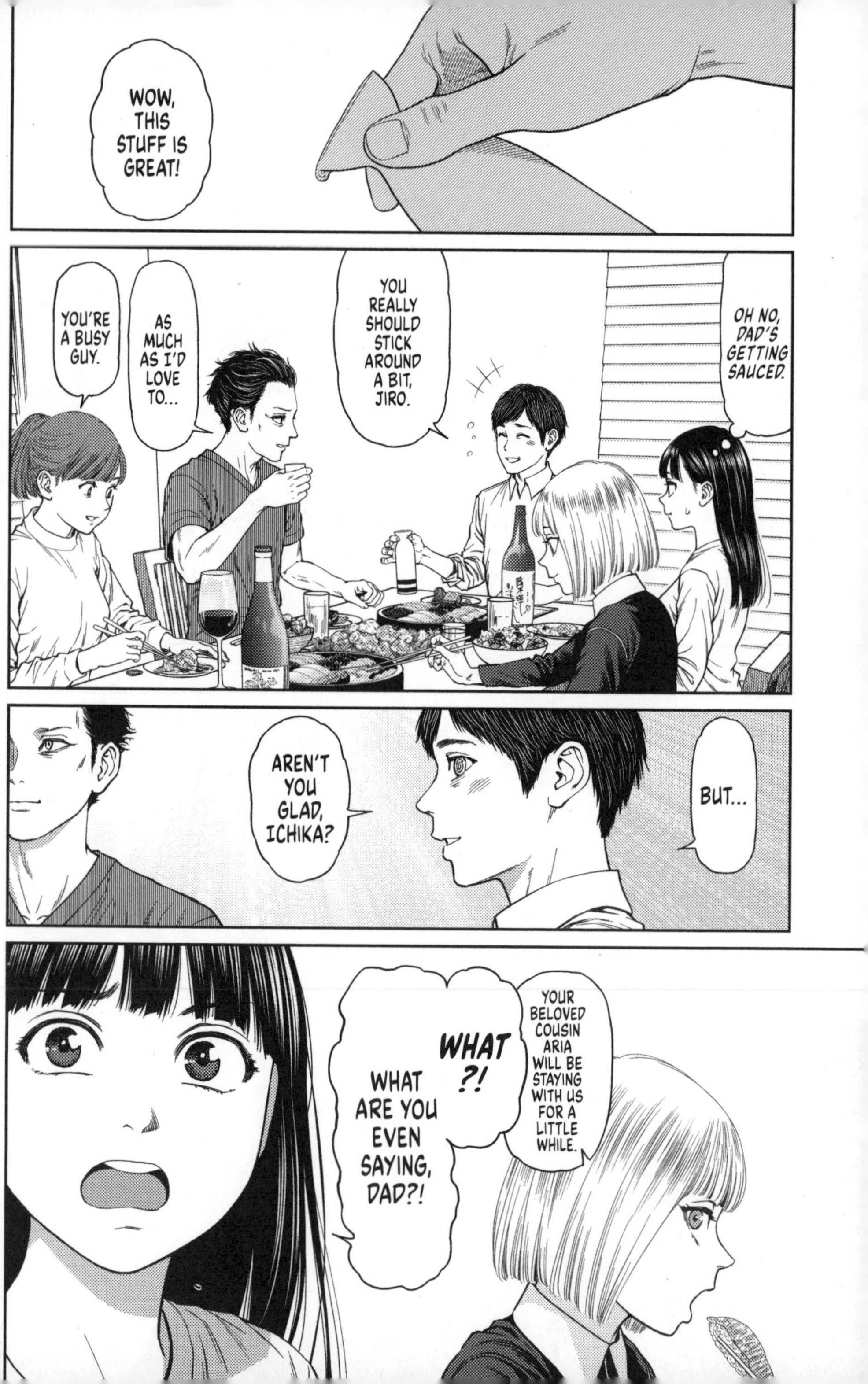
WOW, THIS STUFF IS GREAT!
OH NO, DAD'S GETTING SAUCED.
YOU REALLY SHOULD STICK AROUND A BIT, JIRO.
AS MUCH AS I'D LOVE TO...
YOU'RE A BUSY GUY.
BUT...
AREN'T YOU GLAD, ICHIKA?
YOUR BELOVED COUSIN ARIA WILL BE STAYING WITH US FOR A LITTLE WHILE.
WHAT?!
WHAT ARE YOU EVEN SAYING, DAD?!

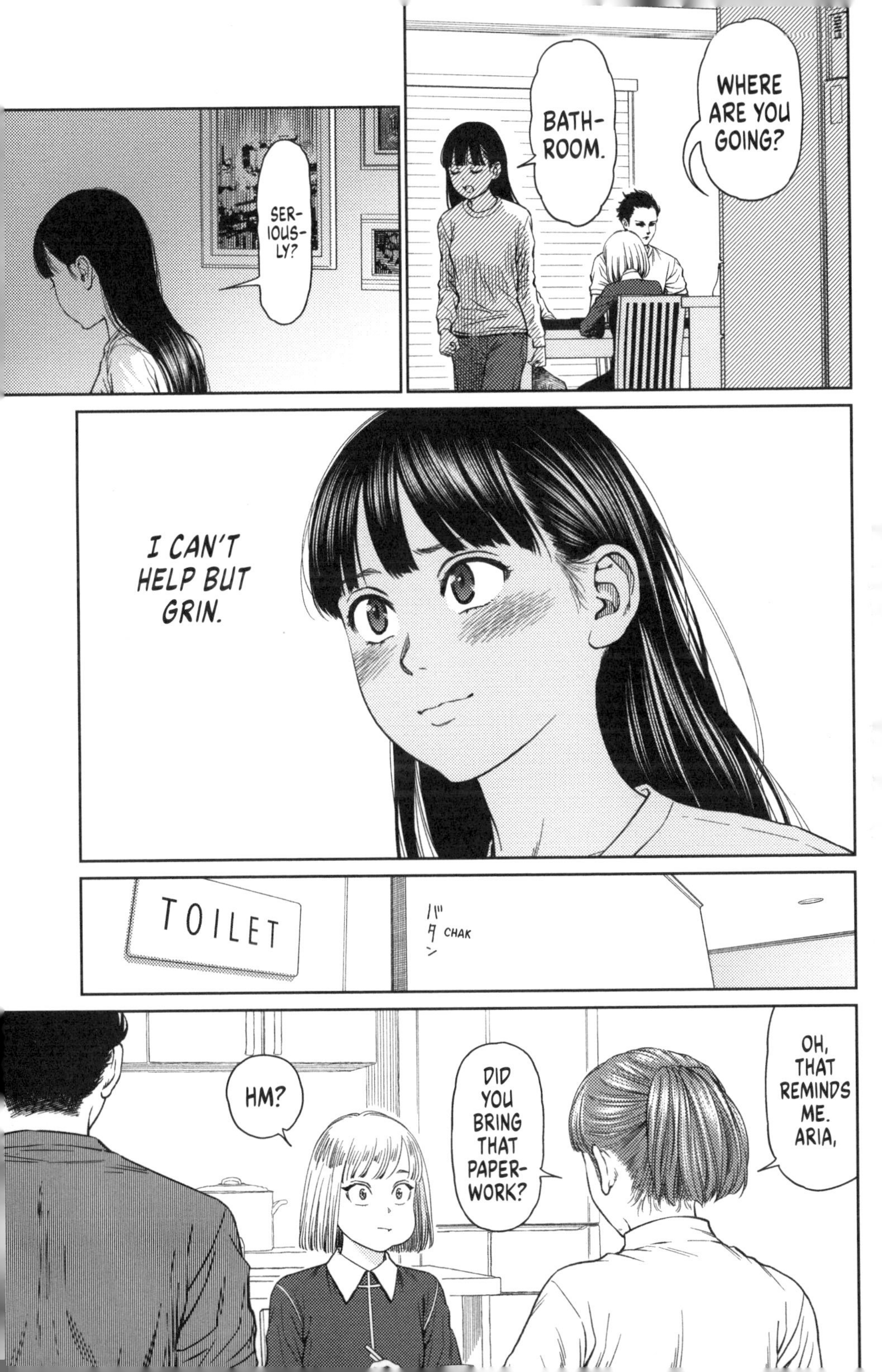
WHERE ARE YOU GOING?
BATH-ROOM.
SER-IOUS-LY?
I CAN'T HELP BUT GRIN.
バタン CHAK
TOILET
OH, THAT REMINDS ME. ARIA,
DID YOU BRING THAT PAPER-WORK?
HM?

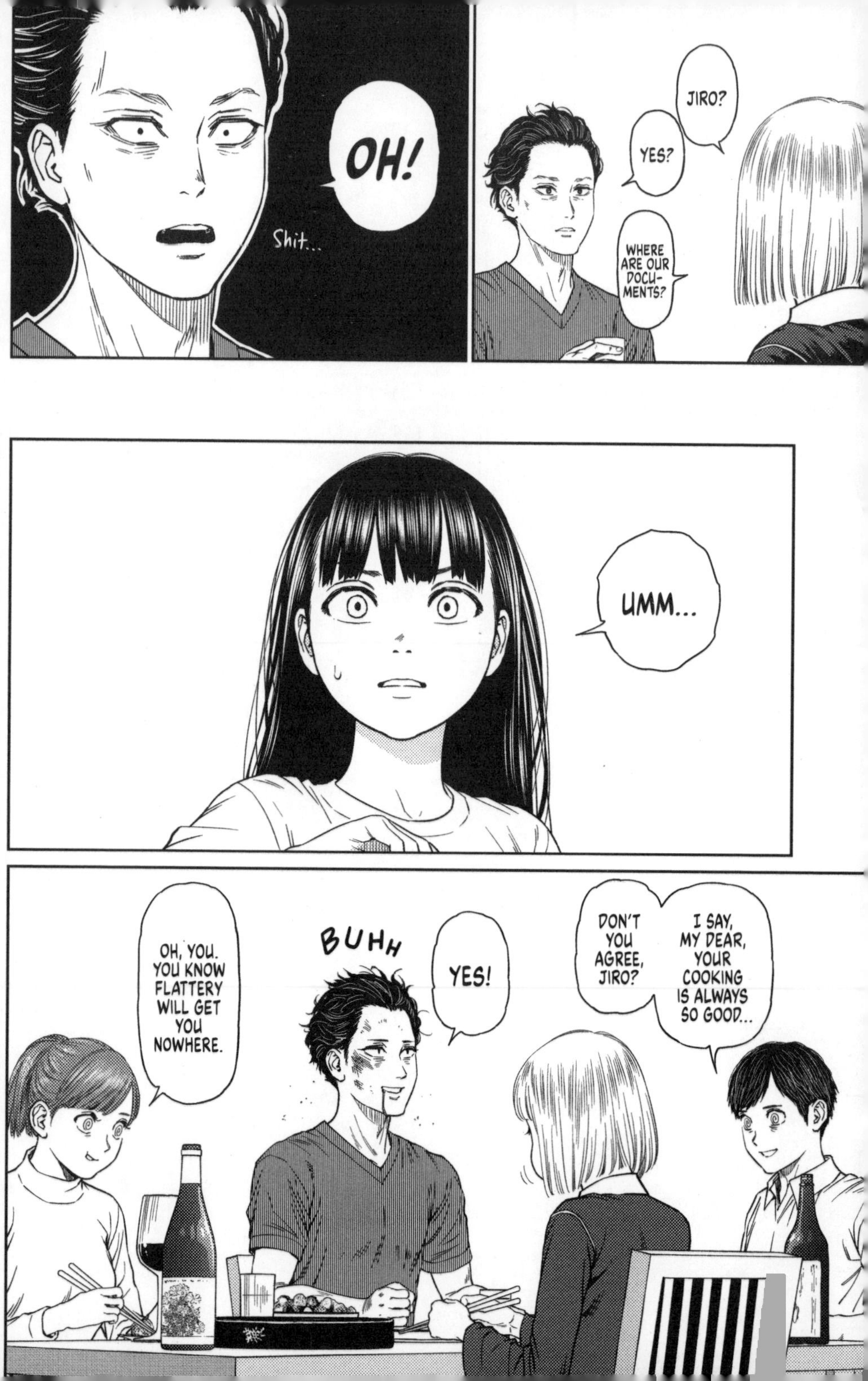
JIRO?
YES?
WHERE ARE OUR DOCUMENTS?
OH!
Shit...
UMM...
I SAY, MY DEAR, YOUR COOKING IS ALWAYS SO GOOD...
DON'T YOU AGREE, JIRO?
YES!
BUHH
OH, YOU. YOU KNOW FLATTERY WILL GET YOU NOWHERE.

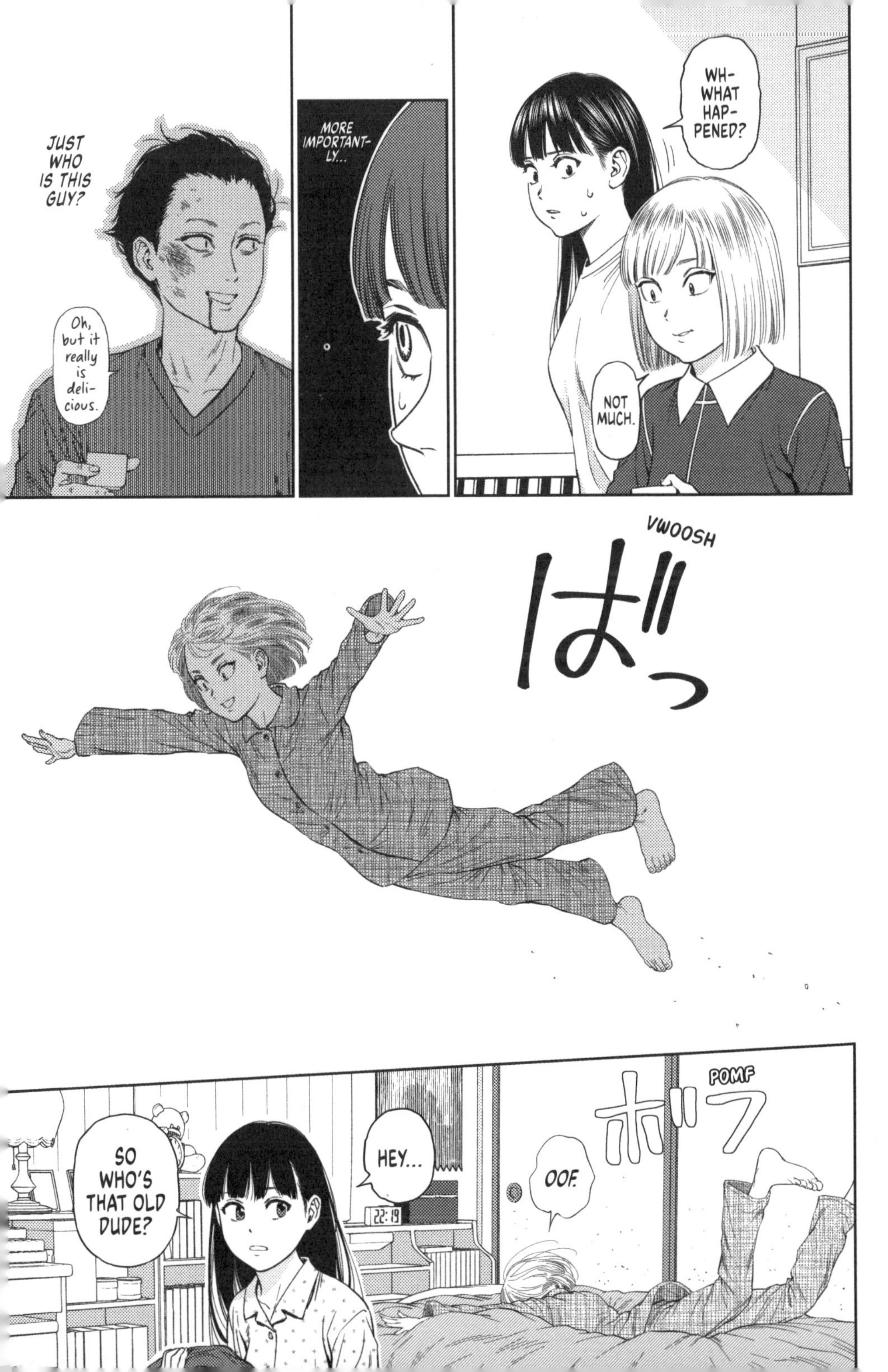
WH-WHAT HAP-PENED?
NOT MUCH.
MORE IMPORTANT-LY...
JUST WHO IS THIS GUY?
Oh, but it really is deli-cious.
VWOOSH
ばっ
POMF
ボフ
OOF.
HEY...
22:19
SO WHO'S THAT OLD DUDE?

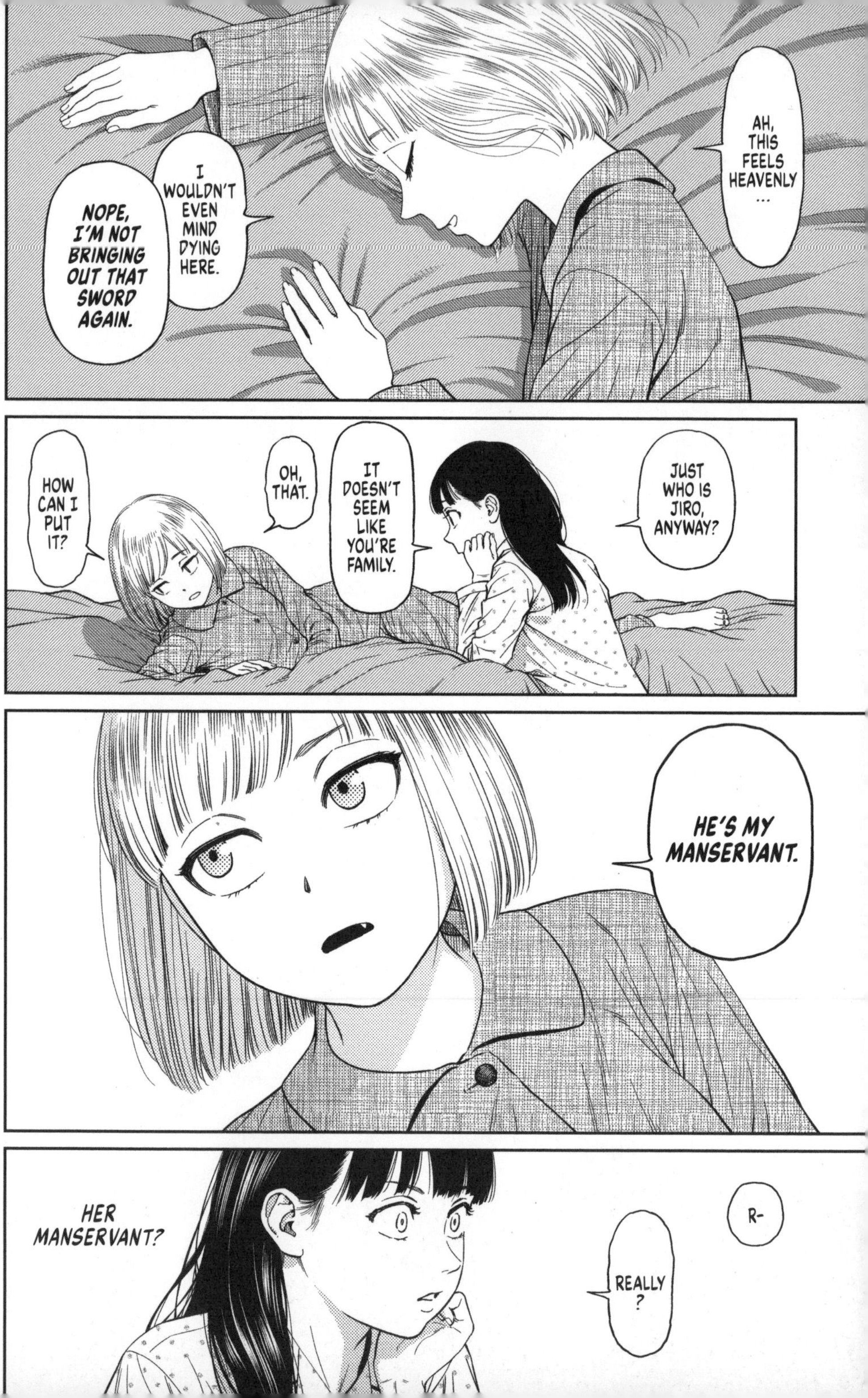
AH, THIS FEELS HEAVENLY...
I WOULDN'T EVEN MIND DYING HERE.
NOPE, I'M NOT BRINGING OUT THAT SWORD AGAIN.
JUST WHO IS JIRO, ANYWAY?
IT DOESN'T SEEM LIKE YOU'RE FAMILY.
OH, THAT.
HOW CAN I PUT IT?
HE'S MY MANSERVANT.
R-
REALLY?
HER MANSERVANT?

HER MANSER-VANT...

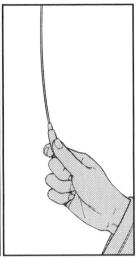

GOOD NIGHT.

FWOOM

FWOOM

OH NO... THAT'S KINDA HOT.

G-GOOD NIGHT.

OH,

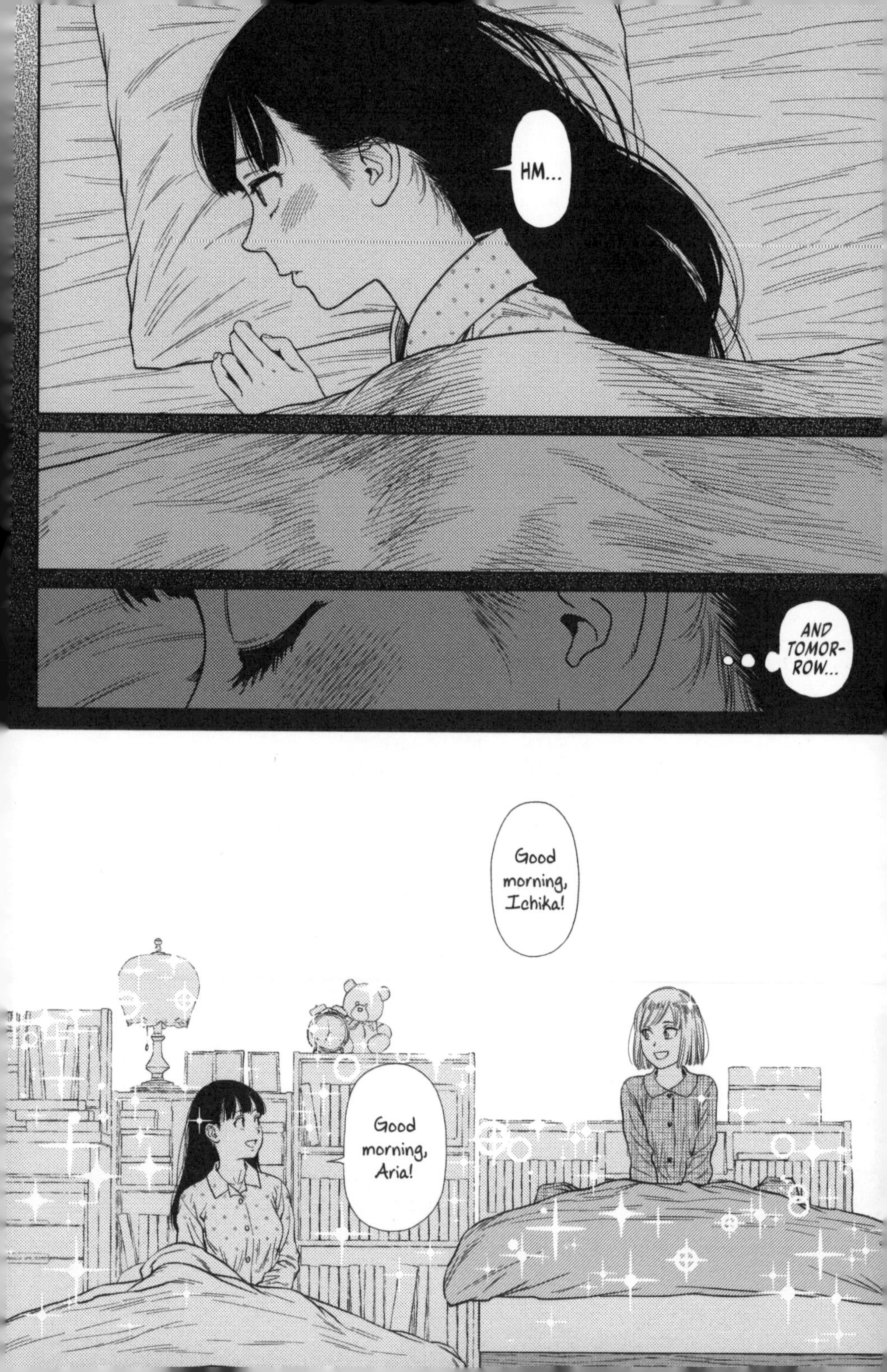
HM...
AND TOMOR-ROW...
Good morning, Ichika!
Good morning, Aria!

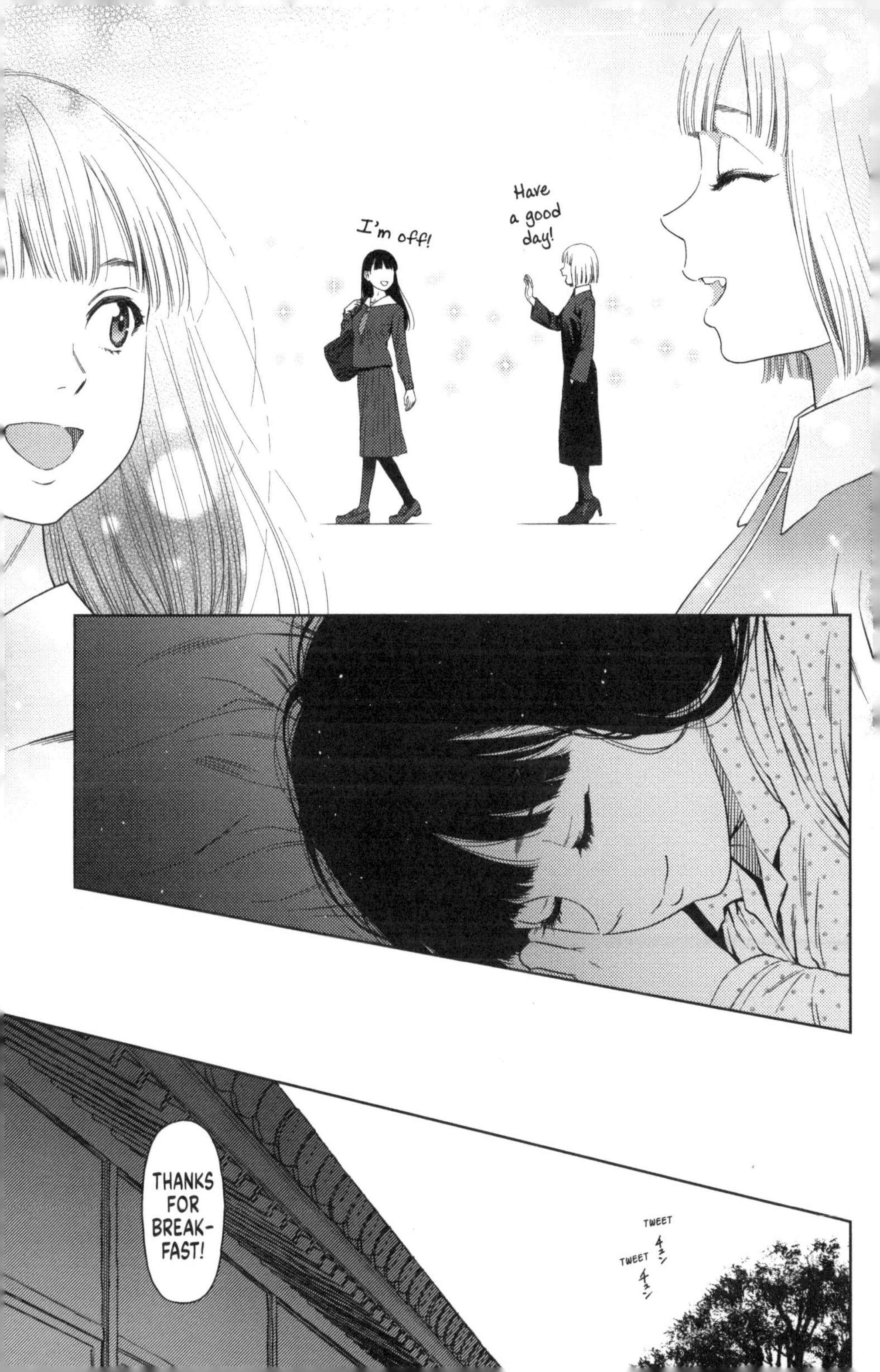
Have a good day!
I'm off!
TWEET
TWEET
THANKS FOR BREAK-FAST!

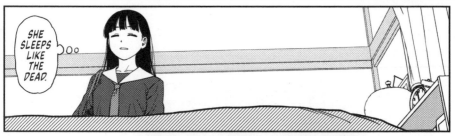

SHE SLEEPS LIKE THE DEAD.

WELL...

Heehee

ANYWAY...

I'M OFF TO SCHOOL.

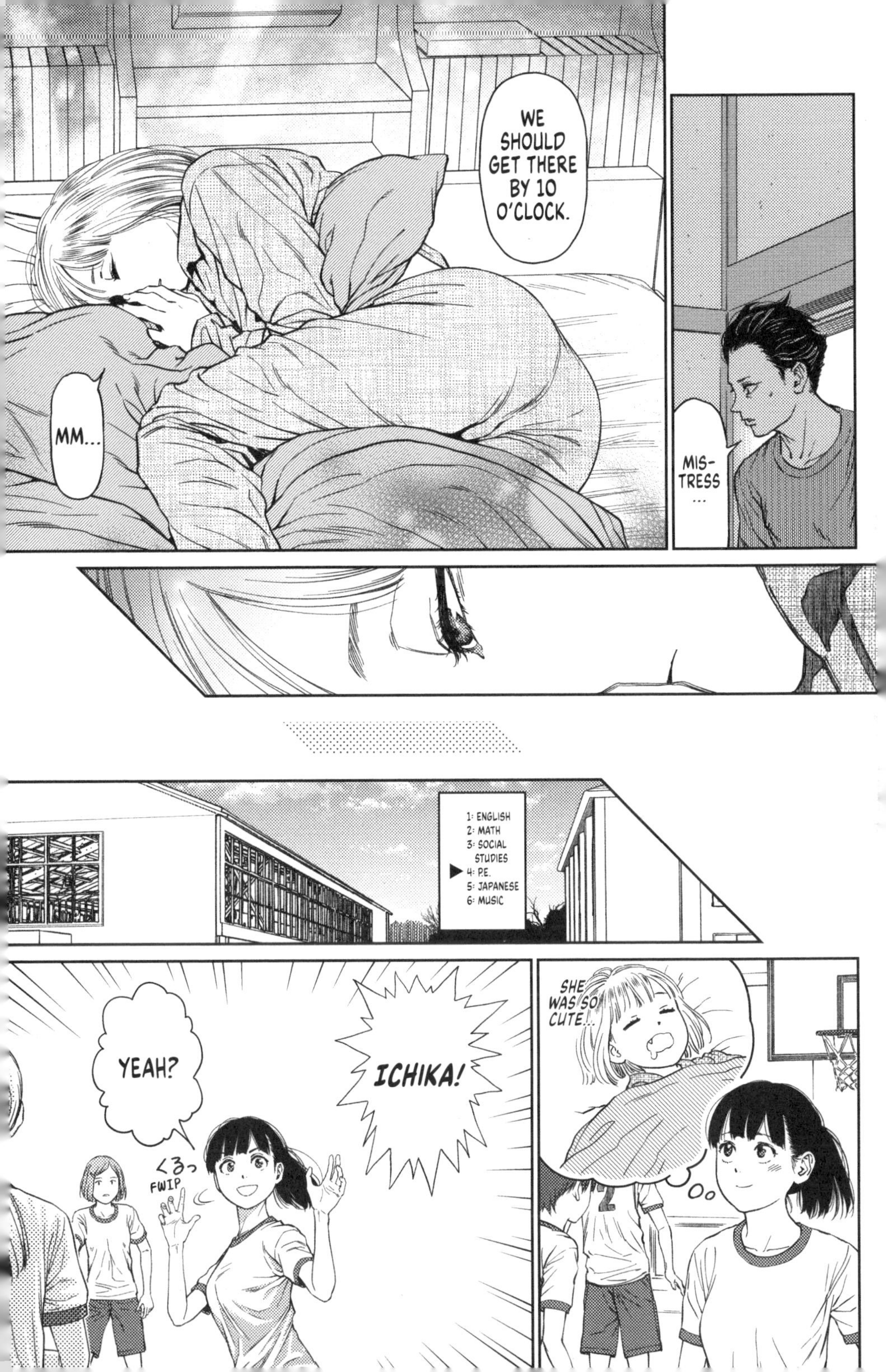
MIS-TRESS ...
WE SHOULD GET THERE BY 10 O'CLOCK.
MM...
1: ENGLISH
2: MATH
3: SOCIAL STUDIES
4: P.E.
5: JAPANESE
6: MUSIC
SHE WAS SO CUTE...
ICHIKA!
YEAH?
くるっ
FWIP

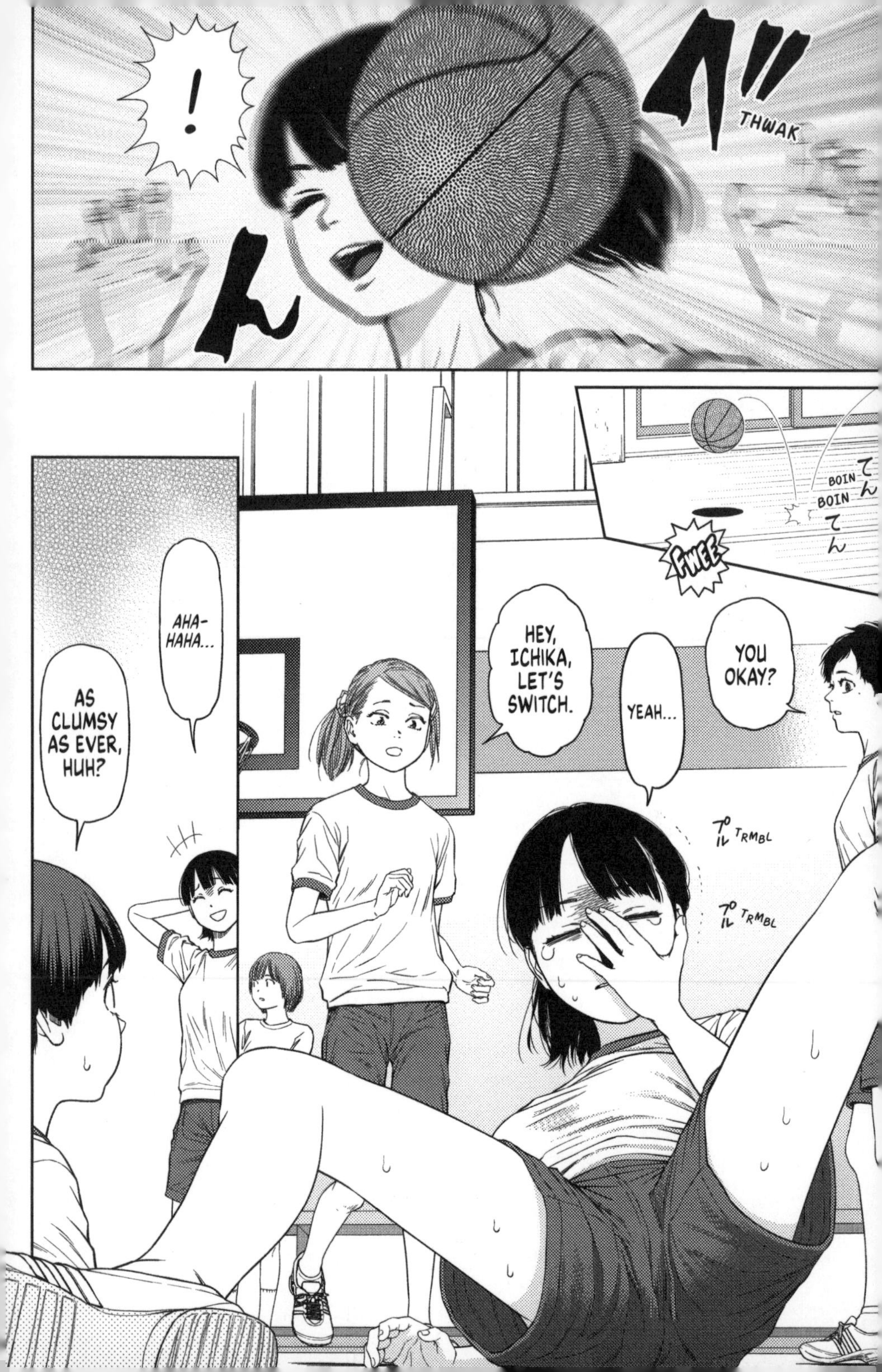
THWAK
!
てん
BOIN
てん
BOIN
てん
FWEE
YOU OKAY?
YEAH...
HEY, ICHIKA, LET'S SWITCH.
プル TRMBL
プル TRMBL
AHA-HAHA...
AS CLUMSY AS EVER, HUH?

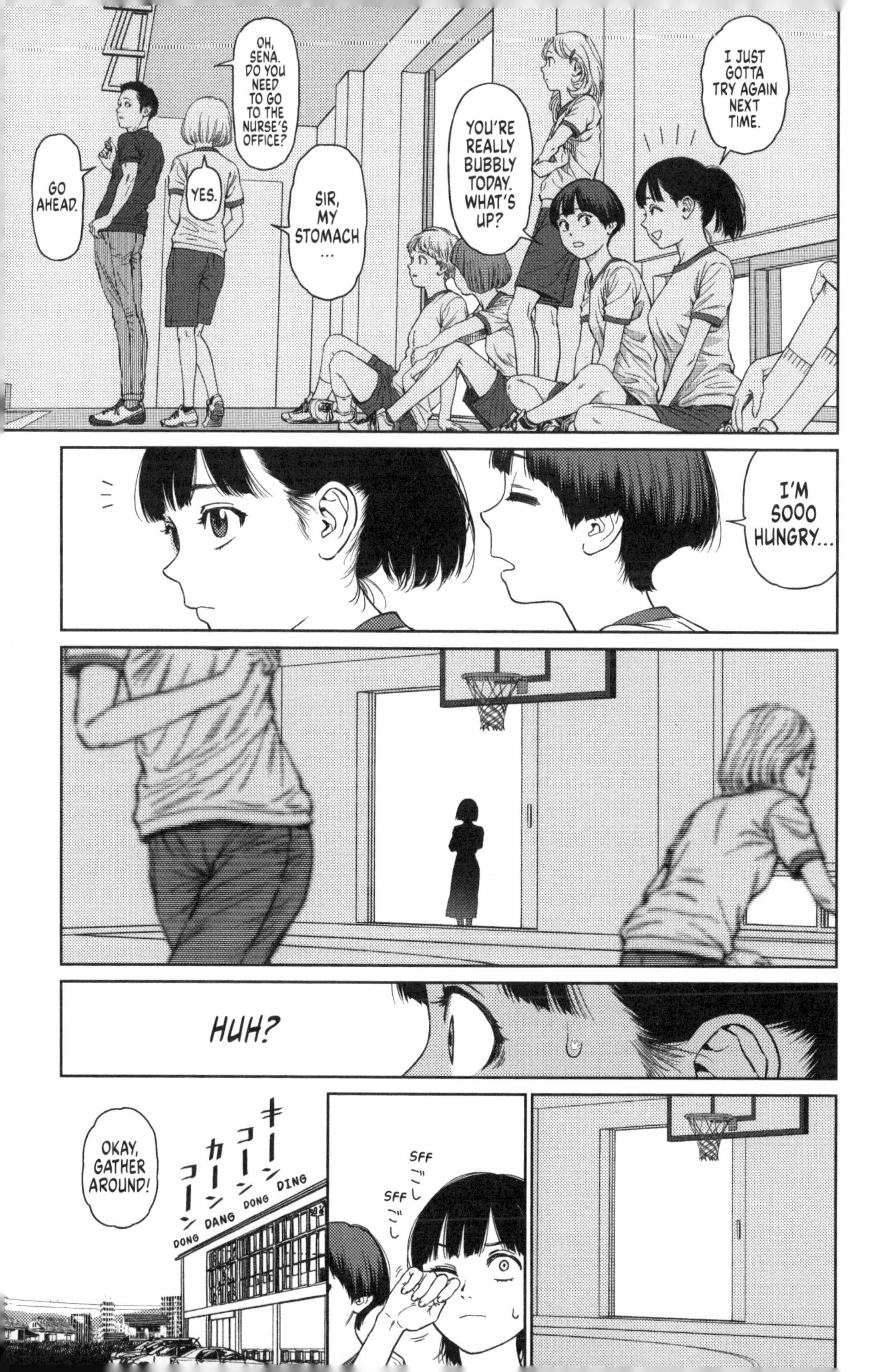
I JUST GOTTA TRY AGAIN NEXT TIME.
YOU'RE REALLY BUBBLY TODAY. WHAT'S UP?
SIR, MY STOMACH ...
OH, SENA. DO YOU NEED TO GO TO THE NURSE'S OFFICE?
YES.
GO AHEAD.
I'M SOOO HUNGRY...
HUH?
SFF ごし
SFF ごし
キーン DING
コーン DONG
カーン DANG
コーン DONG
OKAY, GATHER AROUND!

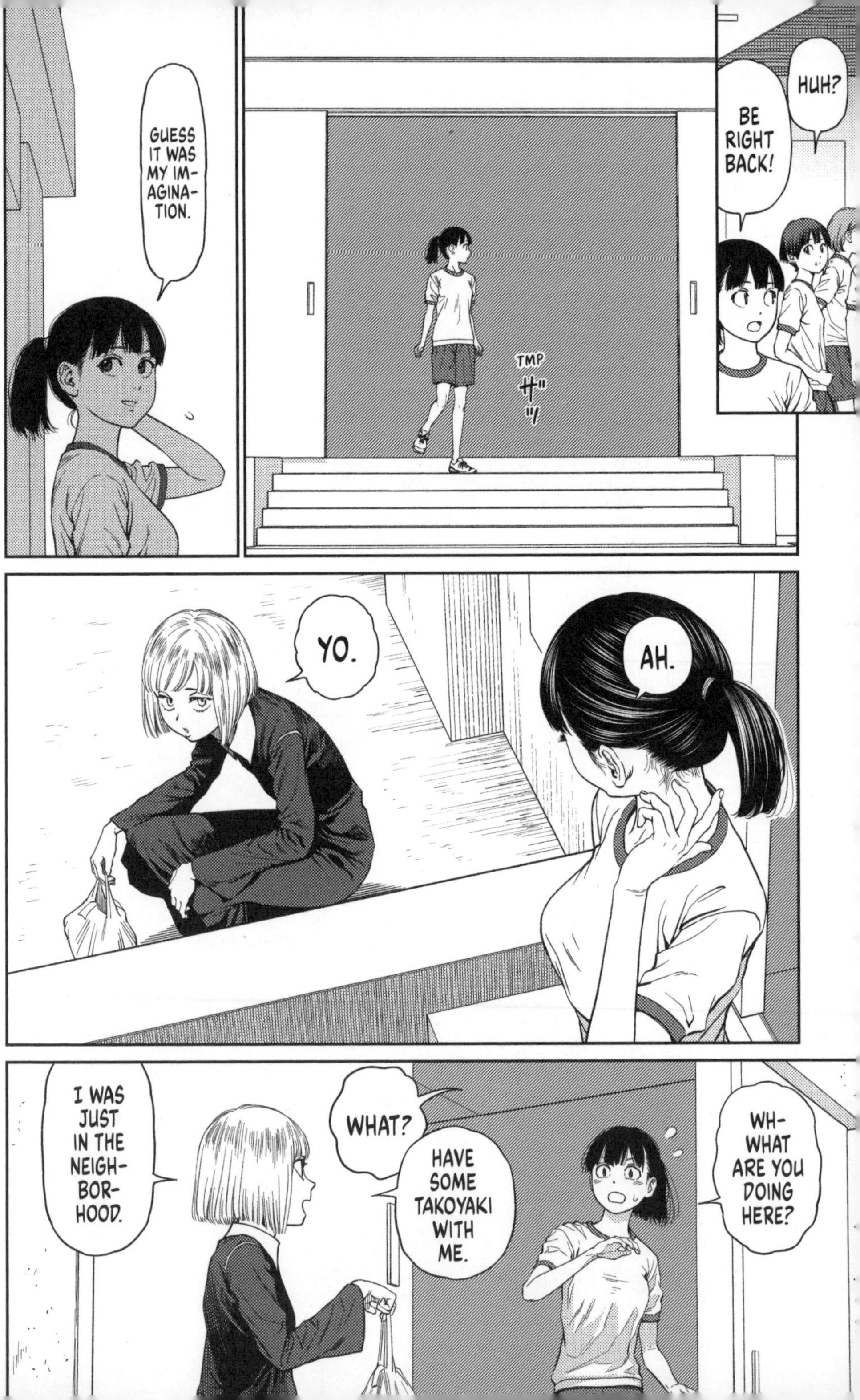
HUH?
BE RIGHT BACK!
TMP
ザッ
GUESS IT WAS MY IMAGINATION.
AH.
YO.
WH-WHAT ARE YOU DOING HERE?
WHAT?
HAVE SOME TAKOYAKI WITH ME.
I WAS JUST IN THE NEIGHBORHOOD.

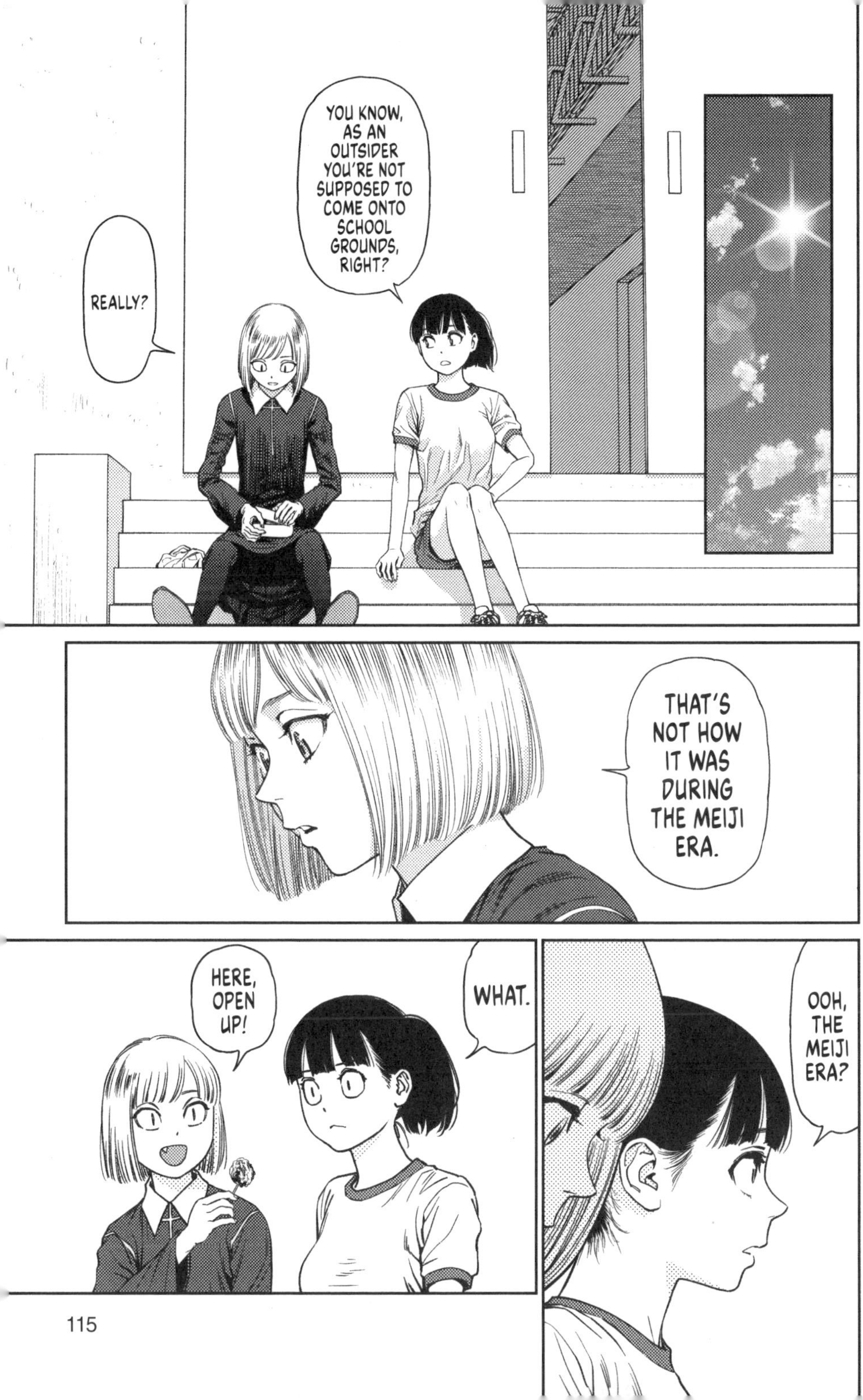
YOU KNOW, AS AN OUTSIDER YOU'RE NOT SUPPOSED TO COME ONTO SCHOOL GROUNDS, RIGHT?
REALLY?
THAT'S NOT HOW IT WAS DURING THE MEIJI ERA.
OOH, THE MEIJI ERA?
WHAT.
HERE, OPEN UP!

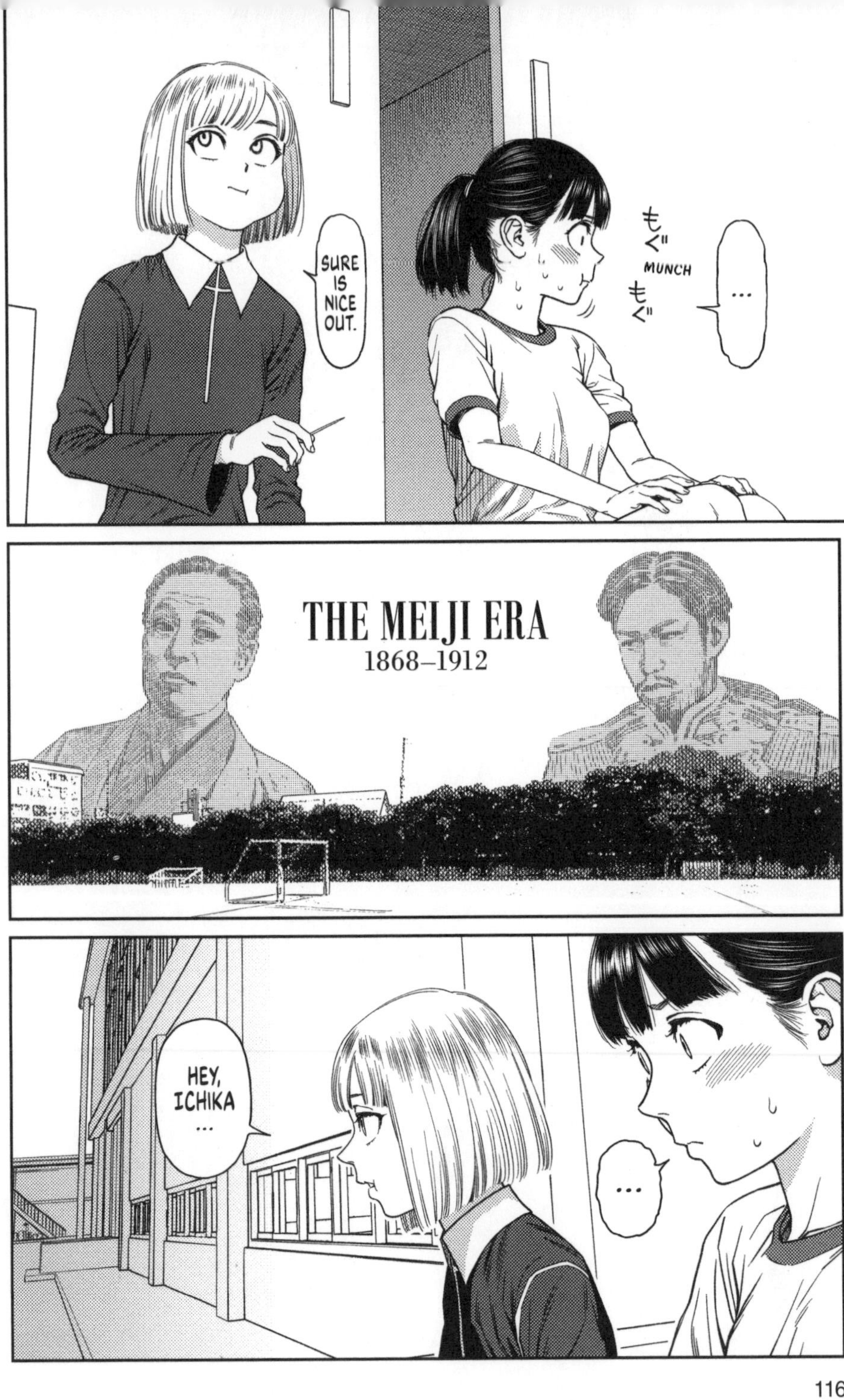
...
もぐ MUNCH もぐ
SURE IS NICE OUT.
THE MEIJI ERA
1868–1912
...
HEY, ICHIKA ...

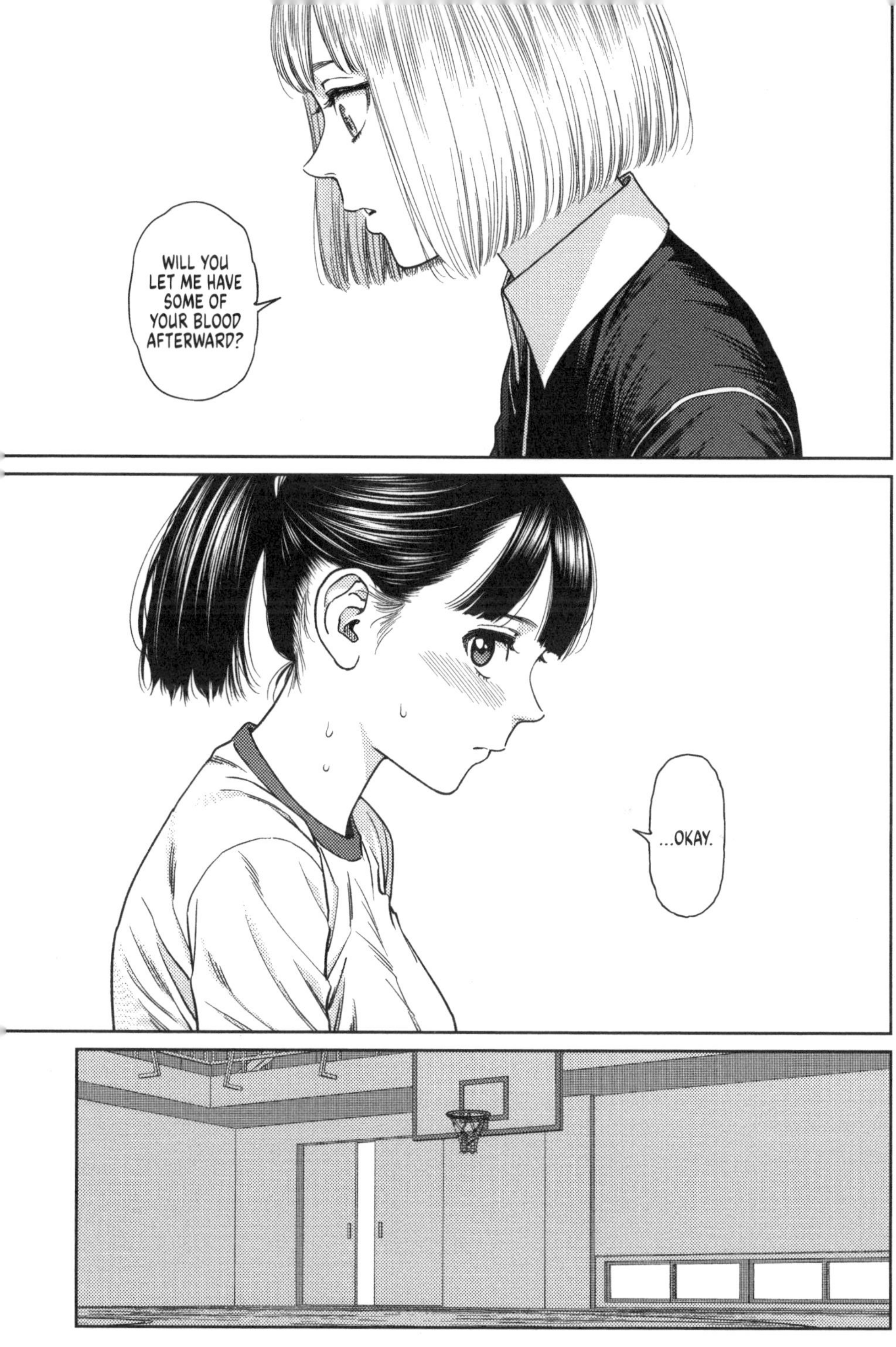
WILL YOU LET ME HAVE SOME OF YOUR BLOOD AFTERWARD?
...OKAY.

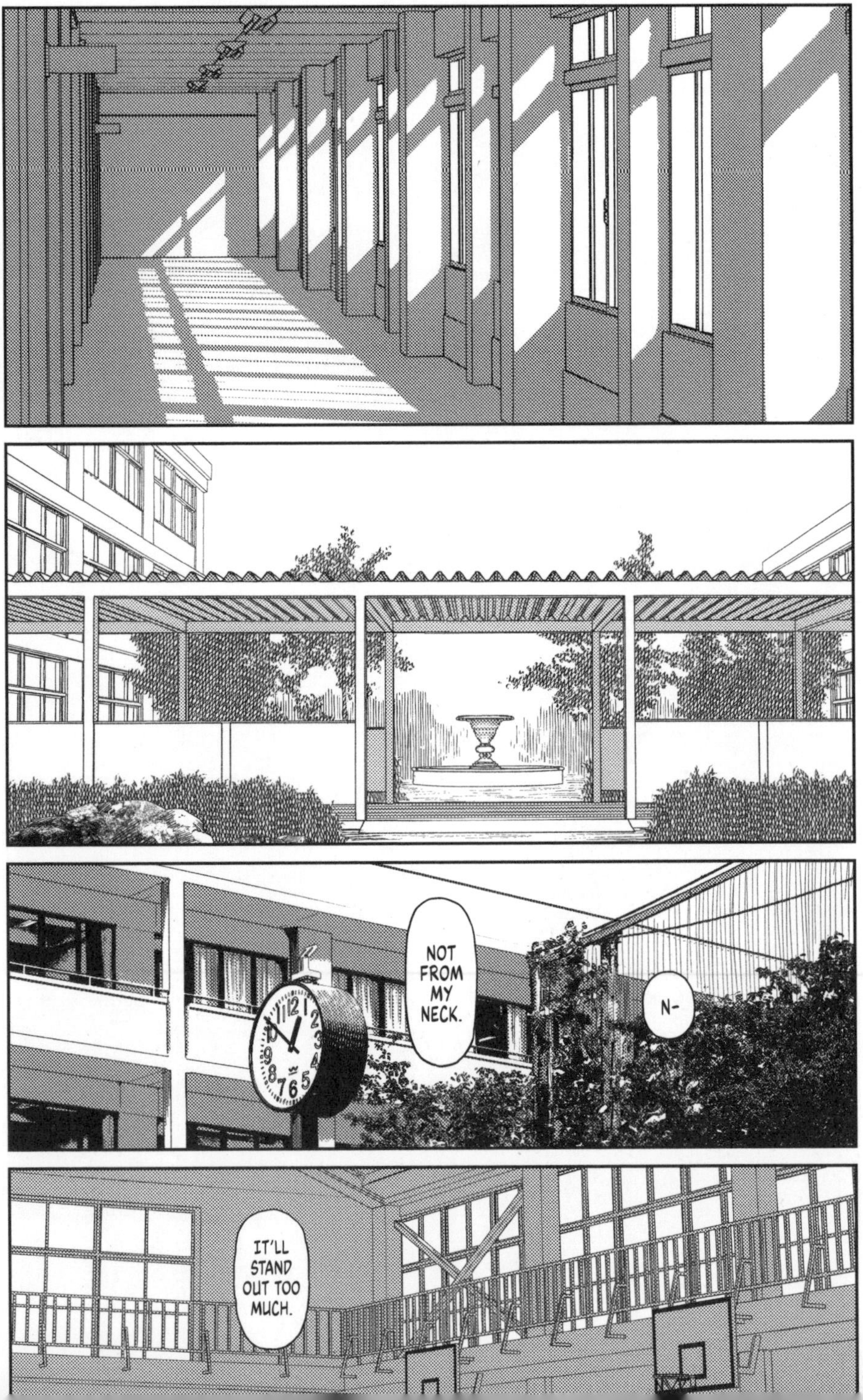
N-
NOT FROM MY NECK.
IT'LL STAND OUT TOO MUCH.

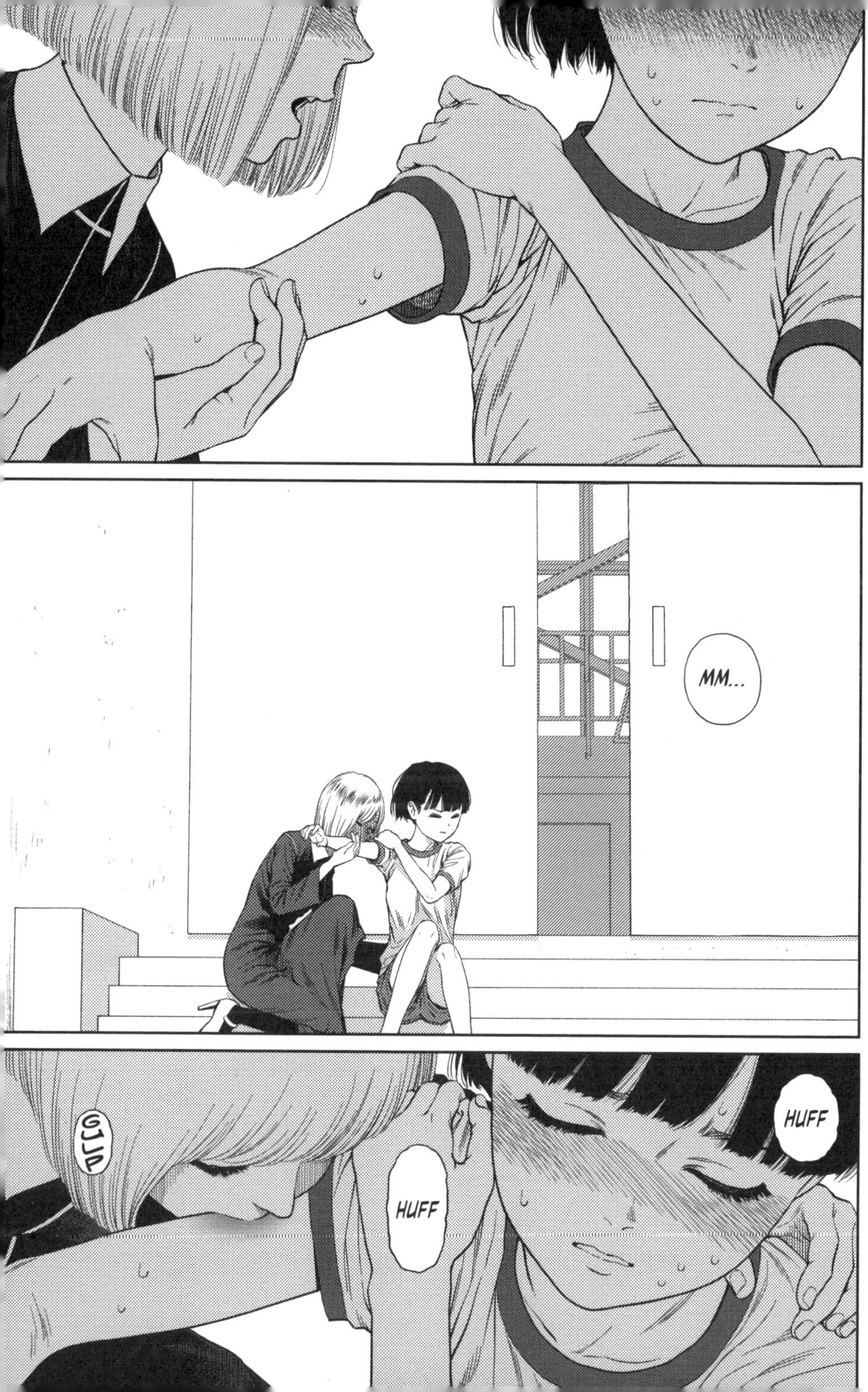
MM...
HUFF
HUFF
GULP

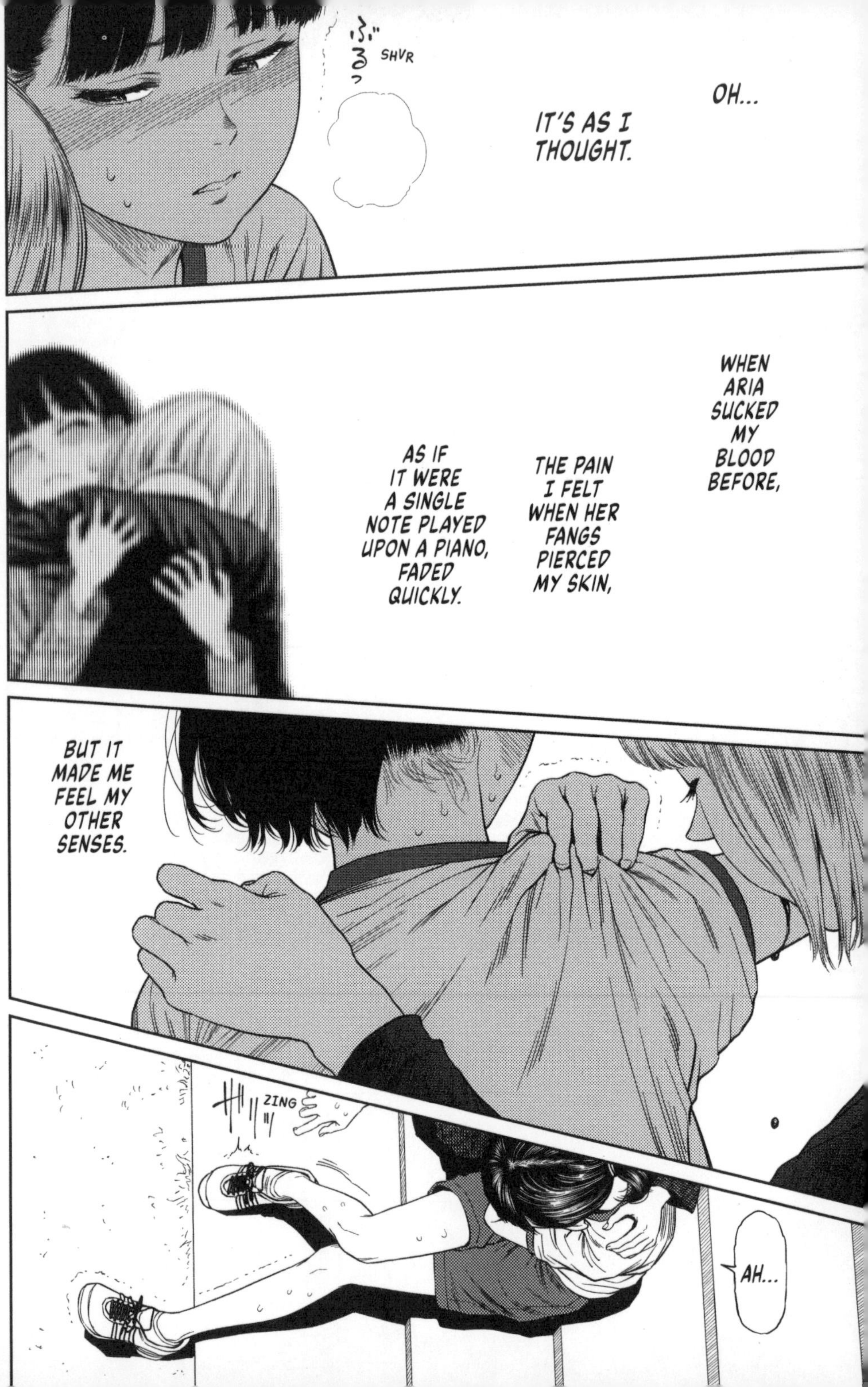
OH...
IT'S AS I THOUGHT.
ぶるっ
SHVR
WHEN ARIA SUCKED MY BLOOD BEFORE,
THE PAIN I FELT WHEN HER FANGS PIERCED MY SKIN,
AS IF IT WERE A SINGLE NOTE PLAYED UPON A PIANO, FADED QUICKLY.
BUT IT MADE ME FEEL MY OTHER SENSES.
AH...
ZING

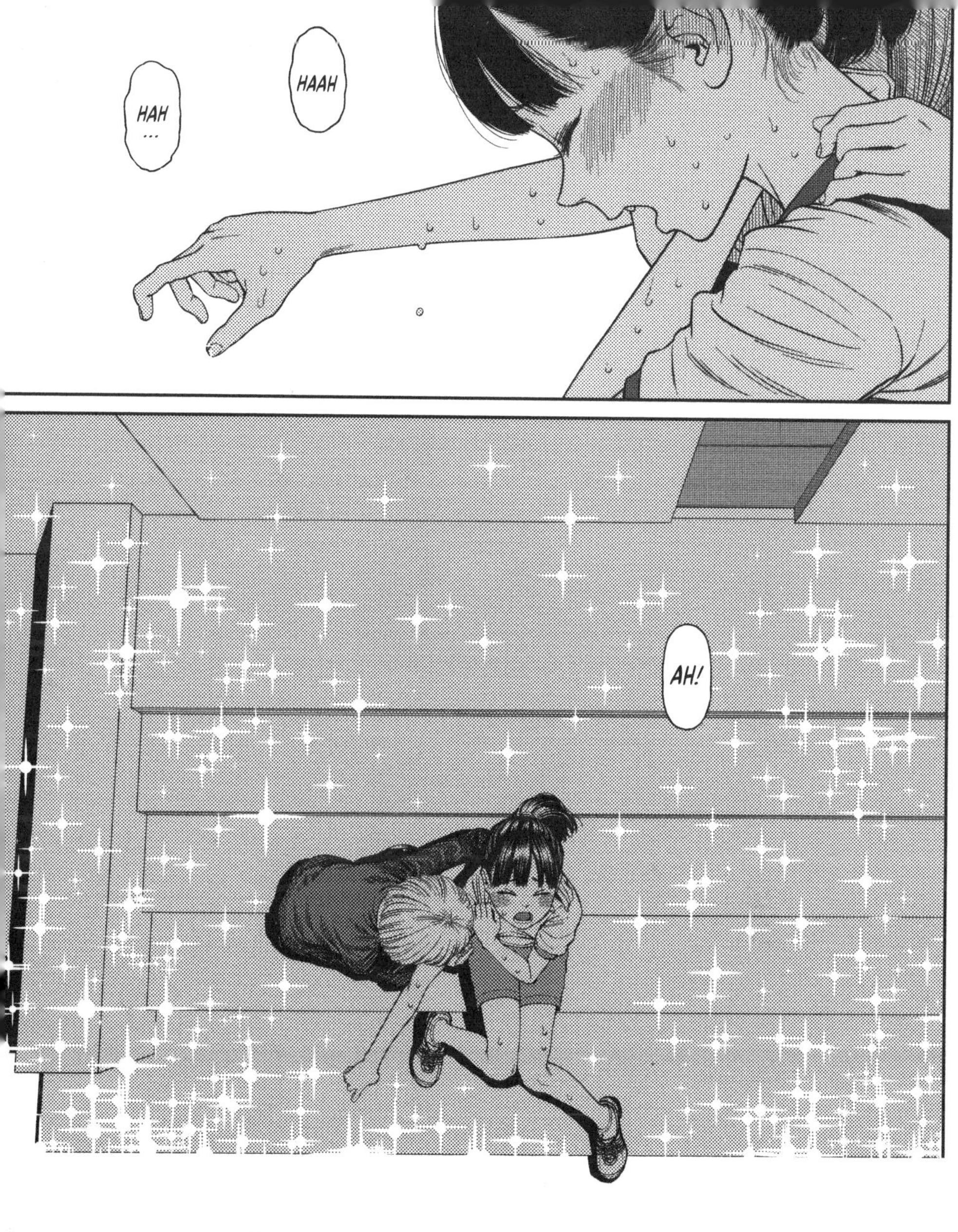
HAAH
HAH ...
AH!

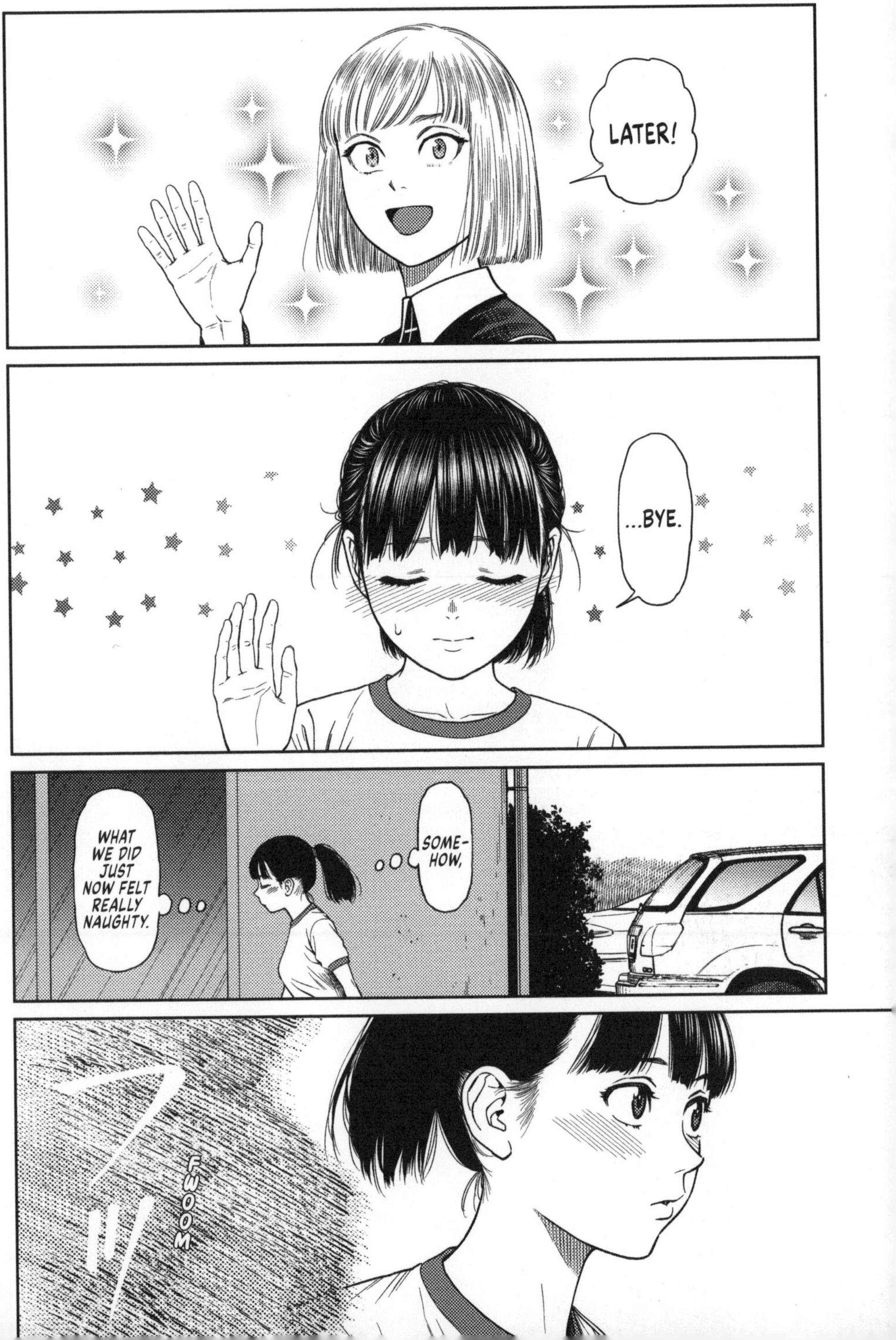
LATER!
...BYE.
SOME-HOW,
WHAT WE DID JUST NOW FELT REALLY NAUGHTY.
FWOOM

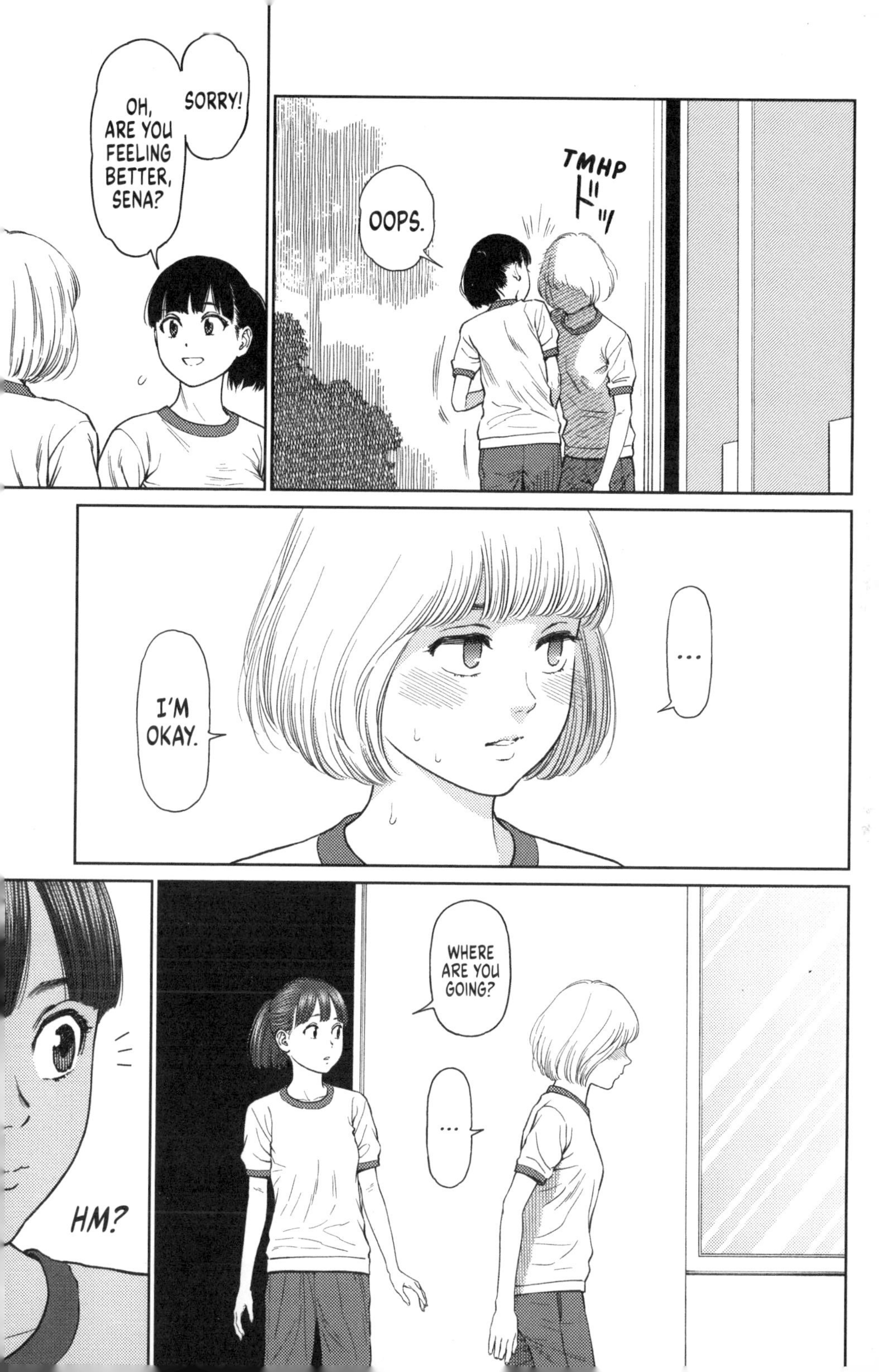
TMHP
ドッ
OOPS.
SORRY!
OH, ARE YOU FEELING BETTER, SENA?
...
I'M OKAY.
WHERE ARE YOU GOING?
...
HM?

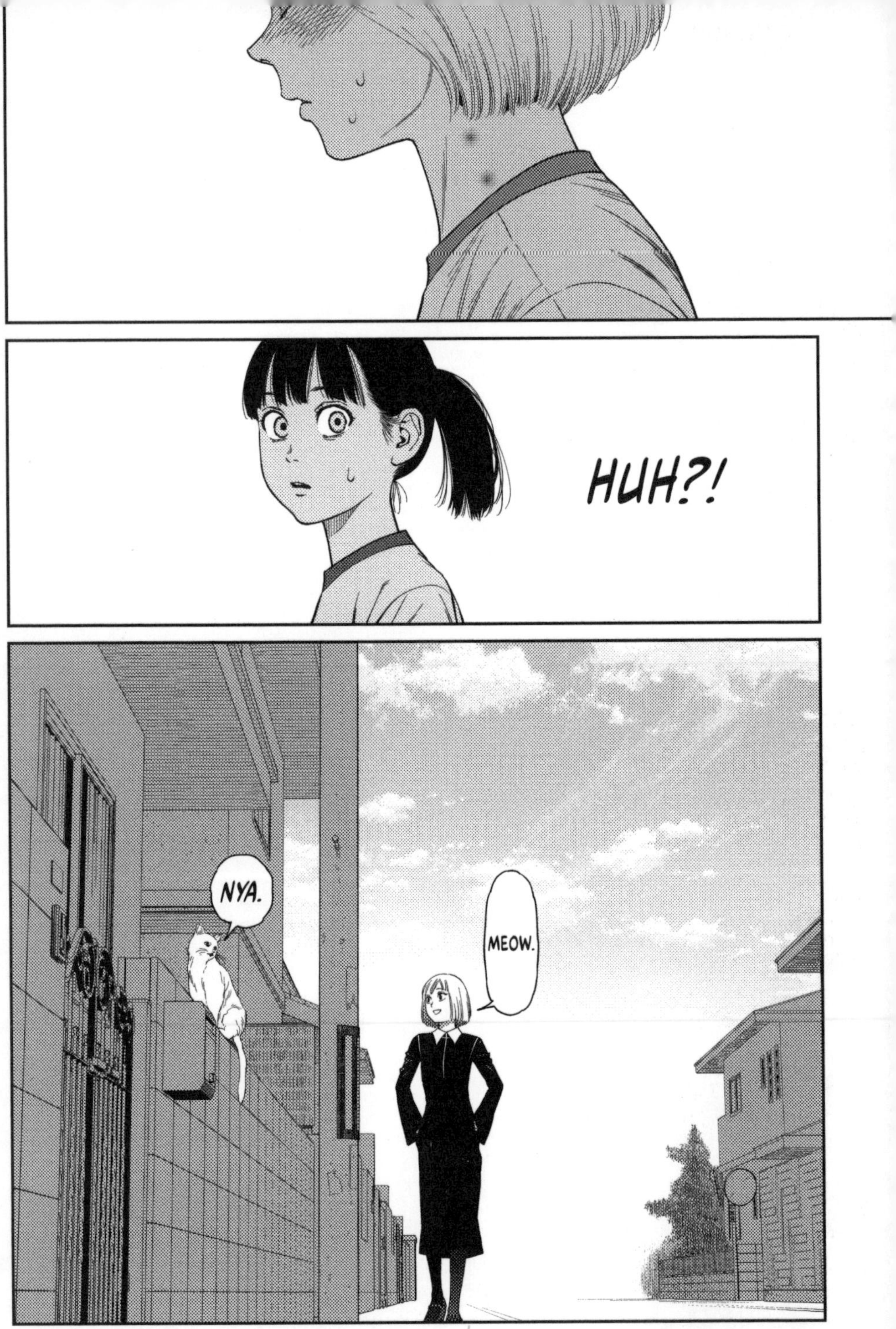
HUH?!
MEOW.
NYA.

#5 PEERS

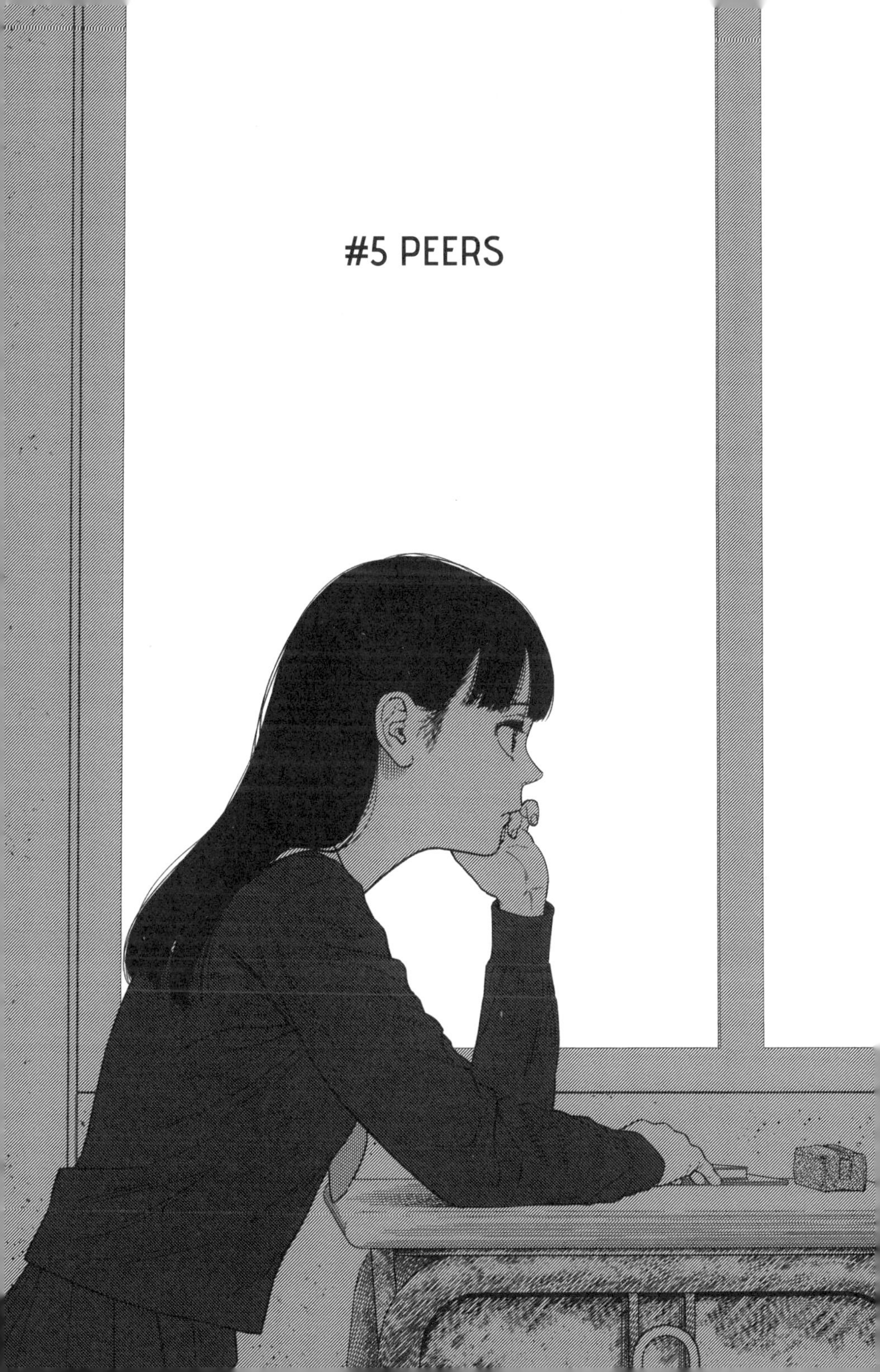

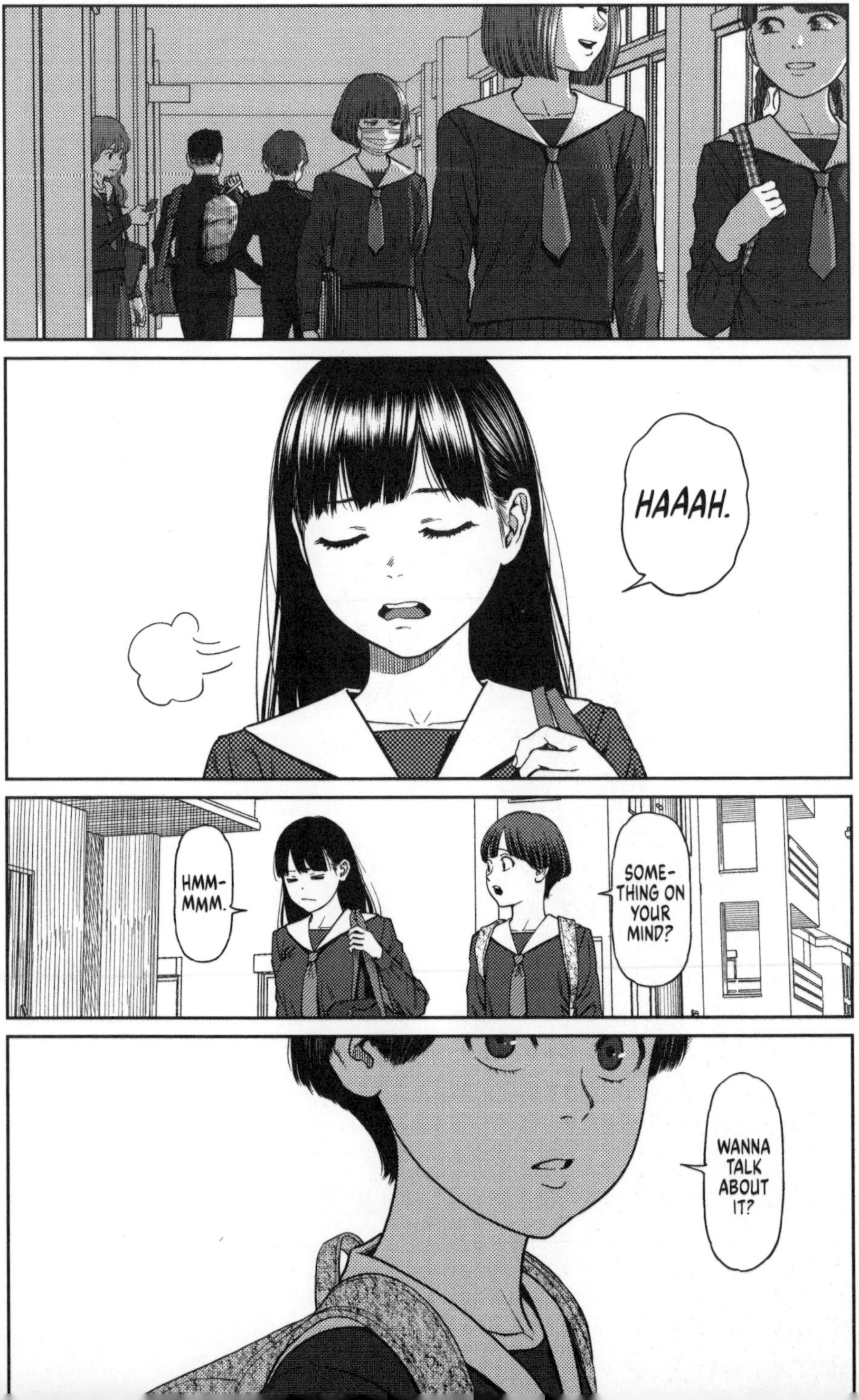
HAAAH.
SOME- THING ON YOUR MIND?
HMM- MMM.
WANNA TALK ABOUT IT?

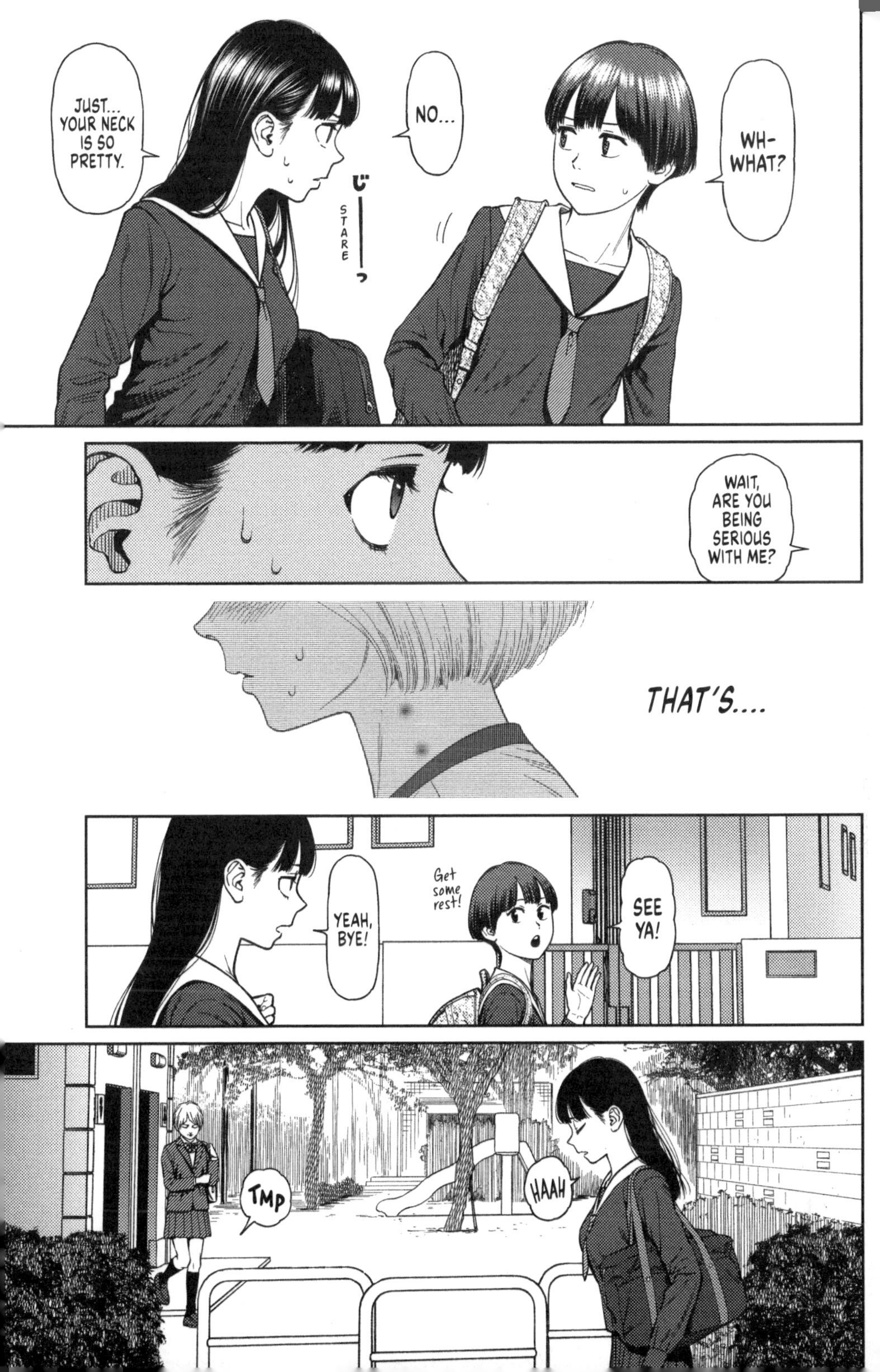
WH- WHAT?
NO...
じーっ
STARE
JUST... YOUR NECK IS SO PRETTY.
WAIT, ARE YOU BEING SERIOUS WITH ME?
THAT'S....
SEE YA!
Get some rest!
YEAH, BYE!
HAAH
TMP

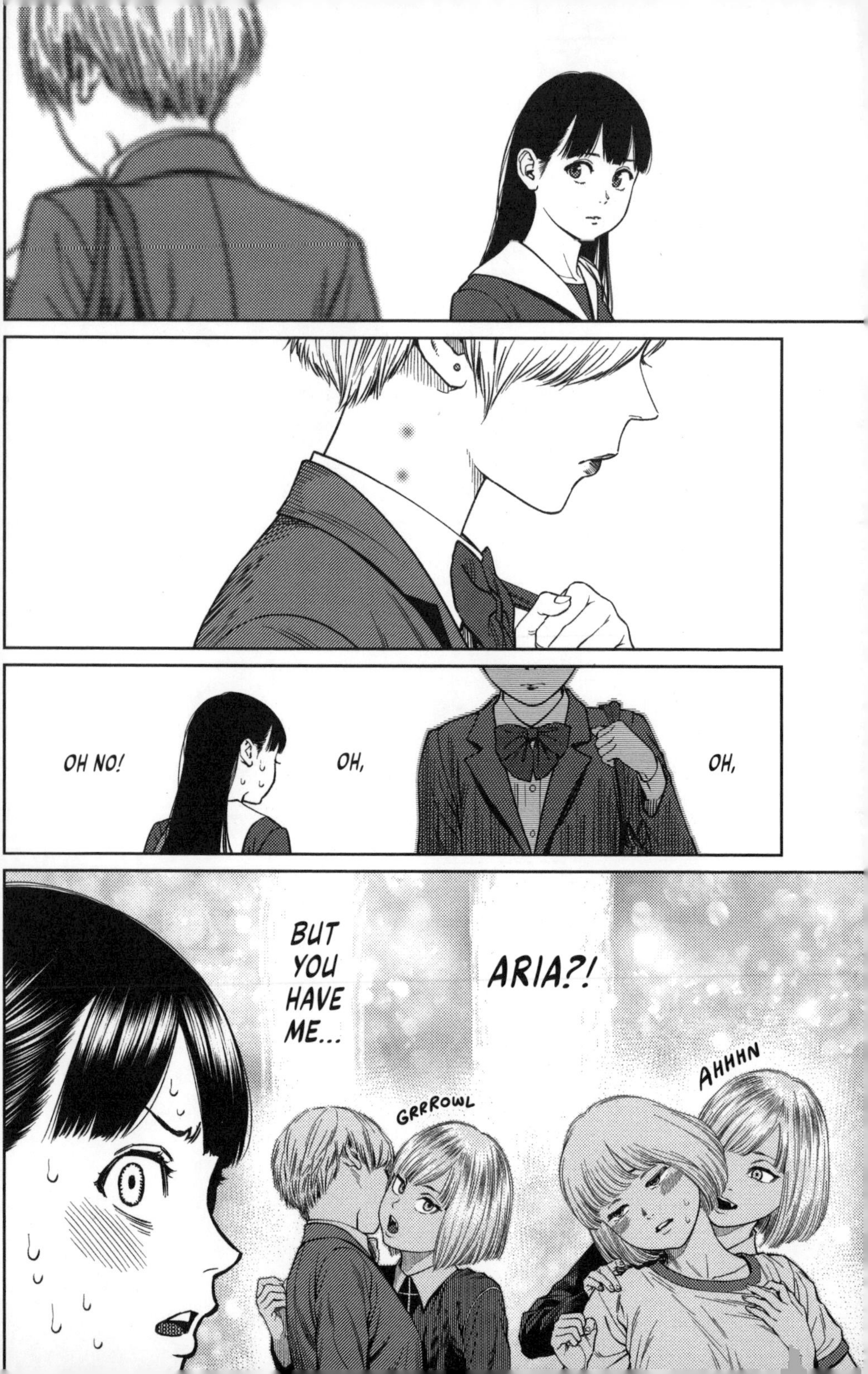
OH,
OH,
OH NO!
ARIA?!
BUT YOU HAVE ME...
AHHHN
GRRROWL

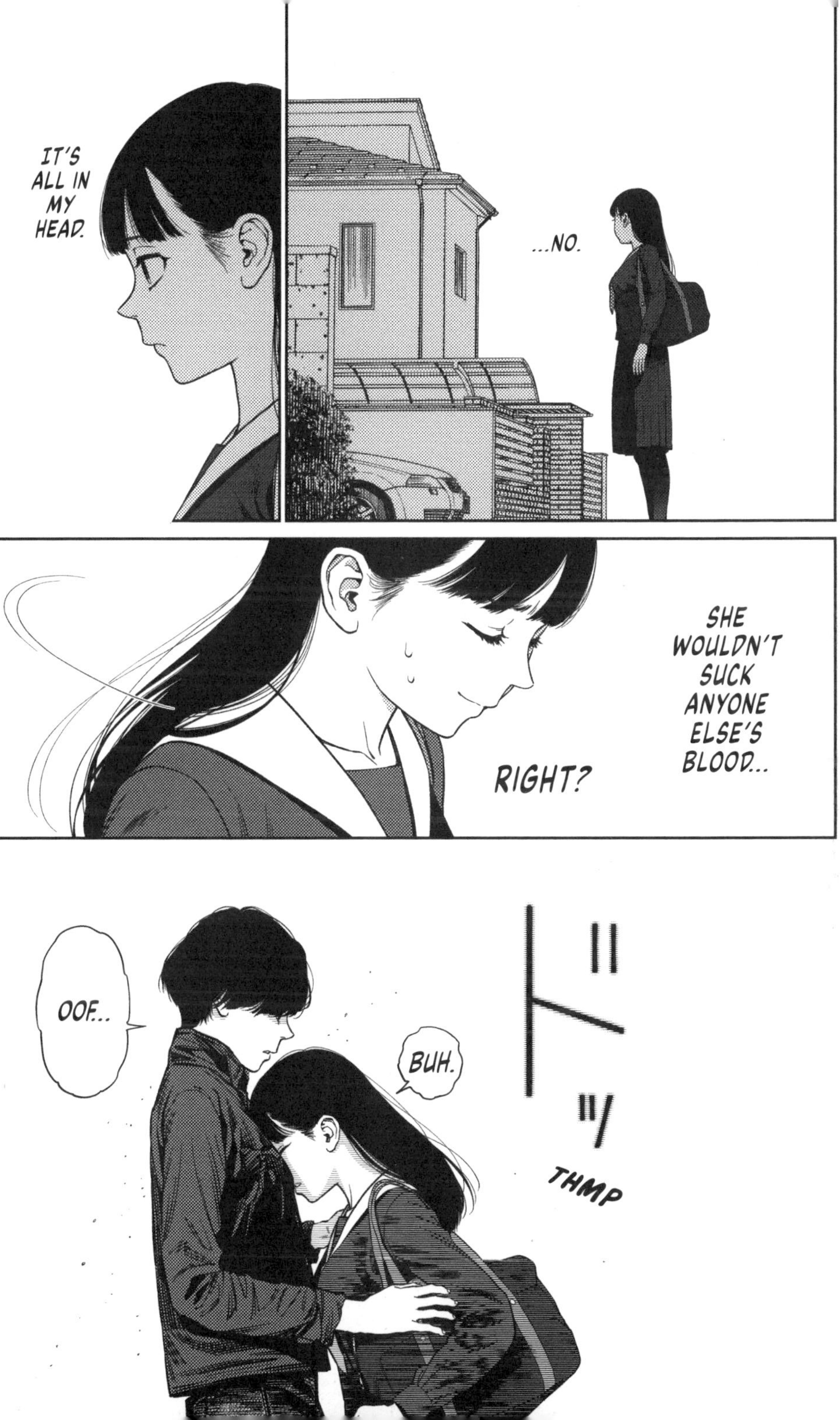
...NO.
IT'S ALL IN MY HEAD.
SHE WOULDN'T SUCK ANYONE ELSE'S BLOOD...
RIGHT?
ドッ
THMP
BUH.
OOF...

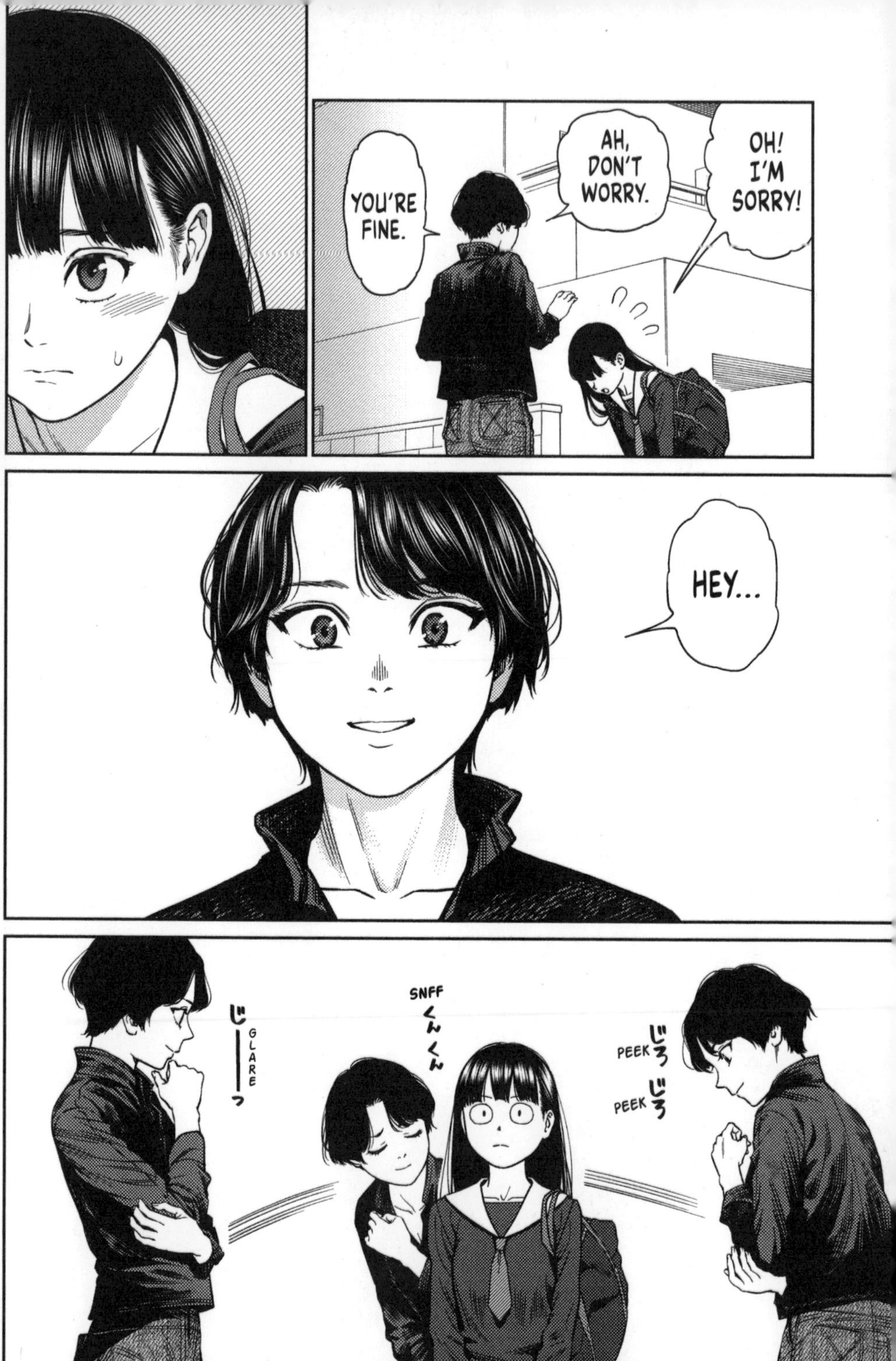
OH! I'M SORRY!
AH, DON'T WORRY.
YOU'RE FINE.
HEY...
PEEK じろ
PEEK じろ
SNFF くんくん
じーっ GLARE

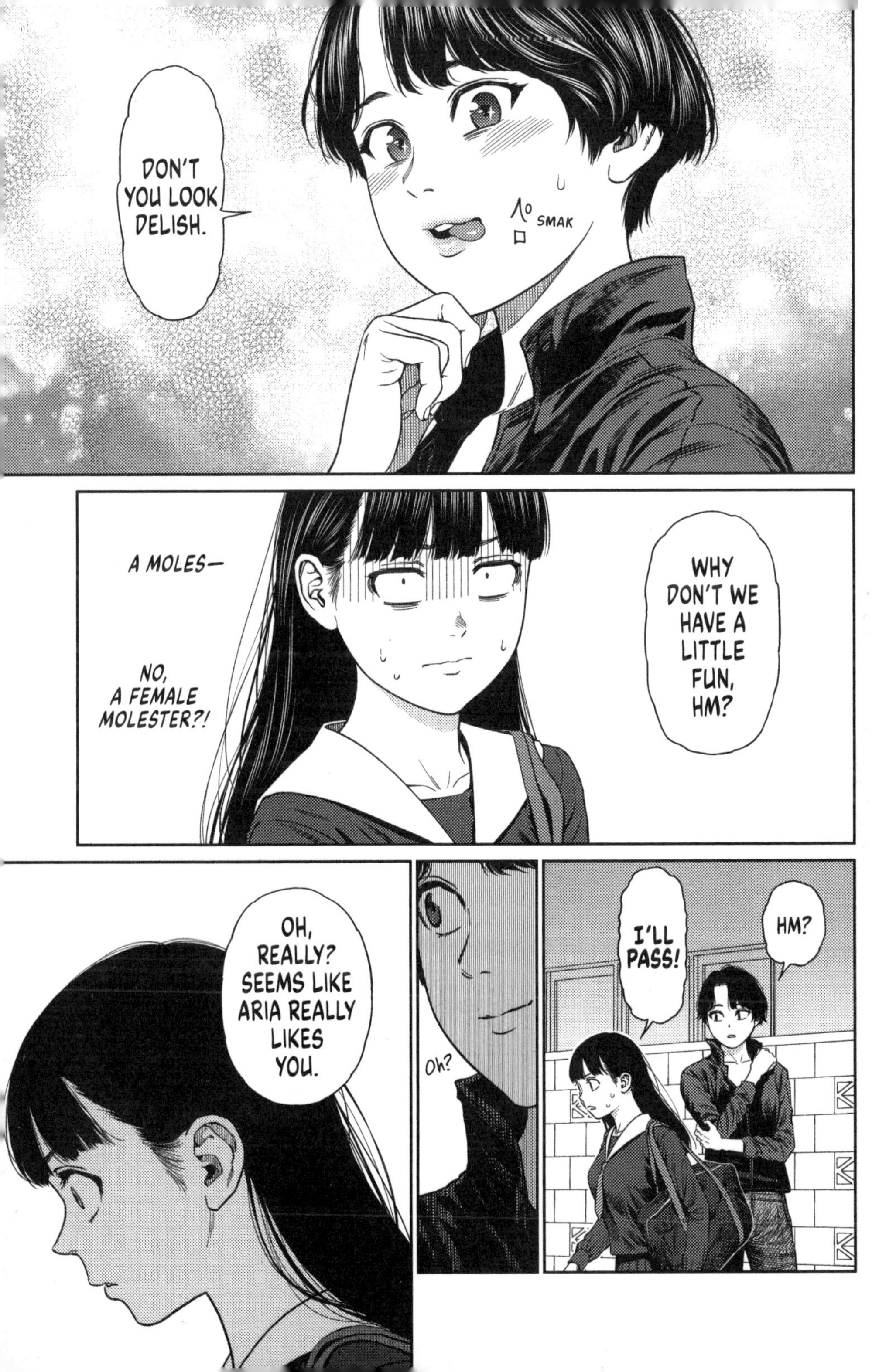
DON'T YOU LOOK DELISH.
ペロ
SMAK
WHY DON'T WE HAVE A LITTLE FUN, HM?
A MOLES—
NO, A FEMALE MOLESTER?!
HM?
I'LL PASS!
Oh?
OH, REALLY? SEEMS LIKE ARIA REALLY LIKES YOU.

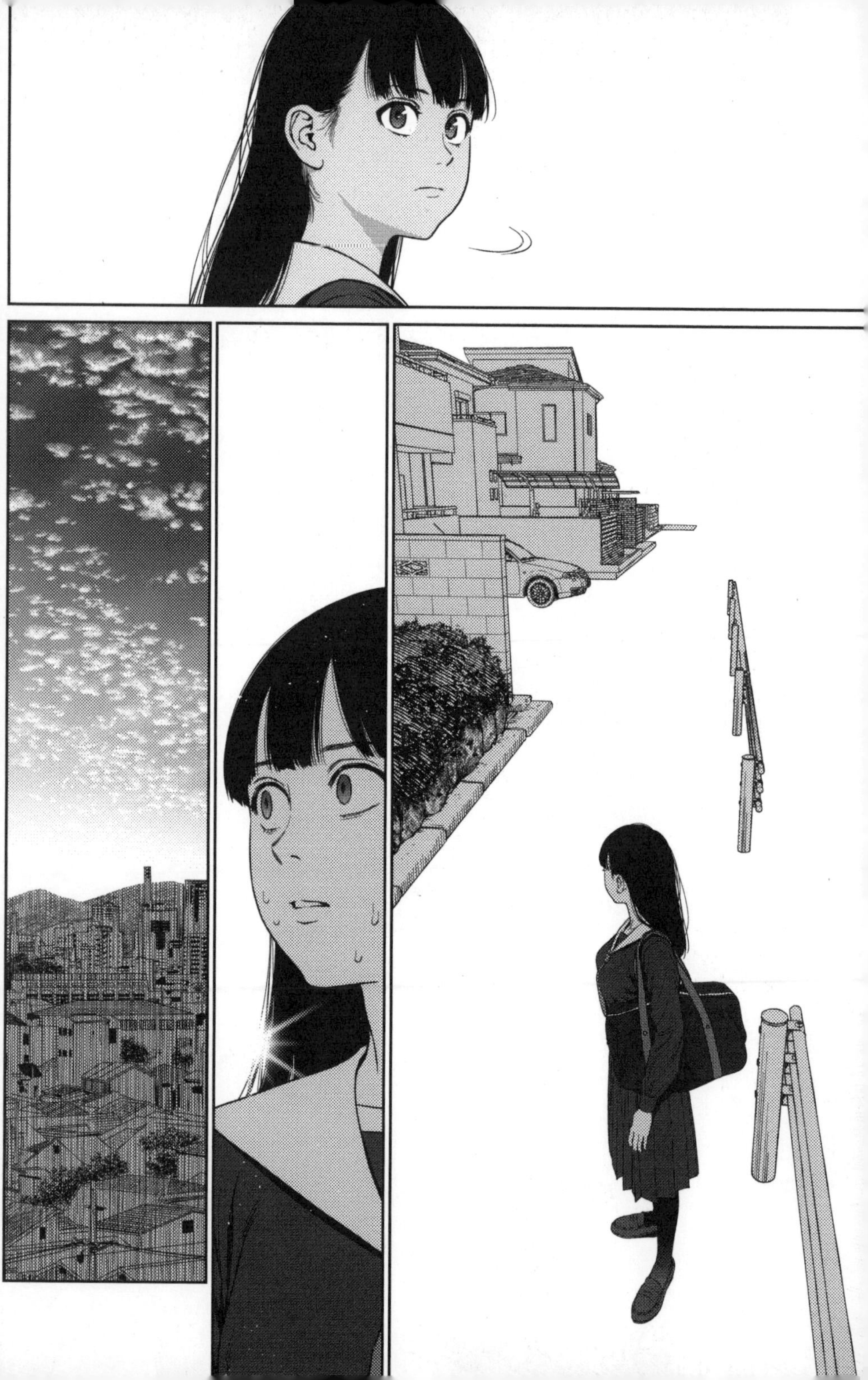

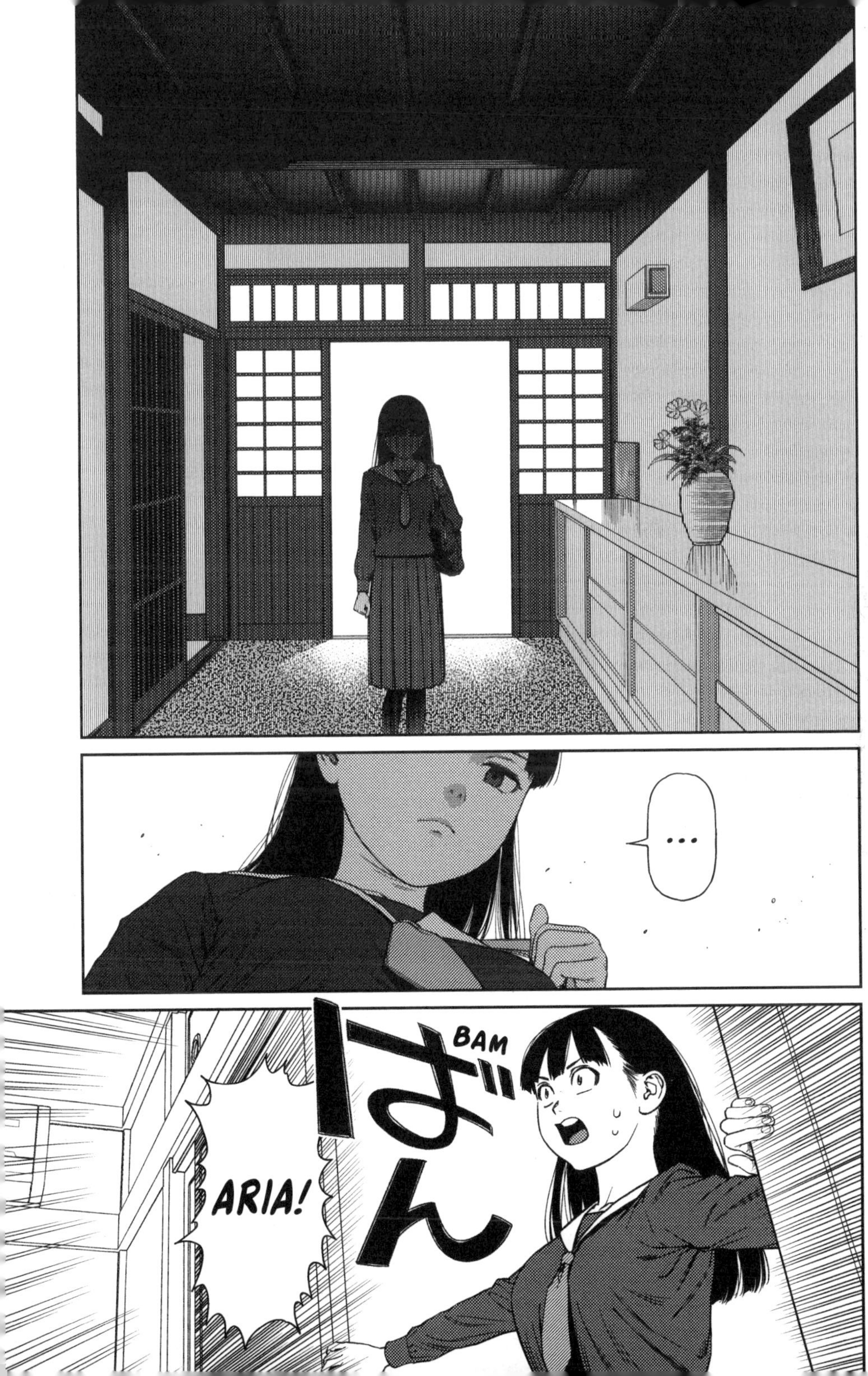
...
ばん
BAM
ARIA!

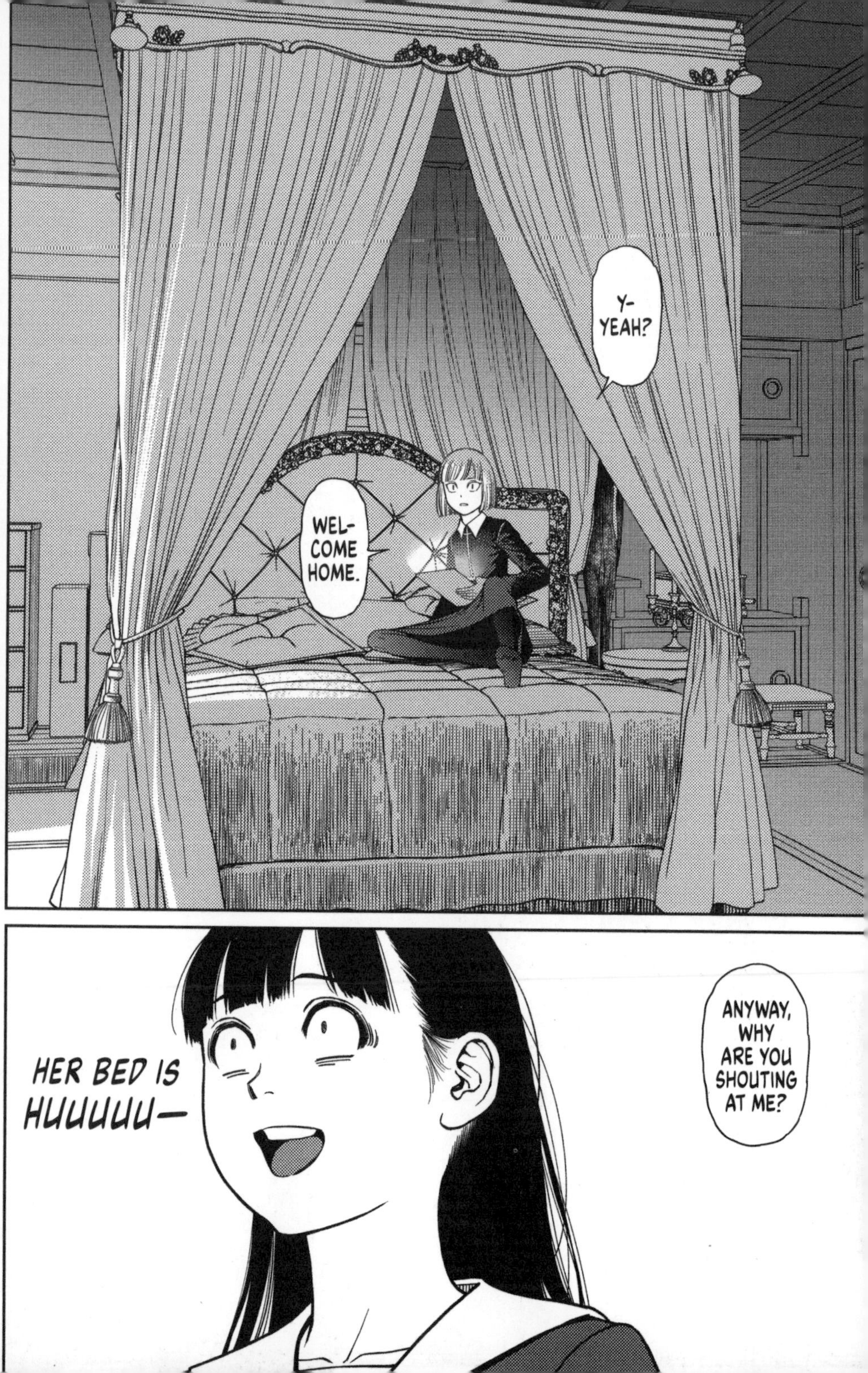
Y-YEAH?
WEL-COME HOME.
ANYWAY, WHY ARE YOU SHOUTING AT ME?
HER BED IS HUUUUU—

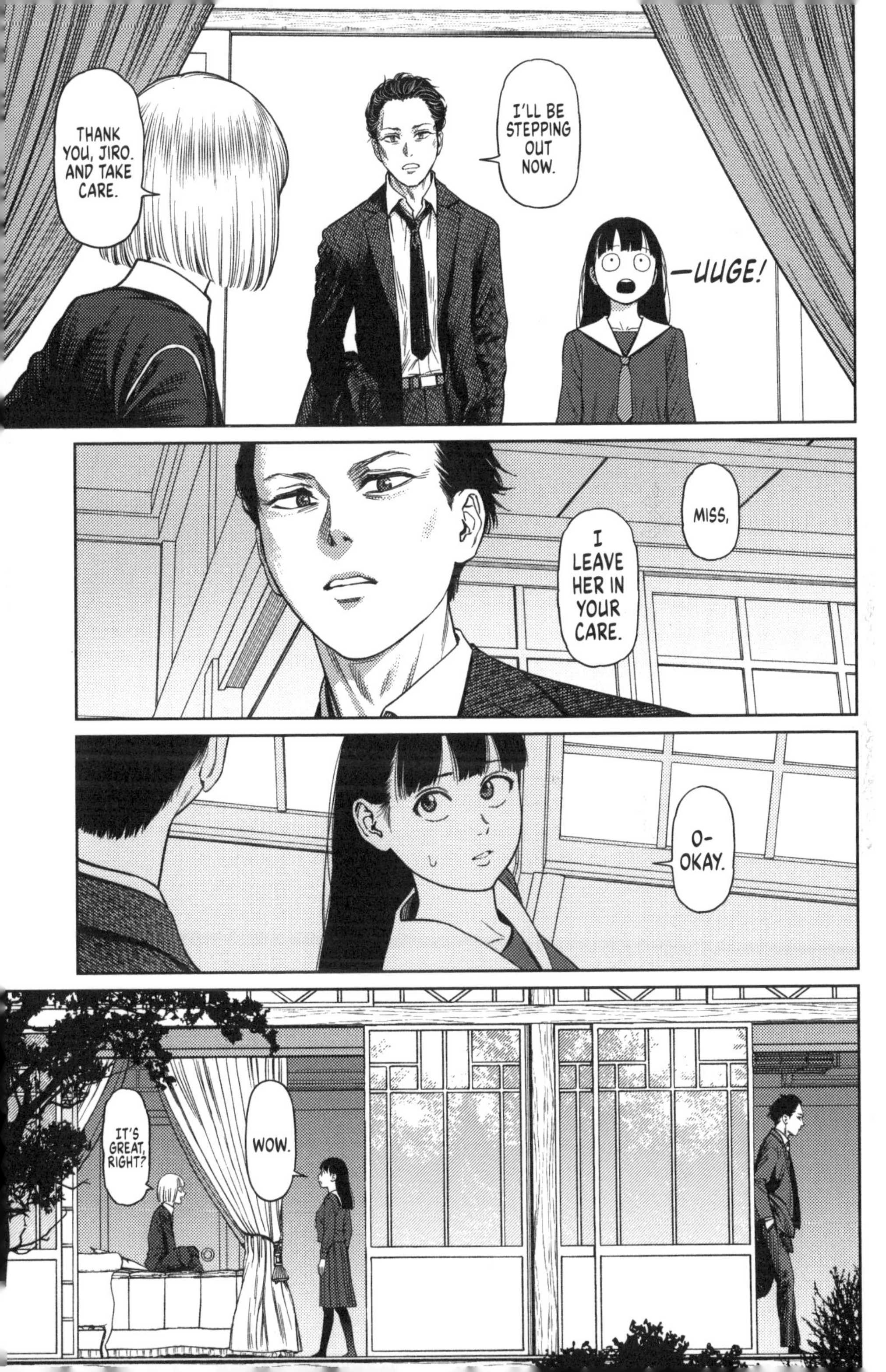
I'LL BE STEPPING OUT NOW.
THANK YOU, JIRO. AND TAKE CARE.
—UUGE!
MISS,
I LEAVE HER IN YOUR CARE.
O-OKAY.
WOW.
IT'S GREAT, RIGHT?

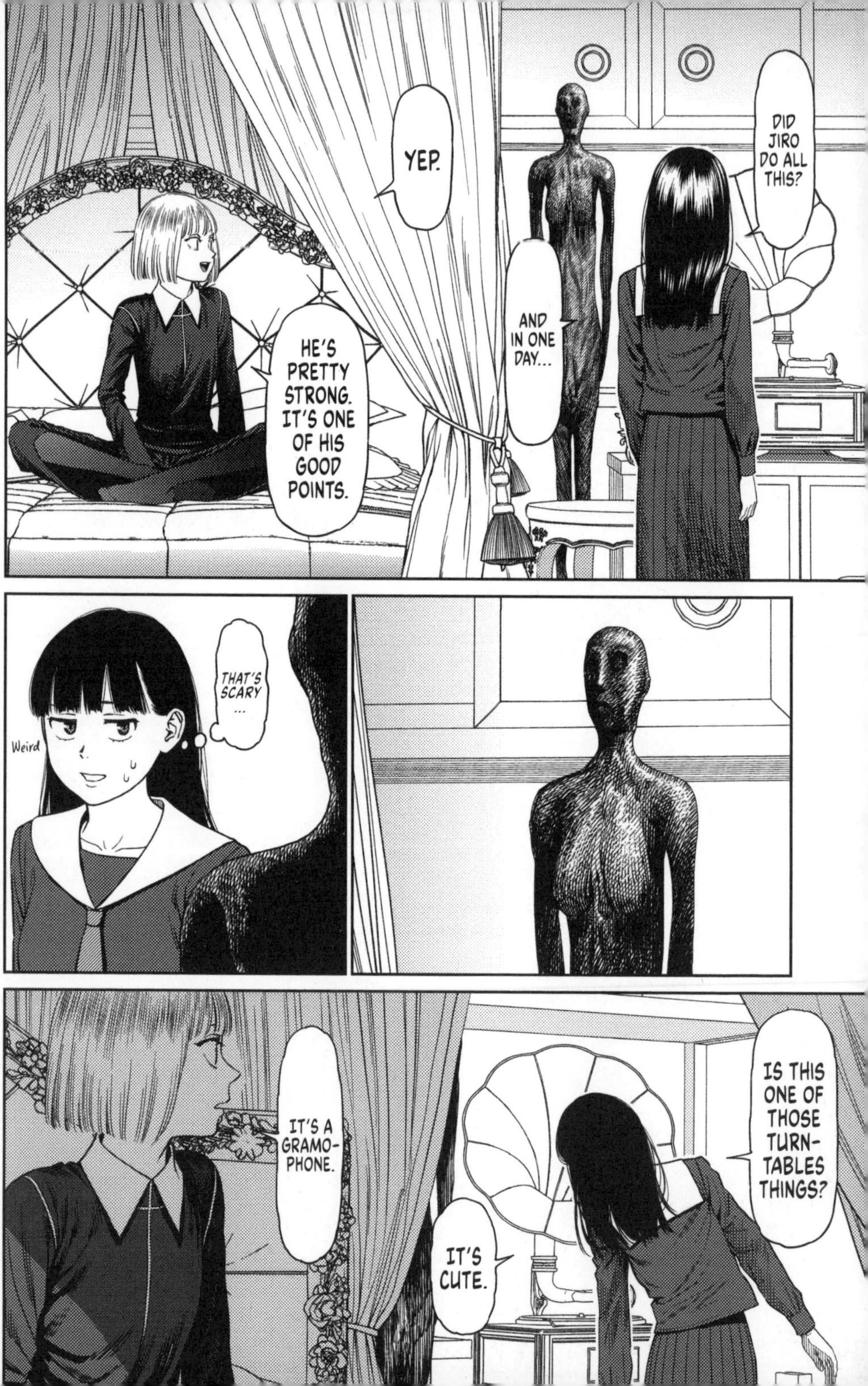
DID JIRO DO ALL THIS?
YEP.
AND IN ONE DAY...
HE'S PRETTY STRONG. IT'S ONE OF HIS GOOD POINTS.
THAT'S SCARY...
Weird
IS THIS ONE OF THOSE TURN-TABLES THINGS?
IT'S CUTE.
IT'S A GRAMO-PHONE.

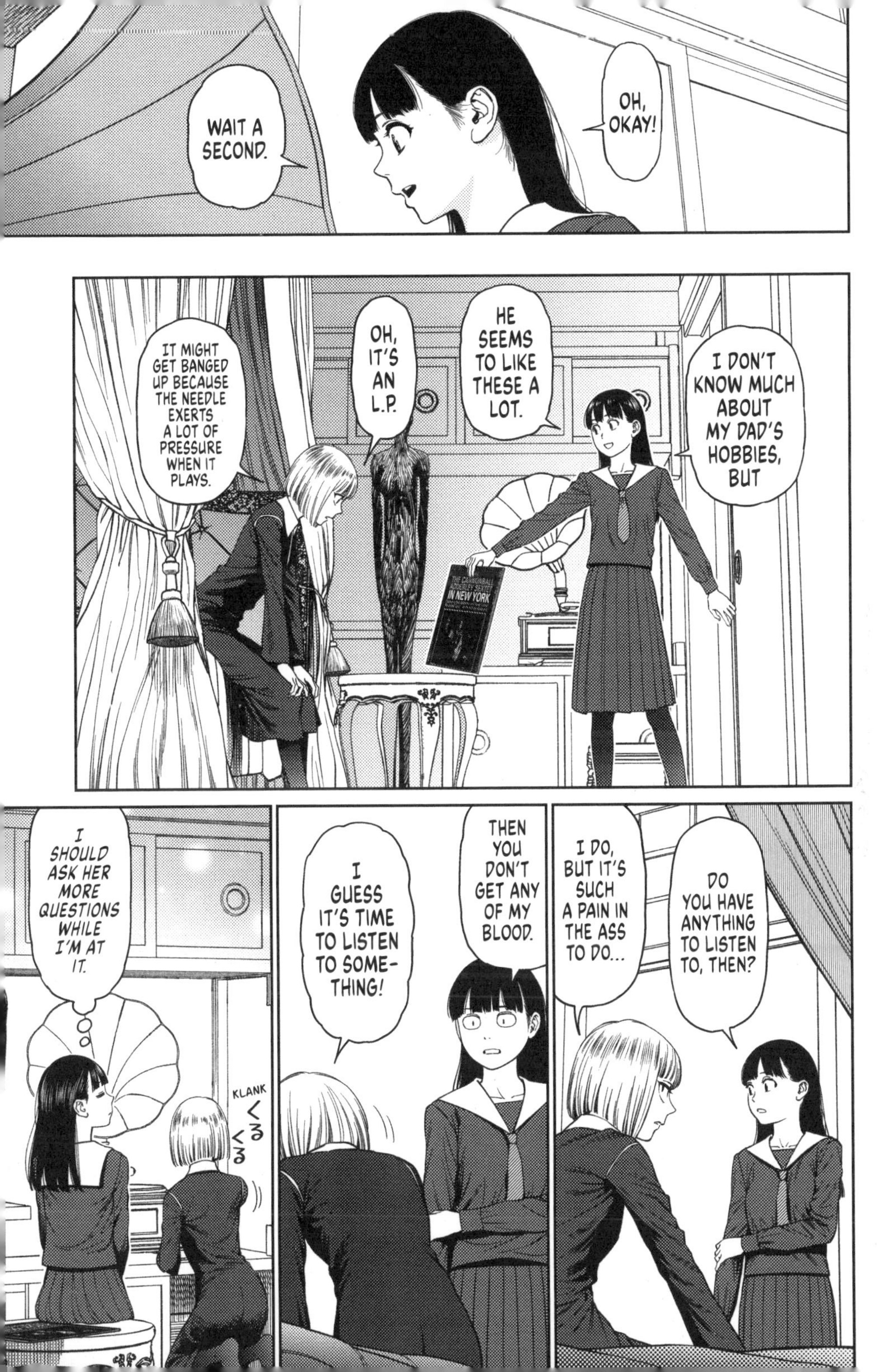
OH, OKAY!
WAIT A SECOND.
I DON'T KNOW MUCH ABOUT MY DAD'S HOBBIES, BUT
HE SEEMS TO LIKE THESE A LOT.
OH, IT'S AN L.P.
IT MIGHT GET BANGED UP BECAUSE THE NEEDLE EXERTS A LOT OF PRESSURE WHEN IT PLAYS.
THE CANNONBALL ADDERLEY SEXTET
IN NEW YORK
DO YOU HAVE ANYTHING TO LISTEN TO, THEN?
I DO, BUT IT'S SUCH A PAIN IN THE ASS TO DO...
THEN YOU DON'T GET ANY OF MY BLOOD.
I GUESS IT'S TIME TO LISTEN TO SOME-THING!
I SHOULD ASK HER MORE QUESTIONS WHILE I'M AT IT.
KLANK
くるくる

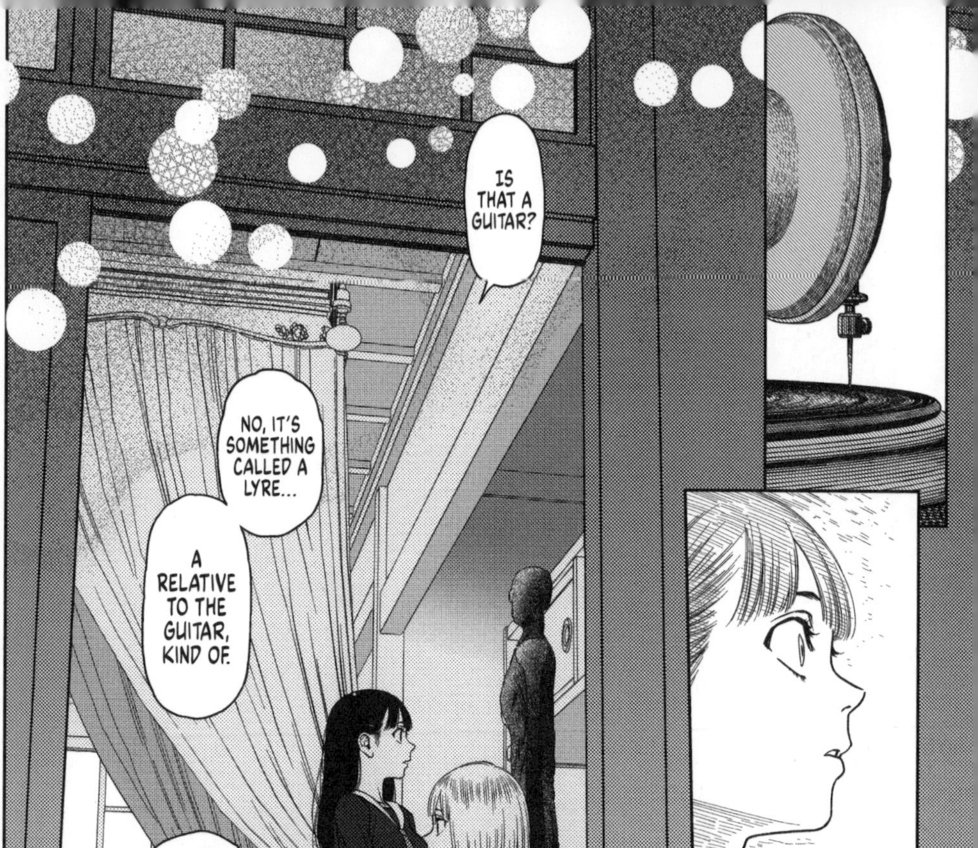
IS THAT A GUITAR?
NO, IT'S SOMETHING CALLED A LYRE...
A RELATIVE TO THE GUITAR, KIND OF.
IT'S LIKE IT'S BEING PLAYED RIGHT HERE.

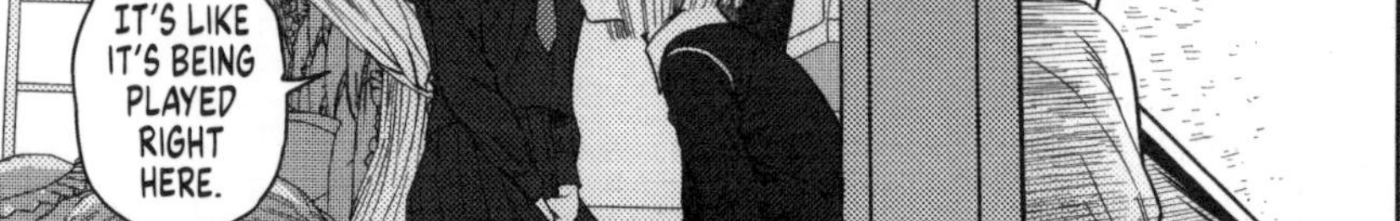

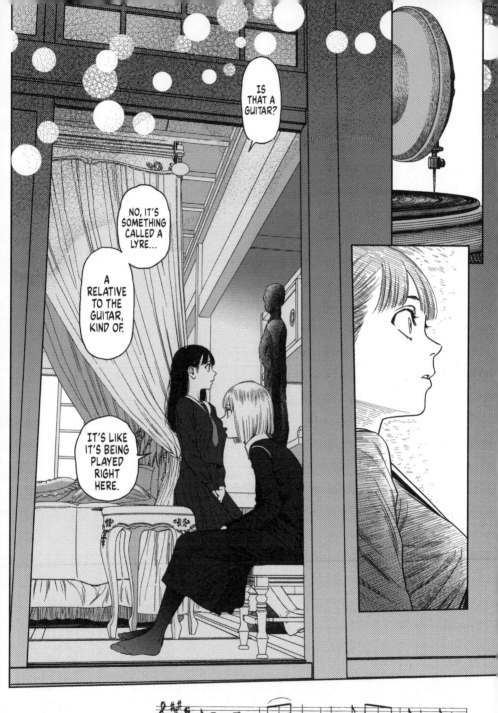

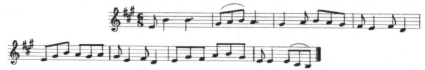

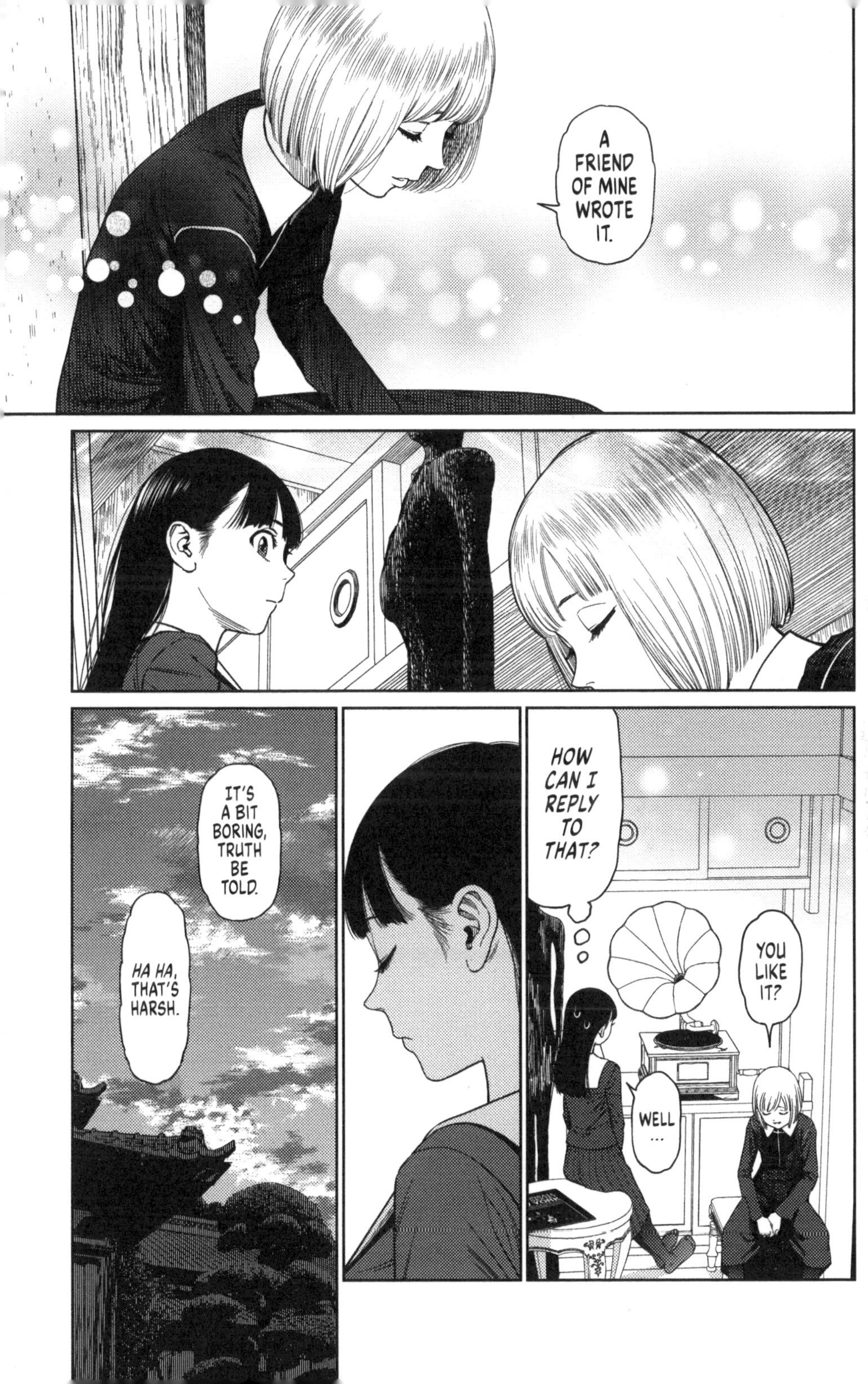
A FRIEND OF MINE WROTE IT.
HOW CAN I REPLY TO THAT?
YOU LIKE IT?
WELL ...
IT'S A BIT BORING, TRUTH BE TOLD.
HA HA, THAT'S HARSH.

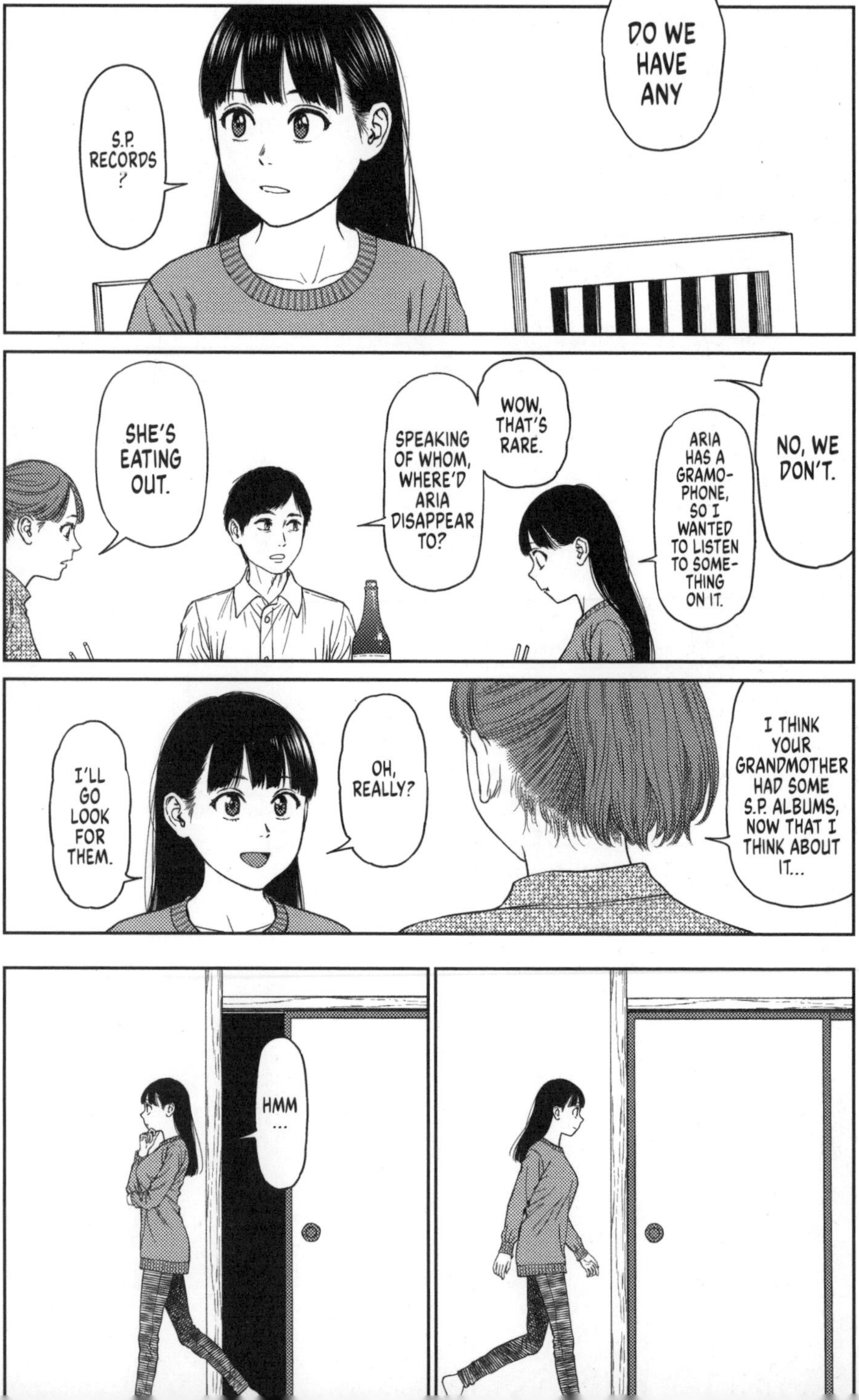
DO WE HAVE ANY
S.P. RECORDS ?
NO, WE DON'T.
ARIA HAS A GRAMO-PHONE, SO I WANTED TO LISTEN TO SOME-THING ON IT.
WOW, THAT'S RARE.
SPEAKING OF WHOM, WHERE'D ARIA DISAPPEAR TO?
SHE'S EATING OUT.
I THINK YOUR GRANDMOTHER HAD SOME S.P. ALBUMS, NOW THAT I THINK ABOUT IT...
OH, REALLY?
I'LL GO LOOK FOR THEM.
HMM ...

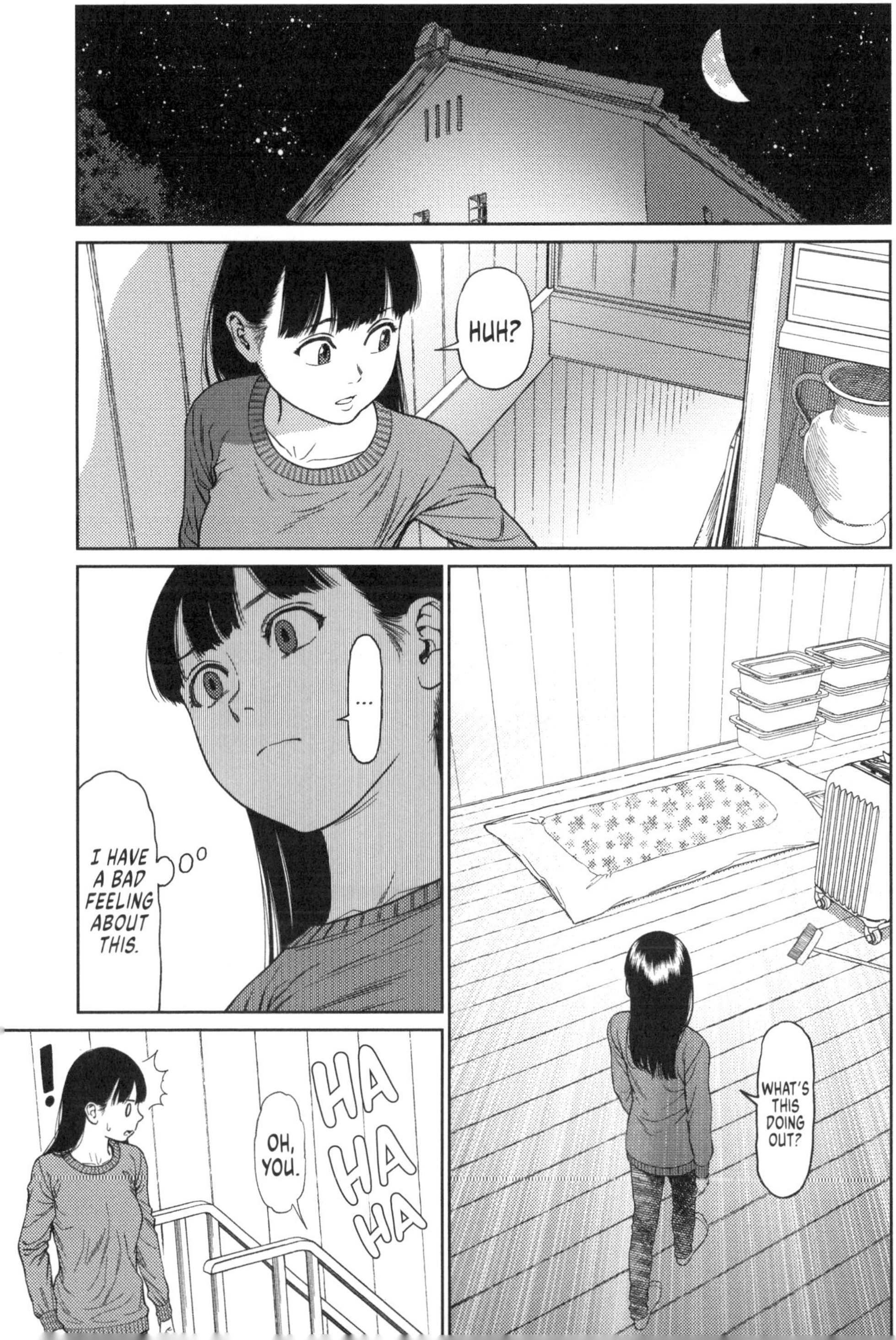
HUH?
WHAT'S THIS DOING OUT?
...
I HAVE A BAD FEELING ABOUT THIS.
HA HA HA HA
OH, YOU.
!

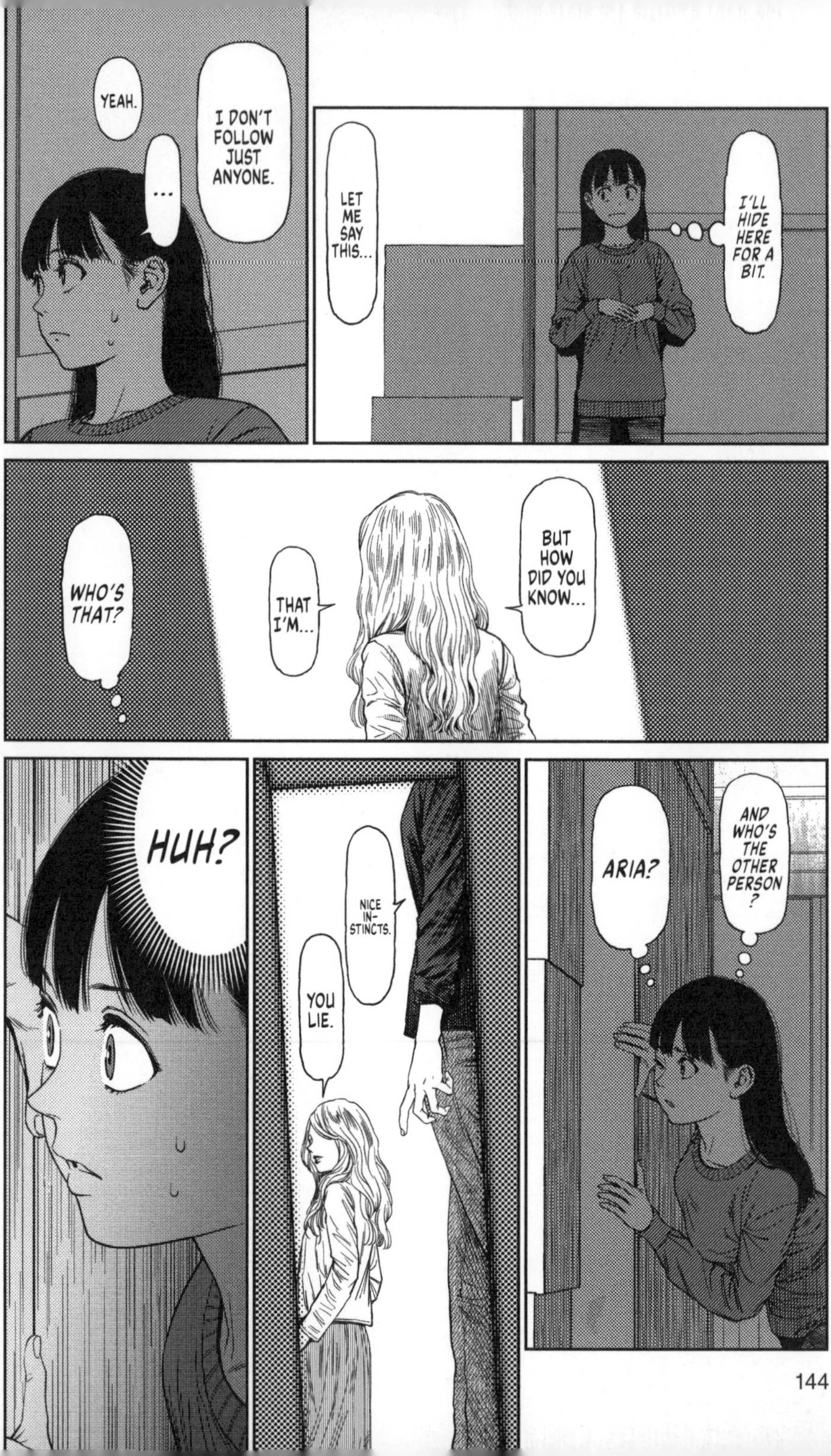
I'LL HIDE HERE FOR A BIT.
LET ME SAY THIS...
I DON'T FOLLOW JUST ANYONE.
YEAH.
...
BUT HOW DID YOU KNOW...
THAT I'M...
WHO'S THAT?
AND WHO'S THE OTHER PERSON?
ARIA?
NICE IN-STINCTS.
YOU LIE.
HUH?

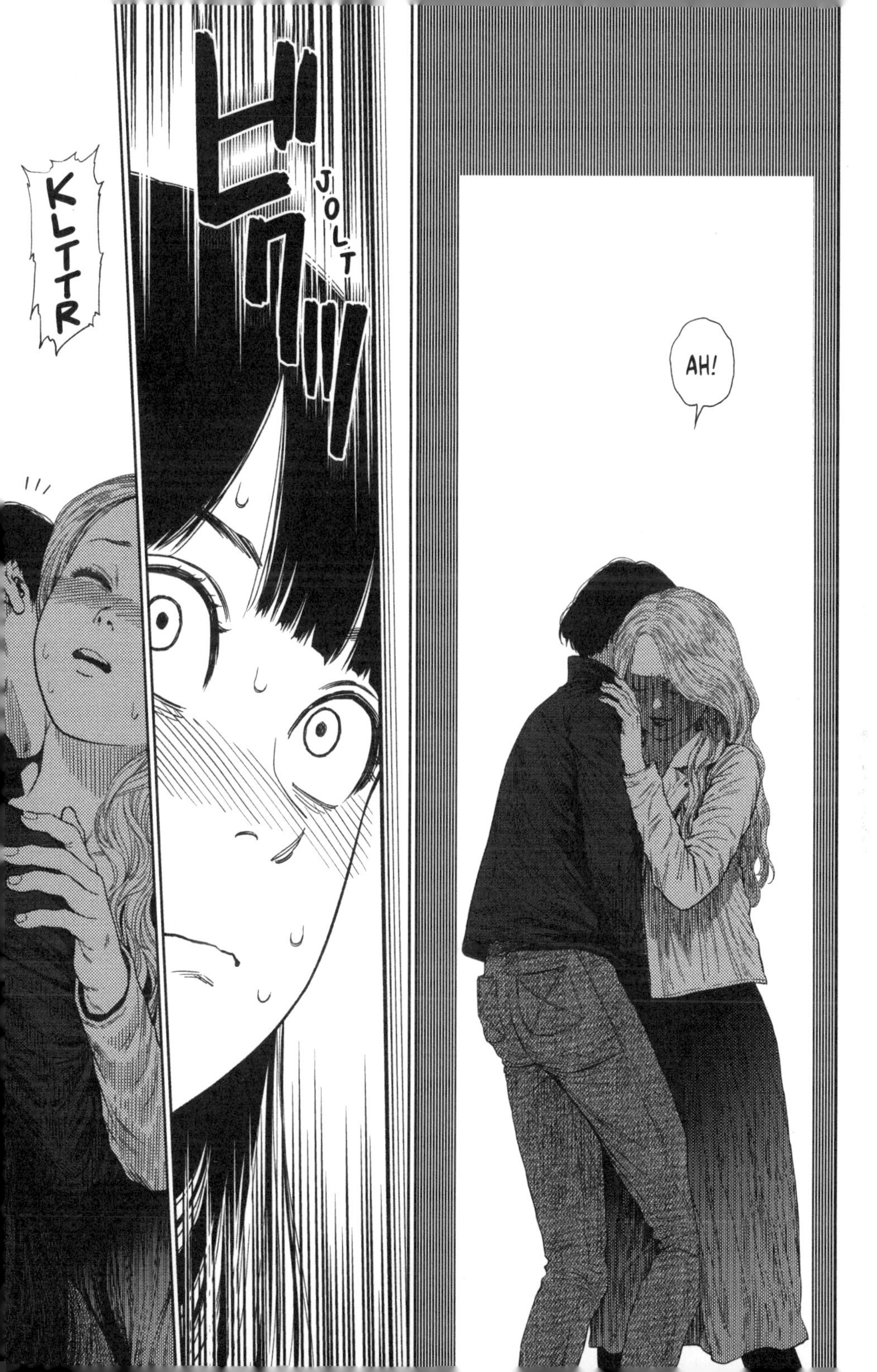

AH!
ビクッ
JOLT
KLTTR

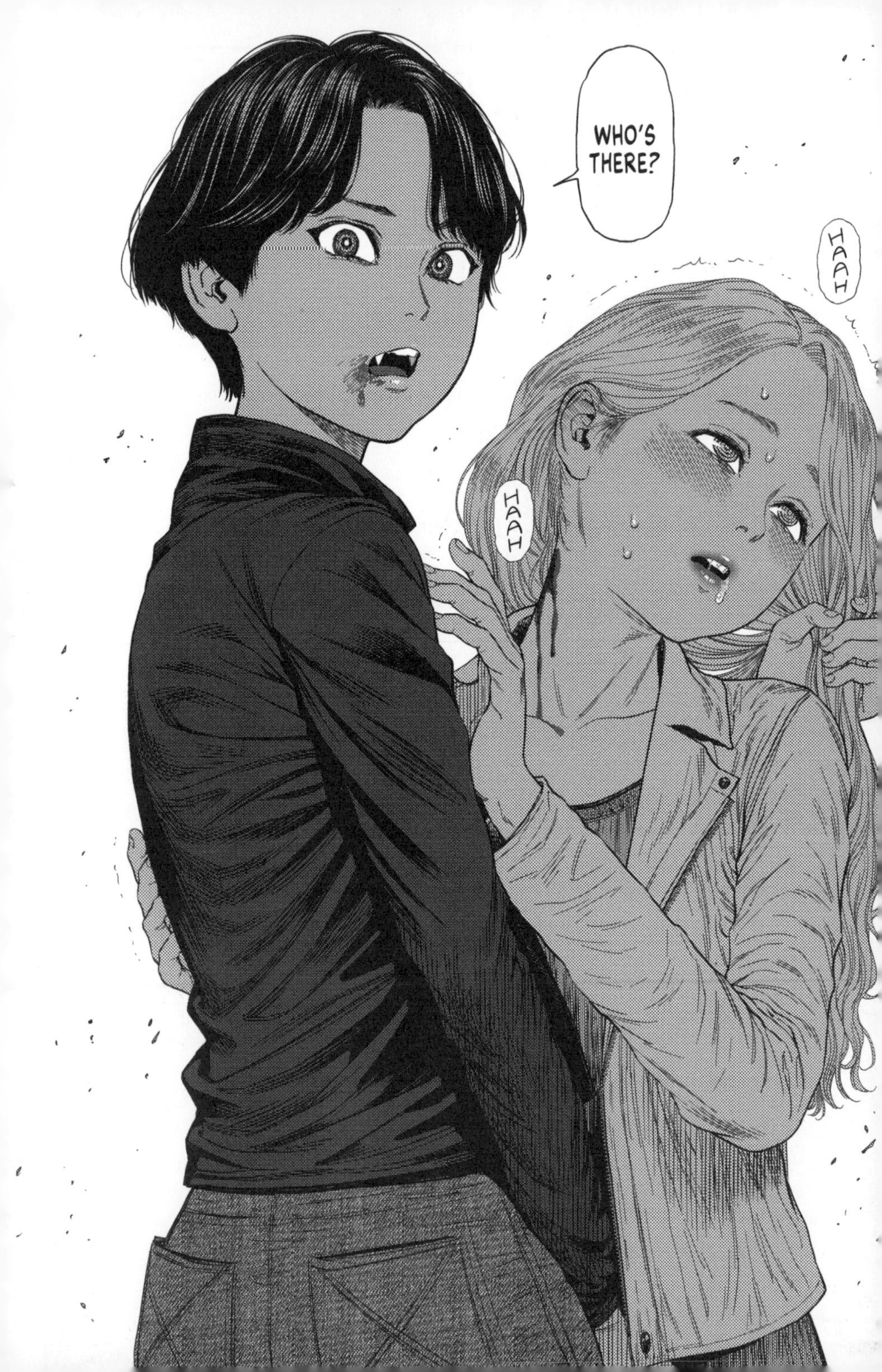
WHO'S THERE?
HAAH
HAAH

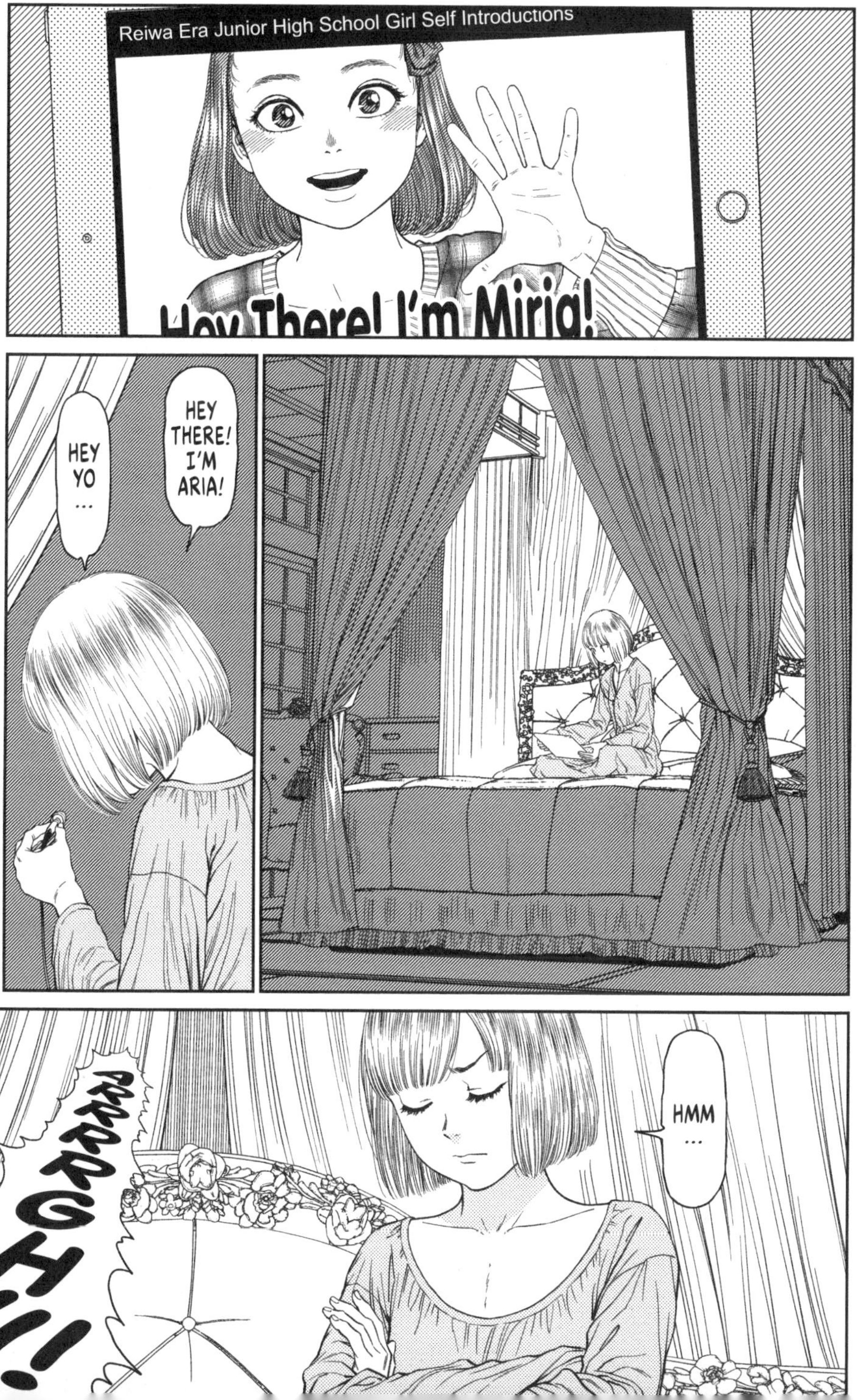
Reiwa Era Junior High School Girl Self Introductions
Hey There! I'm Miria!
HEY THERE! I'M ARIA!
HEY YO ...
HMM ...
PRRRRGHH!!!

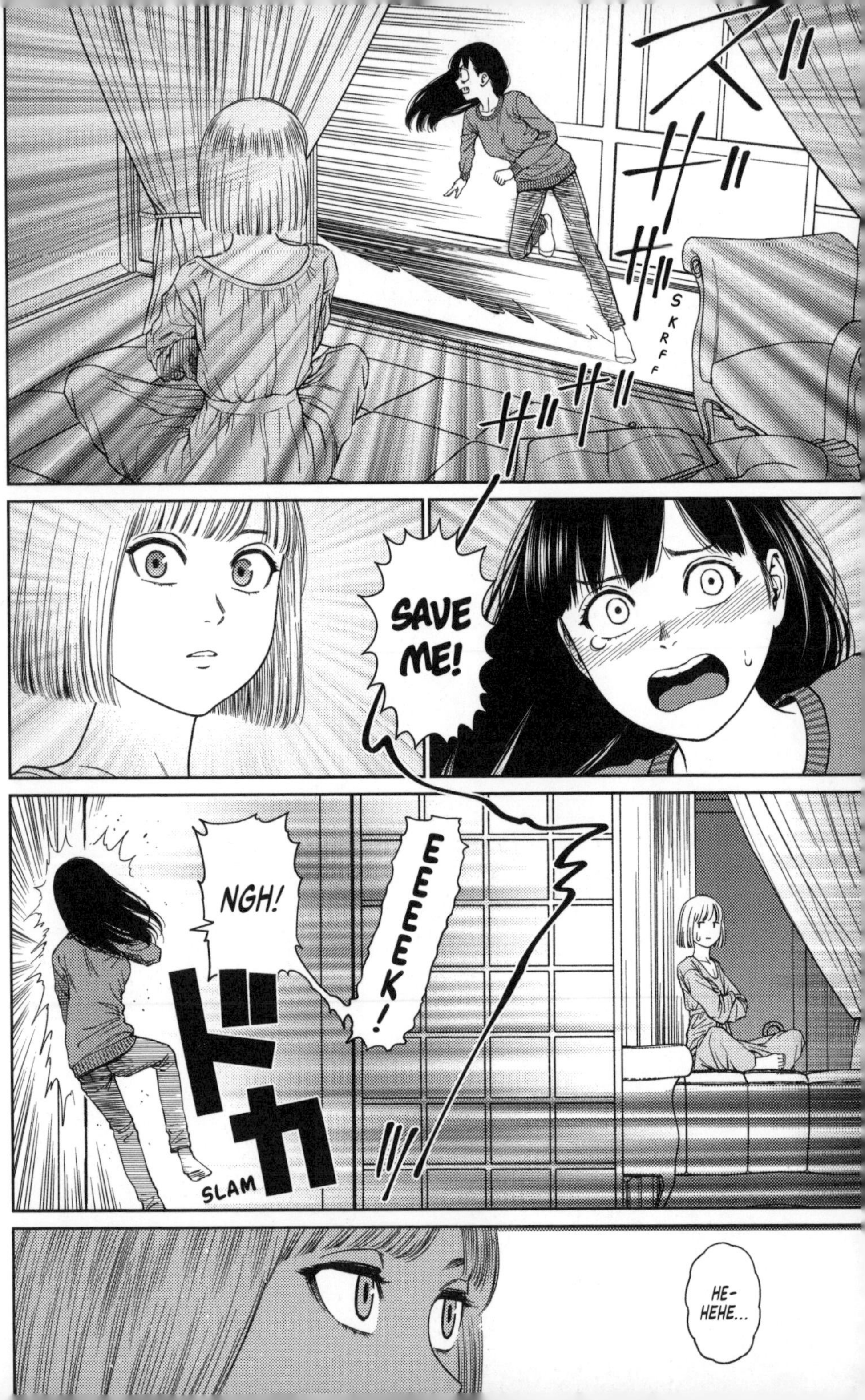
SKRFF
SAVE ME!
EEEEEK!
NGH!
SLAM
HE-HEHE...

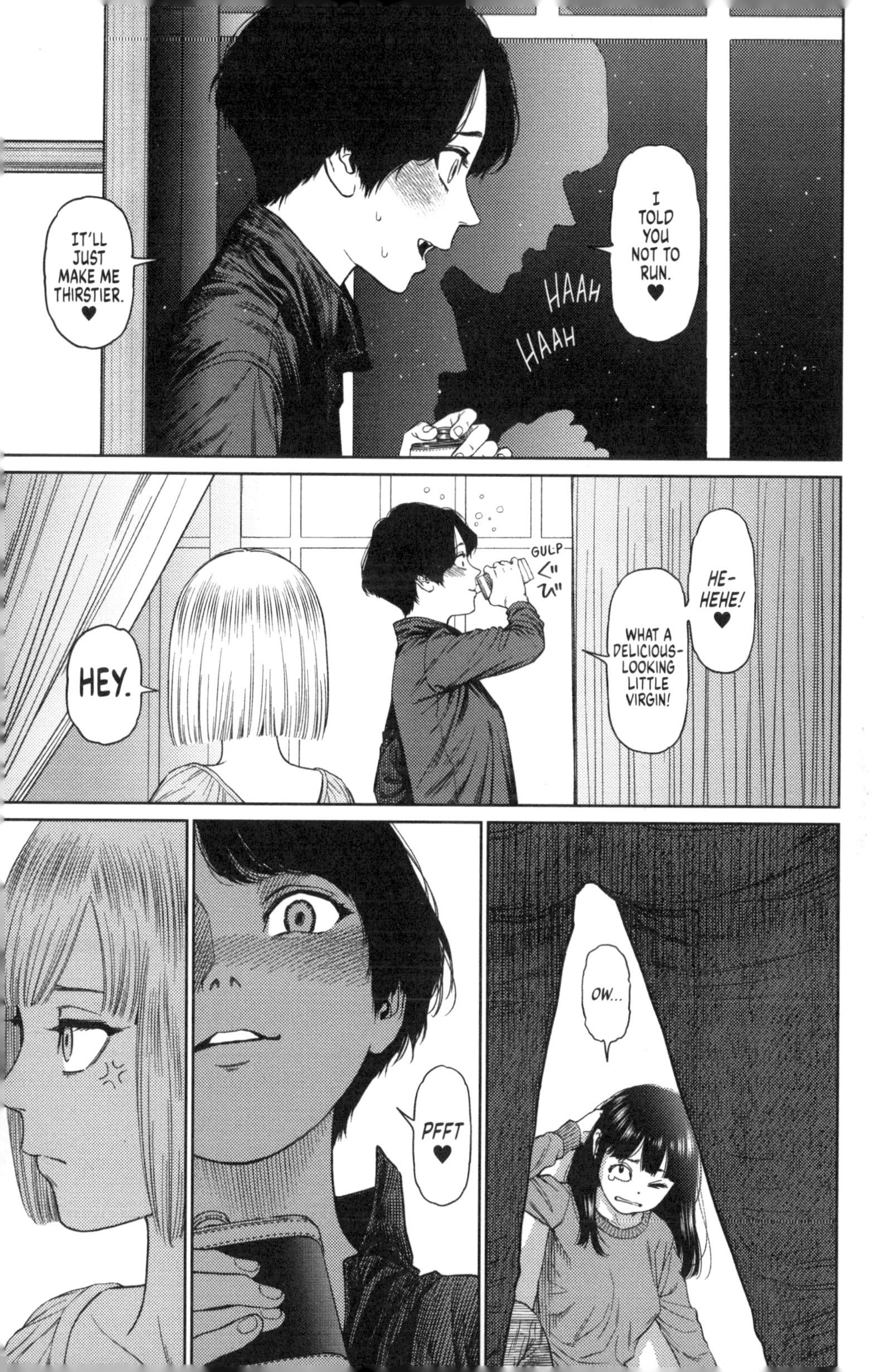
I TOLD YOU NOT TO RUN. ♥
HAAH
HAAH
IT'LL JUST MAKE ME THIRSTIER. ♥
HE-HEHE! ♥
WHAT A DELICIOUS-LOOKING LITTLE VIRGIN!
GULP
ぐび
HEY.
OW...
PFFT ♥

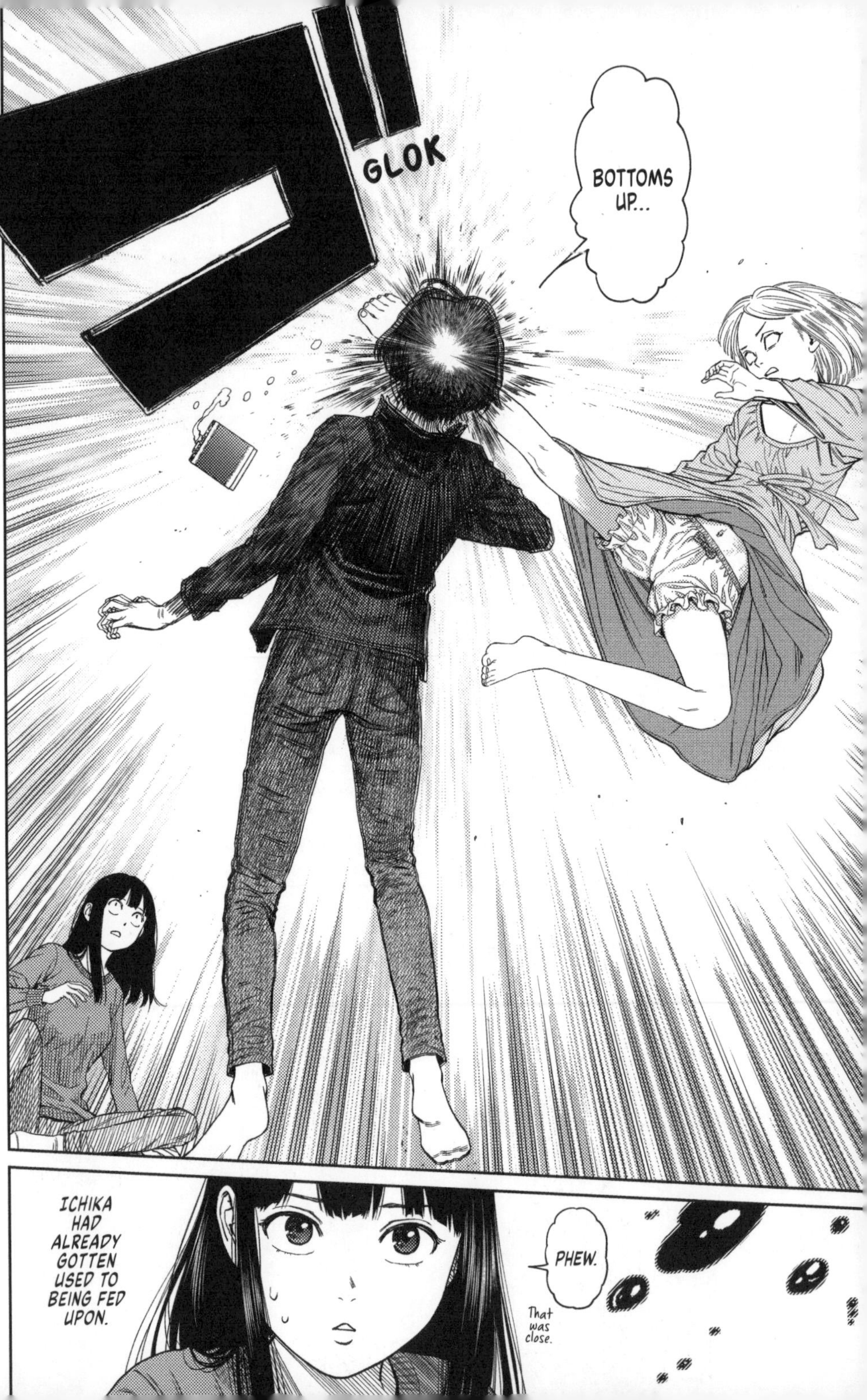
BOTTOMS UP...
GLOK
PHEW.
That was close.
ICHIKA HAD ALREADY GOTTEN USED TO BEING FED UPON.

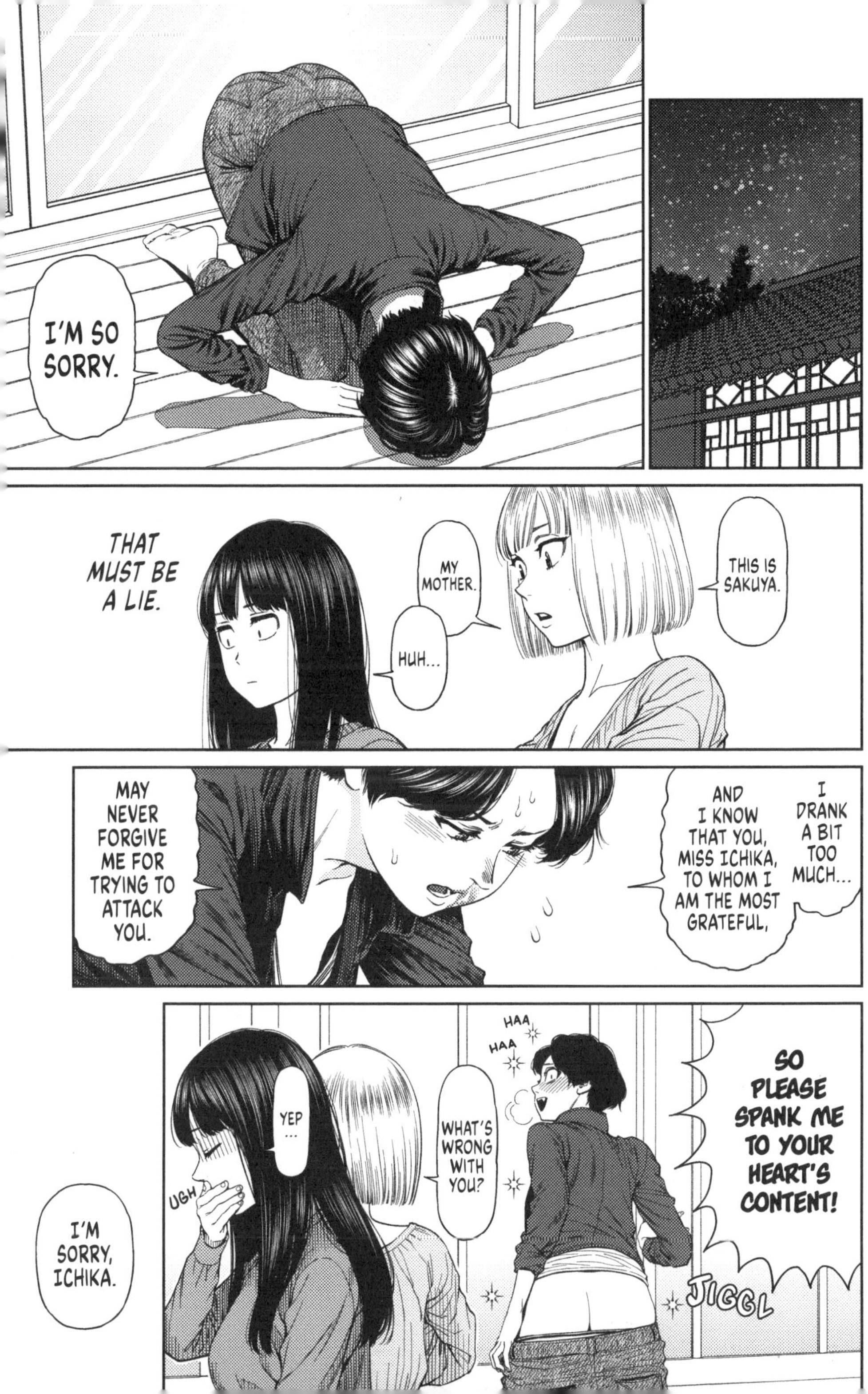
I'M SO SORRY.
THIS IS SAKUYA.
MY MOTHER.
HUH...
THAT MUST BE A LIE.
I DRANK A BIT TOO MUCH...
AND I KNOW THAT YOU, MISS ICHIKA, TO WHOM I AM THE MOST GRATEFUL,
MAY NEVER FORGIVE ME FOR TRYING TO ATTACK YOU.
SO PLEASE SPANK ME TO YOUR HEART'S CONTENT!
HAA HAA
JIGGL
WHAT'S WRONG WITH YOU?
YEP...
UGH
I'M SORRY, ICHIKA.

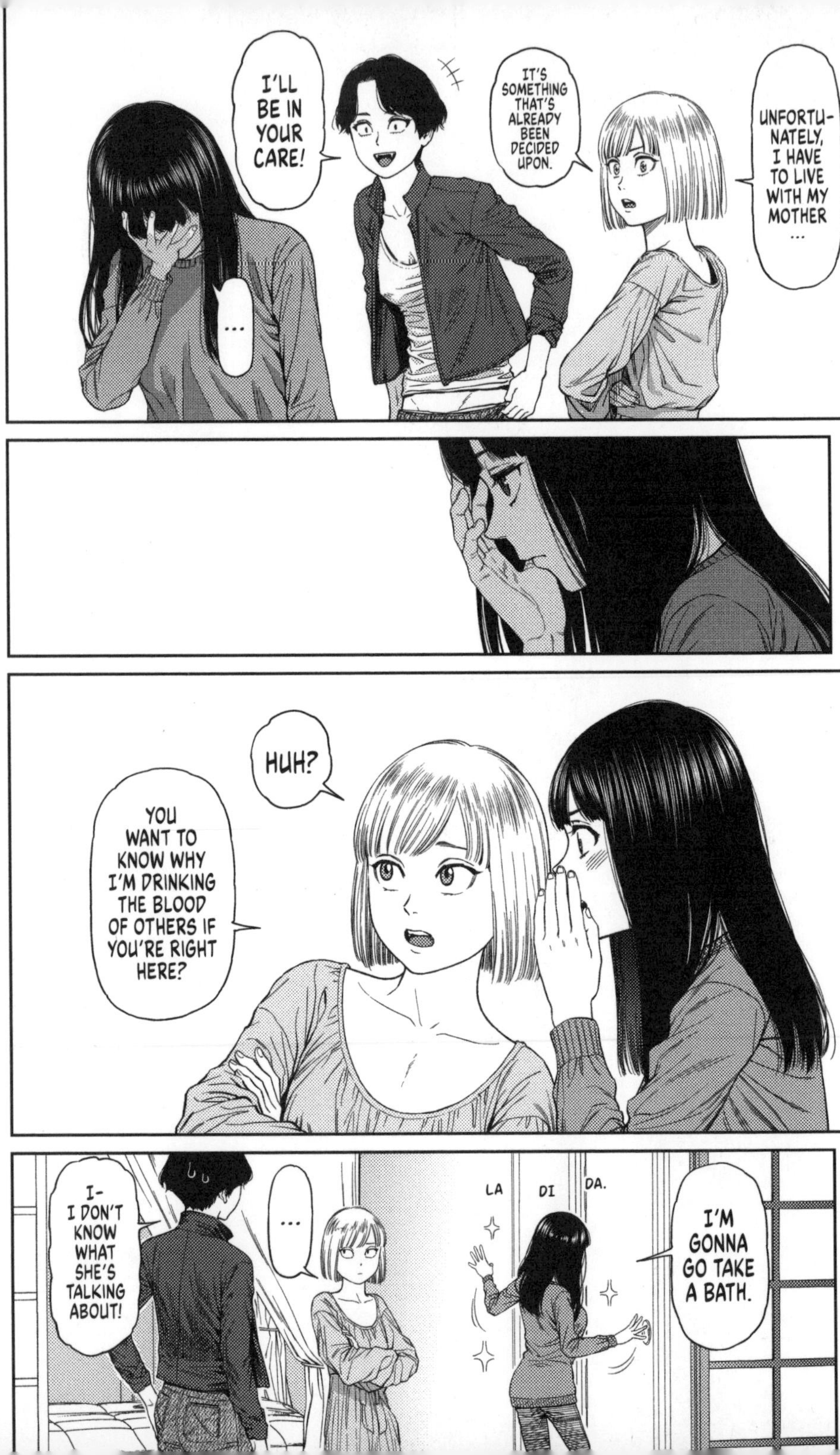
UNFORTU-NATELY, I HAVE TO LIVE WITH MY MOTHER ...
IT'S SOMETHING THAT'S ALREADY BEEN DECIDED UPON.
I'LL BE IN YOUR CARE!
...
HUH?
YOU WANT TO KNOW WHY I'M DRINKING THE BLOOD OF OTHERS IF YOU'RE RIGHT HERE?
I'M GONNA GO TAKE A BATH.
LA DI DA.
...
I- I DON'T KNOW WHAT SHE'S TALKING ABOUT!

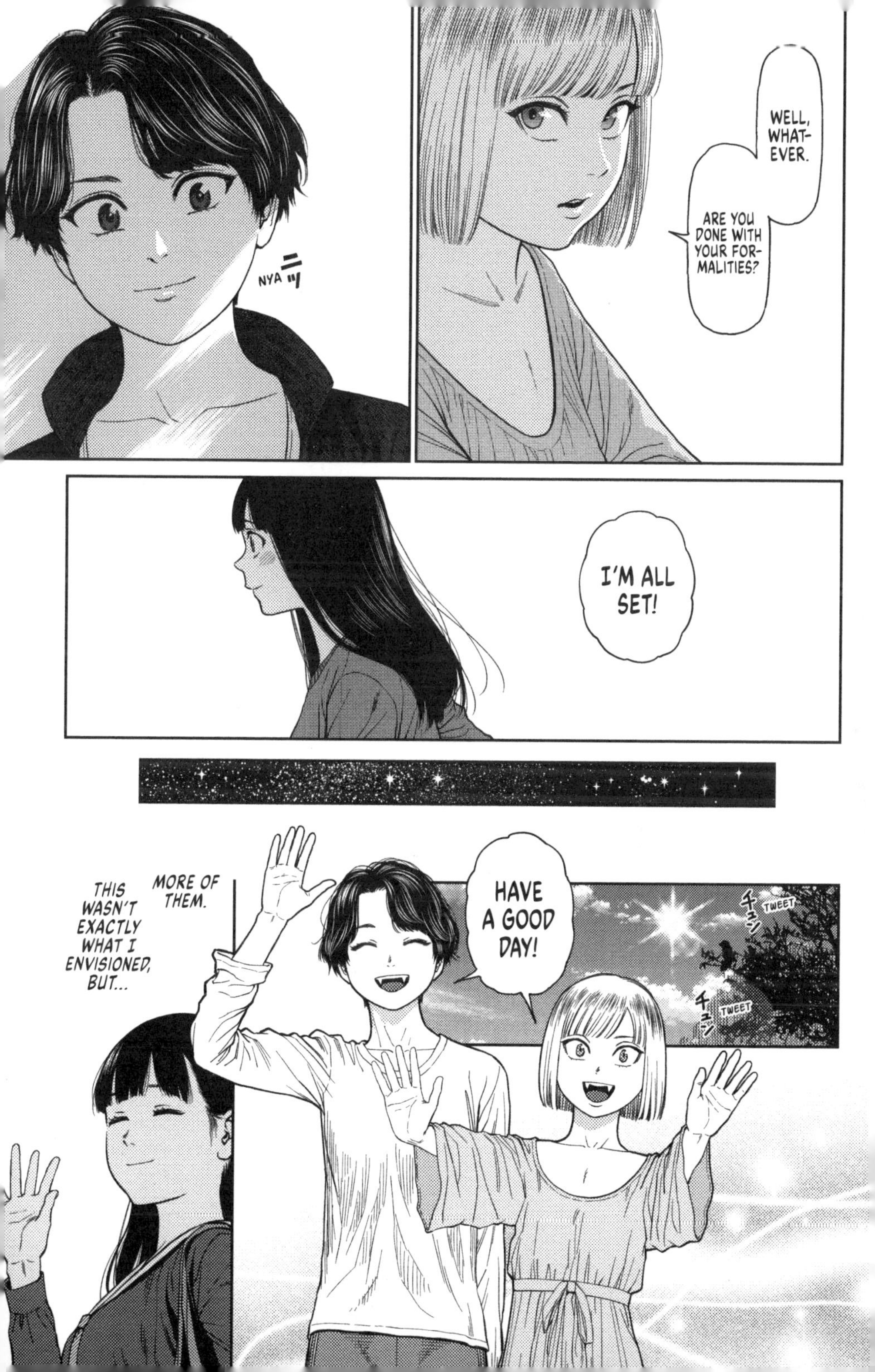
WELL, WHAT-EVER.
ARE YOU DONE WITH YOUR FOR-MALITIES?
NYA ニッ
I'M ALL SET!
チュン TWEET
チュン TWEET
HAVE A GOOD DAY!
THIS WASN'T EXACTLY WHAT I ENVISIONED, BUT...
MORE OF THEM.

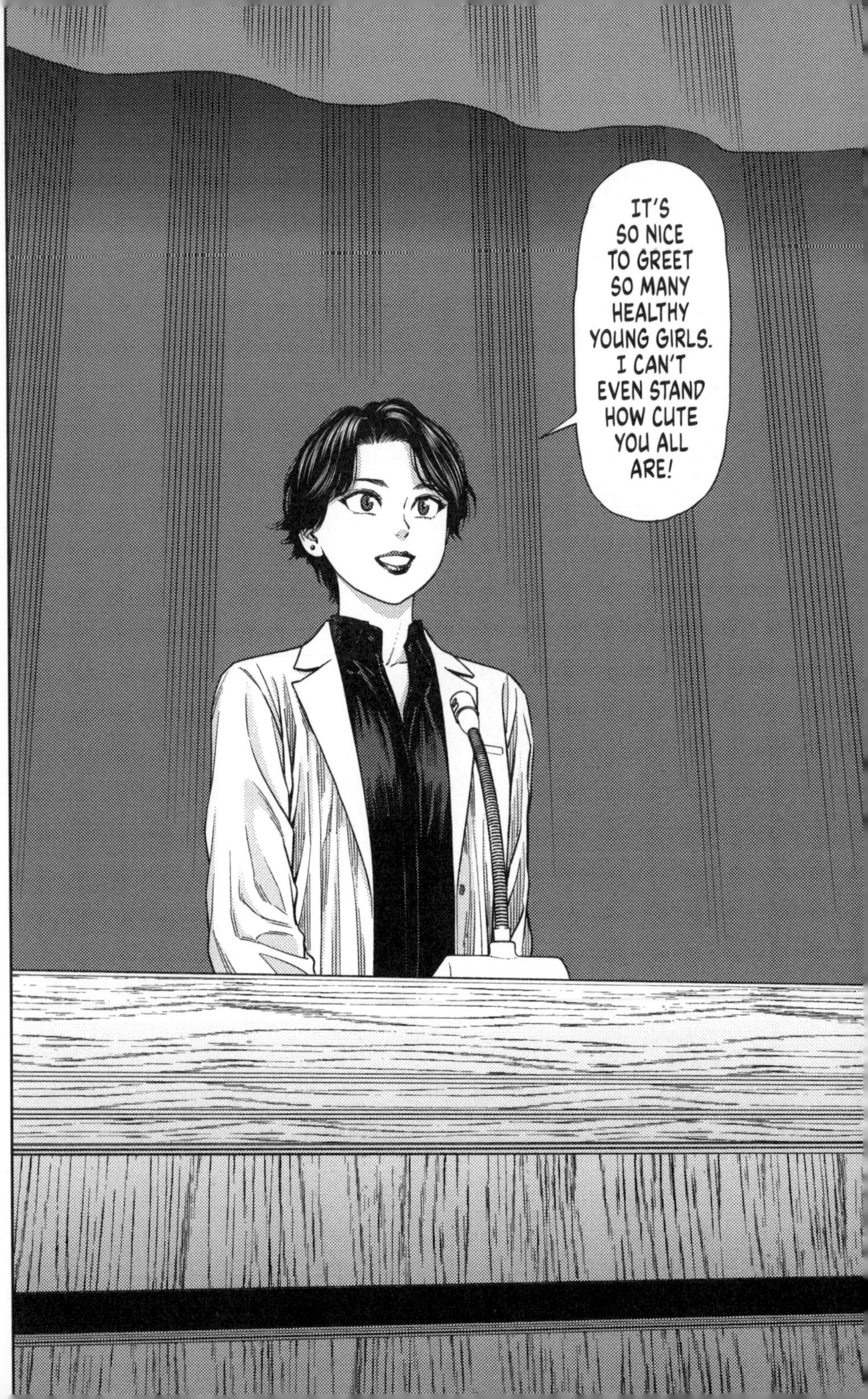
IT'S SO NICE TO GREET SO MANY HEALTHY YOUNG GIRLS. I CAN'T EVEN STAND HOW CUTE YOU ALL ARE!

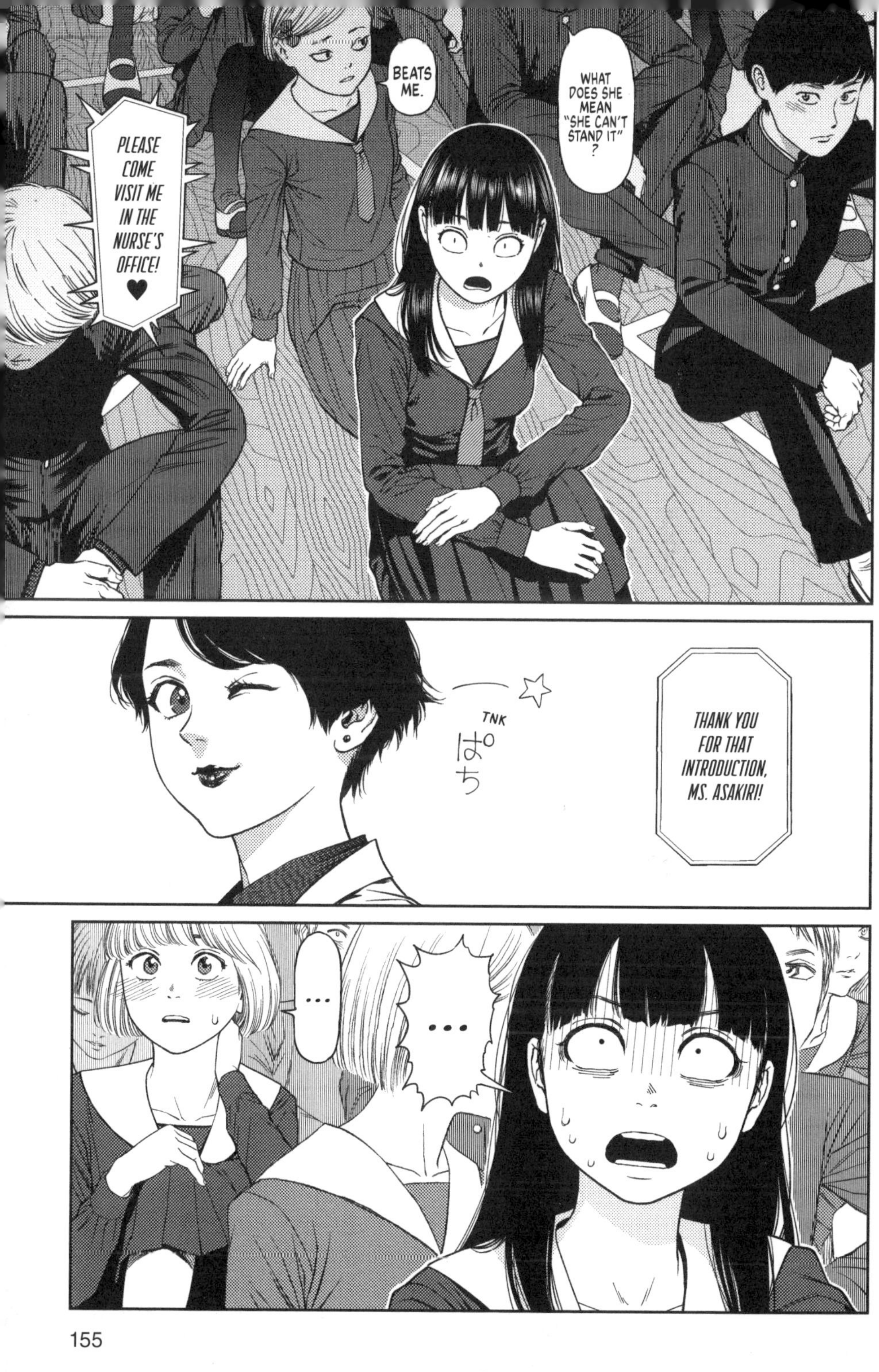
WHAT DOES SHE MEAN "SHE CAN'T STAND IT"?
BEATS ME.
PLEASE COME VISIT ME IN THE NURSE'S OFFICE! ♥
THANK YOU FOR THAT INTRODUCTION, MS. ASAKIRI!
TNK
ぱち
...
...

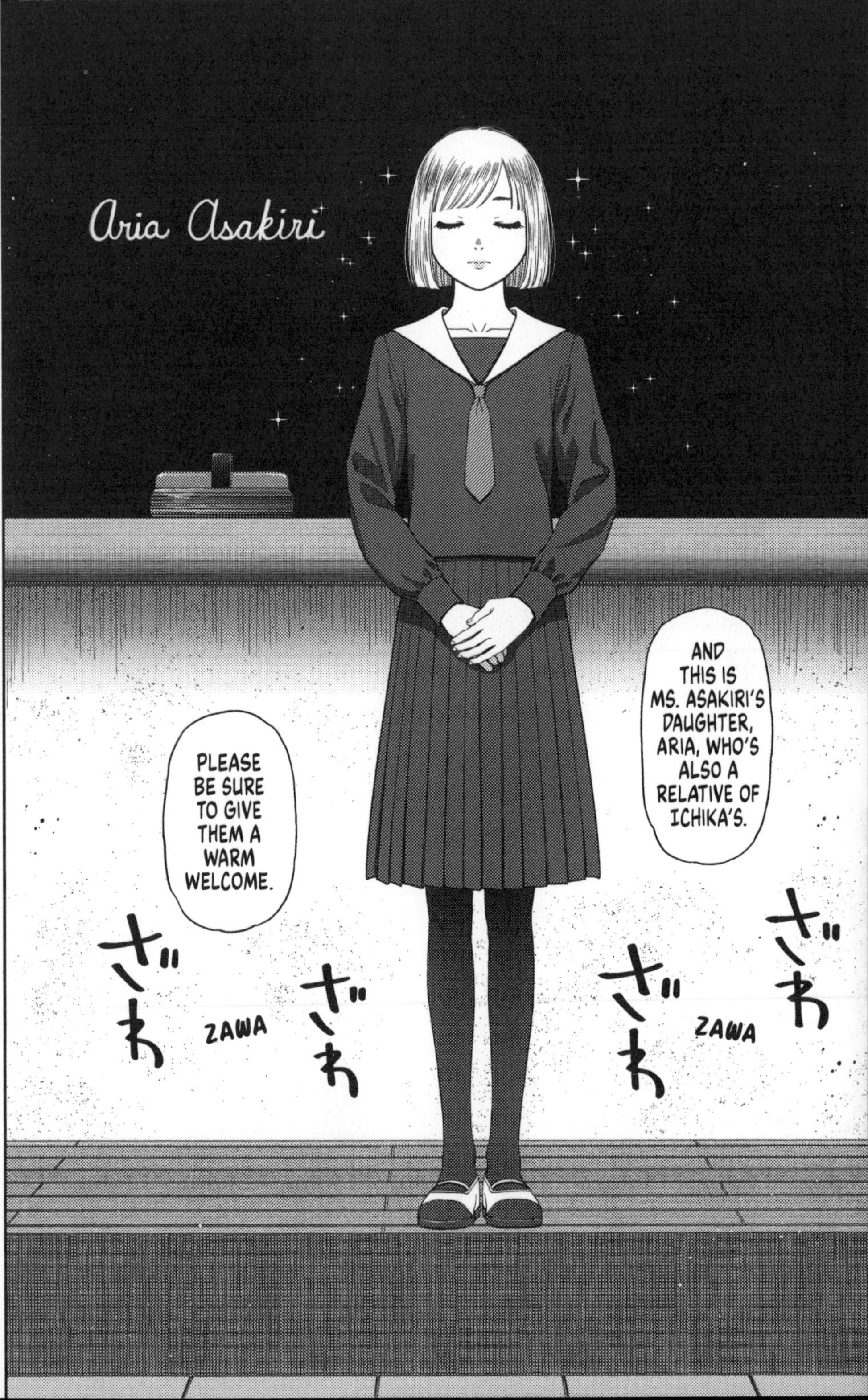
Aria Asakiri
AND THIS IS MS. ASAKIRI'S DAUGHTER, ARIA, WHO'S ALSO A RELATIVE OF ICHIKA'S.
PLEASE BE SURE TO GIVE THEM A WARM WELCOME.
ざわ
ざわ
ZAWA
ざわ
ざわ
ZAWA

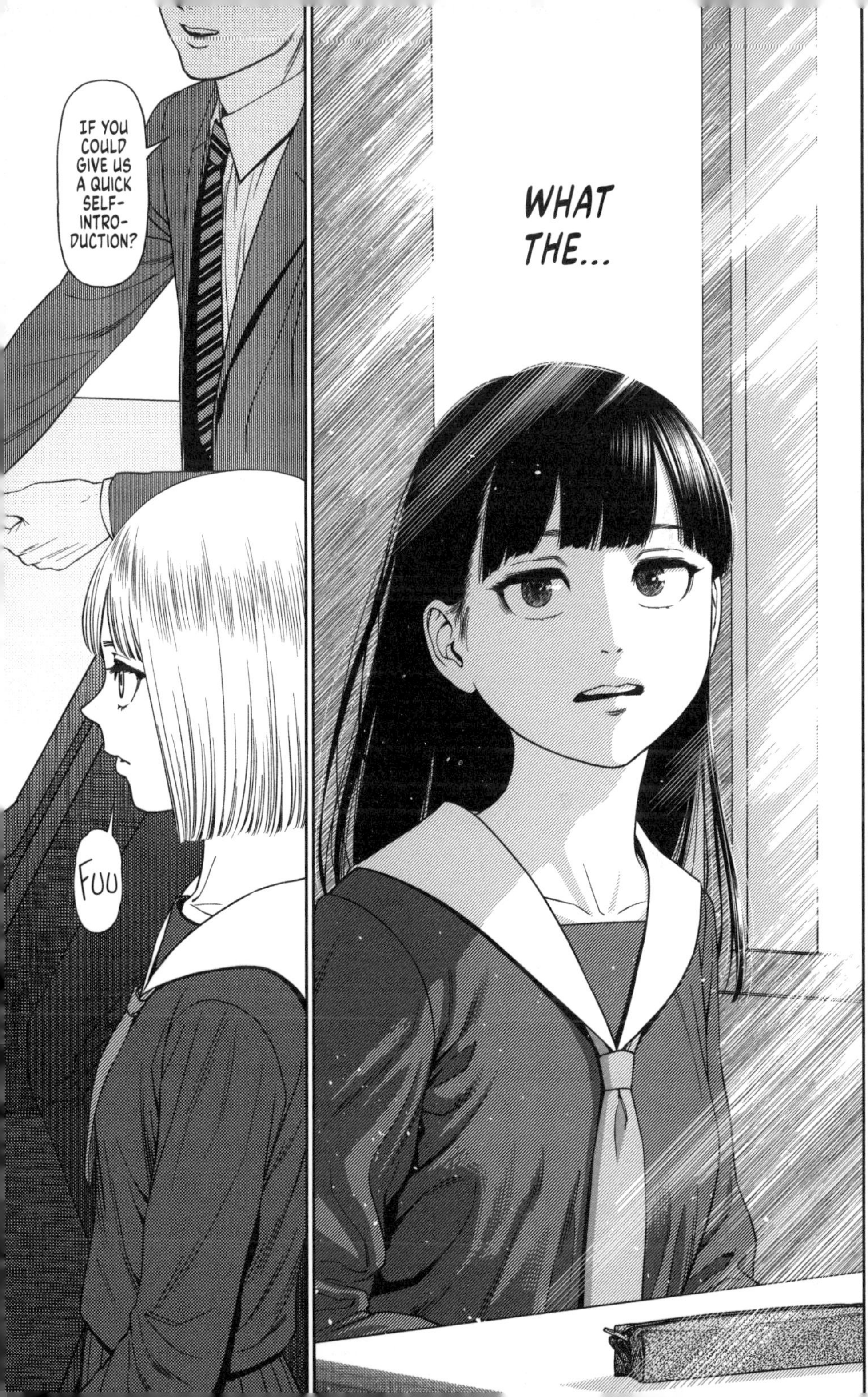
WHAT THE...
IF YOU COULD GIVE US A QUICK SELF-INTRODUCTION?
FUU

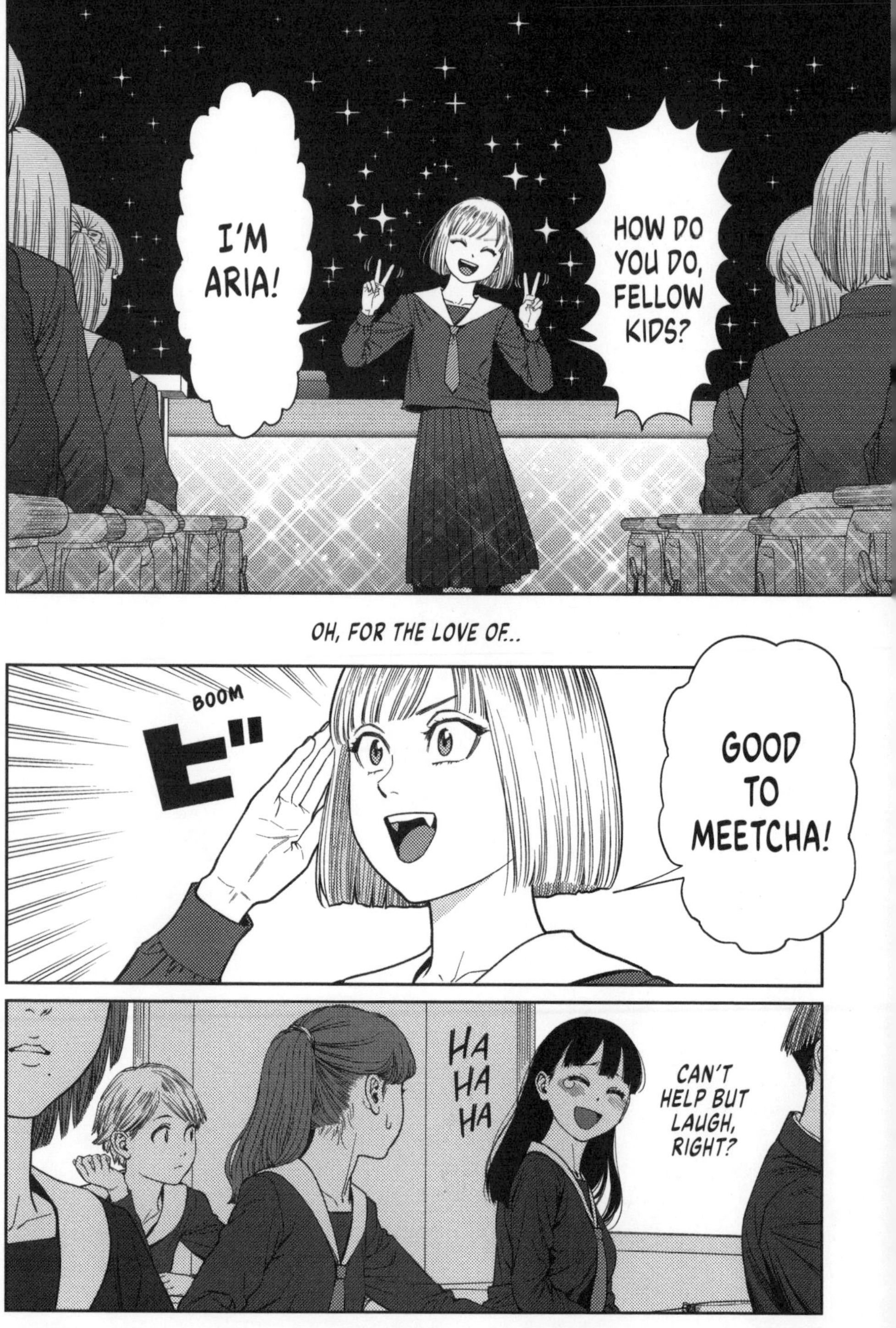
HOW DO YOU DO, FELLOW KIDS?
I'M ARIA!
OH, FOR THE LOVE OF...
GOOD TO MEETCHA!
BOOM
ビ
CAN'T HELP BUT LAUGH, RIGHT?
HA HA HA

Seikilos Epitaph

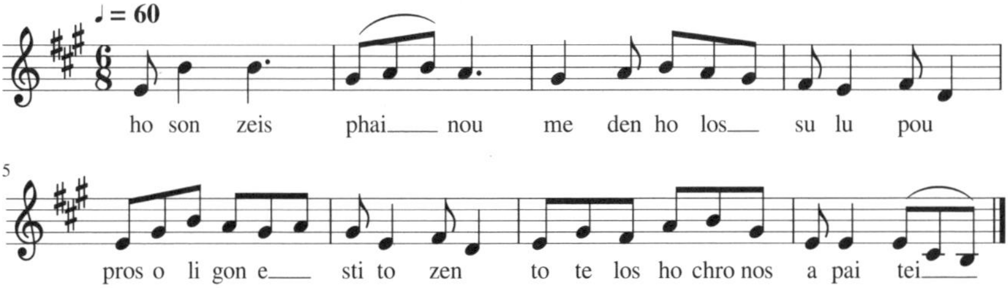
♩ = 60
ho son zeis phai___ nou me den ho los___ su lu pou
5
pros o li gon e___ sti to zen to te los ho chro nos a pai tei___

hóson zêis, phaínou

While you live, shine,

生きている間は輝いてください

mēdèn hólōs sù lupoû

have no grief at all;

決して思い悩んだりしないでください

pròs olígon ésti tò zên

life exists only for a short while,

人生はほんのつかの間ですから

tò télos ho chrónos apaiteî.

and Time demands its toll.

時はいずれ終わりを求めてくるものですから

VAMPEERZ

MY PEER VAMPIRES

Volume 1

Translator: Molly Rabbitt
Proofreading: Patrick Sutton
Production: Glen Isip
Nicole Dochych
Mo Harrison
Original Cover SALIDAS
Design:

VAMPEERZ Vol.1
by AKILI
©2019 AKILI
All rights reserved.
Original Japanese edition published by SHOGAKUKAN.
English translation rights in the United States of America, Canada,
the United Kingdom, Ireland, Australia and New Zealand arranged with
SHOGAKUKAN through Tuttle-Mori Agency, Inc.
Published in English by DENPA, LLC., Portland, Oregon 2022

Originally published in Japanese as *VAMPEERZ*
by SHOGAKUKAN 2019
VAMPEERZ originally serialized in *Shonen Sunday GX* by SHOGAKUKAN 2019.

This is a work of fiction.

ISBN-13: 978-1-63442-933-7
Library of Congress Control Number: 2021952063
Printed in China

First Edition

Denpa, LLC.
625 NW 17th Ave
Portland, OR 97209
www.denpa.pub